Halloween Horror Nights Unofficial: The Story & Guide 2018

Christopher Ripley

Every effort has been undertaken to ensure the accuracy of the information presented within this book including the author's own experiences, research and external references, all of which at the time of print are believed to be correct. Nevertheless, the publishers and author accept no responsibility for any omissions or errors within the book, should they exist, or for any subsequent changes or events outside of our mutual control. No obligation is required to follow the details of this book or have any reliance on the contents of the book, so no responsibility can be derived from these actions from both the publisher and author. Assessments and descriptions of the events and attractions reported are via the research undertaken and the author's own experiences or taken from references; therefore the book is wholly the opinion of the author and the sponsored publisher (Eskdale Publishing), which may or may not wholly or otherwise dictate the reader's own experience of the events and attractions presented with no liability placed on either party for their accounting of the events and attractions they have seen and researched. If the book is used for guide purposes for any potential vacations by any readers then all information presented in this book should be checked prior to travel to ensure it is best represented.

Published by: E&K Publishing

ISBN-10:   978-0-9955362-5-8

Author contact: hhnunofficial@gmail.com

The cover artwork was created by Rob Yeo and the author.

DEDICATION

The Author would like to thank his colleagues Jenny Bentley and Jan Davis, plus Julie Zimmerman, John-Paul Geurts, Ron Schneider, Jason Surrell, Adrian LePeltier, James-Michael Roddy, Mike Aiello, James Keaton, Michael Rives, Fowl Owlerson, Scott Rifkin, Dr. James Walker, Len Testa and Jim Hill for their kind assistance with creating this book.

THIS BOOK IS SPONSORED BY:

CONTENTS

ACKNOWLEDGMENTS

Thank you for everything Emma.

Introduction by HHN Co-Creator
Julie Zimmerman

Manufactured in Sandusky, Ohio circa the late 1950's, I jumped off the shelf and moved to Los Angeles CA at the tender age of 20 to become a movie star...

Well, I didn't become a movie star but I did work as an improvisational comedian. I spread my comedic wings at a small dance studio near a hamburger stand in West Hollywood and became a member of the long-running improvisational comedy group, *Off the Wall*. In that little hole in the wall in Hollywood, I was blessed to work with the illustrious Robin Williams, John Ritter, Andy Goldberg and the Emmy Award-winning comedy series writer of *M*A*S*H*, *Cheers*, *The Simpsons* and *Frasier*. Kenny Levine. I retired from performing at the age of 29 years old and moved to a glorious small town in Northern California called Stinson Beach.

After three years in the land of great white sharks and wine spritzers, I responded to a classified job listing in the *San Francisco Chronicle* under "Entertainment Professionals Wanted" and sent my resume off to a PO box with a 91608 zip. Six months later I received a call from Universal Studios Hollywood. They flew me to LA, I met my new boss, Peter Alexander, VP of Shows and Special Effects and within two weeks I moved back to LA and joined *MCA* Planning and Development, now known as Universal Creative.

Universal then relocated the entire project team to Orlando to build Universal Studios Florida. I found myself looking at a small tropical jungle filled with alligators, swirling pools of mosquito-infested water and snakes. I remember saying to myself, "I have sinned and God is punishing me by sending me to this swamp. What the hell have I done?"

Eventually USF opened and, as the entire world knows, nothing worked. My next adventure was to babysit two non-functioning attractions. My trailer was positioned next to *Jaws* and as we all sat around waiting for Universal to bring in a team to fix the broken shark and gorilla, I would answer the phone as follows: "*Jaws, Kong,* Julie, how can I help you?"

In the late summer of 1991, my dear friend Amy Henry, also part of the original Florida team, asked me if I was interested in a temporary project management position for an event called *Fright Nights.* Of course I said yes.

I moved my borrowed P&D computer and a folding table to an abandoned trailer that had served as the break room for the closed *Fievel* stage show. My first tasks were to find a sword swallower, a fire eater and a human pin cushion. I also had to build a culvert (so Elvis could appear as if he were coming out of a grave) at the Bates Motel for the *Beetlejuice Dead in Concert show,* design a back drop for the *Paul Revere and Raiders show stage* and find someone to design a dress for a woman who was going to be placed in a rat-filled coffin at *The Dungeon of Terror,* which in my opinion is still the scariest haunted house ever created.

Not heavily funded, we begged borrowed and pilfered everything we could find to build the event. *Fright Nights* exceeded everyone's expectations and I actually saw Jay Stein, founding father of Universal Florida, smile. After *Fright Nights* I went on an East Coast promotional tour for the movie *Fievel Goes West* and somehow kept myself employed at Universal picking up little projects here and there, including a re-write of the *Ghostbusters Attraction* and a stint as an actor in *Earthquake.*

One day I received a call asking me to put together some creative ideas for a second *Fright Nights.* I found myself a little space in a trailer, borrowed a computer, set it up on a folding tray table and started typing again.

The treatment for *Bill and Ted's Excellent Halloween Adventure* came first for I really loved the element of time travel associated with the film. I could just see the Terminator and Freddy Krueger coming out of the phone booth as part of the show. I wanted to bring back the hugely successful *Dungeon of Terror* with a new design and improved special effects. I wrote a haunted house treatment for *The People Under the Stairs* based on the Universal Film of the same name for I knew the scenic elements from the film were perfect for a really creepy haunted house. *Fright Night II* needed more scareactors, more entertainment on the streets and just more things that shock us and send chills down our spine.

I turned in my creative brief and thought, okay, they will either like it or think I am just nuts.

They liked it and wanted even more...

I was now the official producer of the newly-branded Halloween Horror Nights. I quickly called on my friend the art director John Paul Geurts to help. He re-designed the *Dungeon* and completely designed *The People Under the Stairs.* My next call was to Project Manager Tony Peugh for I knew we needed a small army of professionals to pull this thing off. And the rest, as they say, is of course history.

I served as the producer of Halloween Horror Nights and many other special events for the next five years. I love Universal Studios Florida and you can trust me when I tell you that part of my DNA is buried in that soil.

After leaving Universal, I acted as a creative consultant in the design/development phase of Universal Japan. I have lived and worked in Las Vegas, Texas and have found my way back to Orlando.

HHN was such an amazing thrill ride for me. We would spend months creating the weirdest and most wonderful experiences we could (and often on a shoestring!). Working closely with the team we had and the team that continues to build our nightmares to this very day, I know they, like us, are just having the best time of their lives. So much blood, sweat and tears go into making this event. That's why we're all so proud of the success it had attracted over the years and just how much love there is out there for what is surely the world's greatest Halloween event.

Thank you, dear reader, and fan of all things Halloween. Thank you for your love and dedication to the best event in the world. I love it too. I always have, and I always will. And I always knew HHN would be a huge success. I just felt it in my bones...

Happy nightmares!

Julie

Julie with her ghouls at HHN (note: the 'dunce' in the background is a very young James Keaton, aka Jack the Clown!)

Gross-ary

Guest: A member of the public.

House/Maze: Haunted house attraction. A temporary built attraction that is built by Universal utilizing the experienced craftsmen and women of the resort. Typically, the whole event takes more than 18 months to plan, design and build. It is noted that Universal Orlando prefers the term 'house' whereas Universal Hollywood prefers the term 'maze'.

Scareactor: This is the term Universal uses to describe any actor trained and deployed within the event for the sole purpose of scaring the guests. This includes actors in both the houses and the streets. I have seen Universal spell it 'Scaractor', 'Scuractor' and 'Scareactor', with the latter being the most widespread, therefore the most used within this book.

Scarezone: An area within the park which is full of scareactors, typically with props and sets to build the story of each scarezone.

Soundstage: A large building within the parks that has been built either for film/TV productions or Halloween Horror Nights.

Icon: The main character of the event who is seen on all marketing and is chiefly portrayed within the event's narrative for that year.

Mascot: A secondary character who is not the main icon but might be involved in the houses or marketing.

Art & Design: The colloquial term for the department within Universal Orlando that is responsible for designing all the scares for the event.

Rat Lady: A lady often encased within glass and covered by rats. She is seen at every event, sometimes within a house or within a casket on wheels on the streets (Note: 2013 & 2014 she was not seen).

Roach Man: Same as the Rat Lady but with roaches and usually not mobile at the event.

Original House: A house that was designed in-house by Universal that is either completely original in its design or inspired by real-life events.

IP House: Intellectual Property House. IP houses are houses that contain characters, sets, props, music from a particular source that are not owned by Universal. An example of an IP house would be a movie or TV show. Universal goes to great lengths to attract the biggest and best properties to their event and as such continually works with outside creatives to create iconic houses and experiences.

Jello-Shot Girl/Nurses: Women employed within the park selling fake blood packs filled with a jello substance colored red and containing alcohol, to mimic the appearance of blood. Usually dressed as vampires or demons with fake blood on them and pulling a stand with a flashing red beacon to denote their presence in a queue.

Blood Day: The day within the calendar prior to opening when the members of Art and Design go around each house with a bucket of fake blood and spray it onto the newly created sets. It's usually 2 weeks before opening.

CAD: Computer aided design, a computer program used to design the houses of the event, including virtual 3D walkthroughs.

IP: Intellectual Property. The term comes from the two different types of houses and scarezones at the event. Original houses are imaged in-house by Universal for the event, IPs are where deals are done to bring outside franchises to the event (such as movies or TV shows). Typically, original houses are favored by the fans and IPs are favored by the general public.

SIF: Stuff In Face, the process of suspending string, wires, fabric or other materials at head-height-level that when touched appear to give the guests the sensation that something might be touching them in the face. The SIF is usually suspended in corridors where there are low light conditions.

AAT: Actor Activated Trigger. Hidden pads, buttons and switches hidden in the houses that scareactors use to activate sounds, special effects or traps.

Blackout Performer: A team member who works behind the scenery in each house. They often wear black clothing and operate large props, special effects or puppets.

Building permits: Applications to build the temporary haunted houses are issued for approval by Universal Orlando to the City of Orlando.

Frequent Fear: A type of pass which allows the owner to attend the event on more than one night.

Gory Getaway: A vacation package which includes tickets to the event and a hotel stay.

Rush of Fear: The same as the frequent fear pass but typically held for guests attending the event in the first two weeks.

RIP Tour: A tour with a tour guide which takes guests to every house and every show in one night.

Express Pass: An extra add-on ticket which can be purchased to enable guests to get into houses more quickly by using a special queue line. The pass works on the basis that it is good for one use per house and can be used multiple times for any open rides.

Behind-the-screams/Unmasking the Horror: A tour that takes guests during the day around some of the houses to see how they were designed and built.

Stay and Scream: People who stay in either the Studios or Islands Park while the event is setting up.   Sometimes special offers are given to guests wanting to do this.

For more information regarding ticket options, please see the official event website at Halloweenhorrornights.com

Opening Scaremonies: A show that is often presented on the opening night of the event, which introduces the event's icon and narrative for the event's duration. It is not held every year.

Streetmosphere: A term created by theme park professionals that encompasses all entertainment types within the areas between the rides, including but not limited to: street performers, street shows, sets, lighting, soundtrack, etc.

E-ticket: A term originally created by Walt Disney to mean the most anticipated ride within a park. It has later been reworked to mean the most thrilling or largest ride within a park. Originally at Disneyland in the 1950s, guests would buy tickets to enter into the attractions that were graded A to E, with E being for the most popular rides and therefore limited in quantity.

Boo-doors: Hatches and apertures within a set from which the scareactors appear, to scare guests. Lately also named Boo-holes.

Sprung Tents: A style of building whose appearance is that of a tent. However these buildings are not as temporary as a tent and are utilized solely for Halloween Horror Nights.

Scare-moving / scare propelling: A means of moving guests from one room to another by scaring them into moving forward.

Red Button: Hidden as 'Easter eggs' through select houses, they often trigger effects when pressed. Universal officially calls them GATs - Guest Activated Triggers.

Hell Week: A week within the calendar when local and out-of-State schools all close for the holidays during the event. This often ties in with South American and European guests (particularly British and German) who also have school closures around this week. This causes the event to be heavily packed with guests. It often occurs around mid to late October.

Chicken Runs: Pathways that are built within scarezones or to the side of scarezones to allow guests who do not want to be scared to move through. These have not always appeared throughout the events.

Fire Crew: A crew of people who are employed at HHN to fill the shoes of anyone that has not arrived at work. So, say someone is ill and can't come in, a member of the fire crew will undertake their role for that night. Members of this team will likely fill the roles of dozens of different actors, performers and operational staff throughout the event's run.

Boo Bucks: Managers at Universal reward great scareactors by giving them 'Boo Bucks' such as coupons for each scare. They can either be kept as a keepsake or given to a draw for weekly prizes. They look like *Monopoly* money and feature the icon of that year's HHN on the front of them. As these are only given out to scareactors, the Bucks are highly prized and often sell on online auction sites for large amounts of money.

Ab-grieve-iations

HHN: Halloween Horror Nights

USF: Universal Studios Resort Orlando

USH: Universal Studios Hollywood

IOA: Islands of Adventure

A&D: Art and Design Department

HRH: Hard Rock Hotel

Author's Introduction

If you've just picked this book up and have no idea what a Halloween Horror Night is, then allow me to explain. It is an annual event held at the Universal Studios Resort in Orlando and in other Universal locations around the world (though this book is mostly concerned with the events in Orlando). It is a separate, after-hours hard ticketed event that is directly aimed at teenagers and adults.

The event has, over the last 25 years, morphed into probably the world's largest most detailed and experiential Halloween party. This rich history of the development of this beloved event is captured within this book, along with a guide towards the end that explains the best means for all attendees to get the most out of their trips.

So sit back, pull up a comfy chair and enjoy reading the Halloween Horror Night Unofficial's Story and Guide for 2018...

Chapter One: Where it all began… on the West Coast

The world's premier Halloween event in Florida had a very long and protracted history even before the actual original *Fright Nights* took place. Our story doesn't even start in Orlando; it starts on the West coast at Universal Studios in Hollywood…

Since October 26th 1973, local theme park and Southern California mainstay Knott's Berry Farm had been running a small Halloween event that had been growing in popularity with local residents. The event, *Knott's Scary Farm*, in 1981, appointed actor and song-parodist Weird Al Yankovic to become the event's icon or center of their marketing, with 1980s glamour-puss Elvira taking on the mantle the following year. Soon the event was bursting with guests and quickly became sold out.

Upstate Universal Studios' parent company head Lew Wasserman was noticing the fleets of guests making their way home early from the park in order to make their way to Knott's Berry Farm, which would simply not do. As early as 1985 plans had been made to create a series of Horror Nights around the popular Halloween holiday to try to combat the perceived loss of trade resulting from the popular event held at Knott's Berry Farm. The plans didn't take off in 1985 mostly due to increased studios' requirements for shooting. Missing their window of 1985 did not deter the company though. The following year a bold decision was made to enable the event to take priority over any filming for the 1986 Halloween holiday season.

On October 8th 1986, *The Los Angeles Times* reported that the local studio would run 'Horror Nights' where 15,000 'frightniks' could part with $14.95 to attend a specially ticketed event to be run in the evenings after park close. The marketing for the event, which included newspaper adverts and radio commercials (*Power 106 FM* and others), promised guests the chance to spend an evening with Dracula, the Mummy, the Wolf Man, the Phantom of the Opera and even Norman Bates' dead mom! Over 70 costumed characters would roam the expansive backlot and the studio tram tour would run at night for the first time in Universal's history (it happened first here in 1986 and not in 2015 as some believe!).

Universal had been the crowned home of horror since the 1920s when Lon Chaney Snr delighted audiences with *The Hunchback of Notre Dame* and, more successfully, *The Phantom of the Opera*. (The set still remained intact on Soundstage 28 on the backlot up until 2015 when it was demolished to make way for park expansion, though most of the surviving set pieces were retained for storage in the studios' expansive prop storage warehouse). Building on Chaney's success, the mantel was passed to British (by patronage) Boris Karloff and Hungarian-born Bela Lugosi, who terrified audiences with *Frankenstein's Monster*, *The Mummy* and *Dracula* movies with all sorts of combinations and sequels. Lon Chaney Jnr joined the franchise in the 1940s with *The Wolf Man*, using detailed makeup, like his father before him, to both delight and terrify audiences in equal measures. This legacy of horror continued well into the 1960s when the ever-increasing series of self-reverential comedy parodies (*Abbott and Costello meet the...* series etc.) allowed for the regular succession of hits to come to a slow end. It was the renewed interest of the *Monster Kids* of the late 1960s and the current 1980s generation, who had not grown up with attending the cinema to see these monster hits, that allowed for a whole new plethora of monster-related serials, merchandise, books and comics to feed into popular culture, once again putting the Universal Monsters center stage of the cultural lexicon.

A Universal spokesman announced to the local media outlets that the event would run from 7pm to midnight on both October 31st and November 1st 1986. They advised that the tickets would be sold on a first-come-first-served basis with a limit on ticket sales of just 7,500 per day. This event would be a one-of-a-kind event utilizing Universal's impressive back catalogue of monster heritage to its full strength.

"We're getting set up to scare up the devil out of people" the spokesman for Universal said, "so please, do not bring your children," he continued.

The plan for the event was to utilize existing park assets such as the Bates Motel, which had recently enjoyed increased popularity with the summer release of *Psycho 3* that year. *Psycho 2* (1983), which had been released a couple of years before had, at that time, been the longest awaited sequel in film history. The newly formed *Psycho* franchise was drawing on the new wave of new 'slasher' and monster movies that were becoming extremely popular. Since creating the genre by definition in 1960 with Sir Alfred Hitchcock's original masterpiece, *Psycho*, the niche genre - a combination of a thriller and horror (usually with a knife-toting psychopath in tow) - had gone from strength to strength in the 1970s and 1980s with classics such as *Friday 13th* (1980), *A Nightmare on Elm Street* (1984) and *Halloween* (1978) proving popular with audiences. Other popular areas included Courthouse Square dressed to look as if a killing spree had occurred and the Court of Miracles made to look like a peasants' revolt. The Court of Miracles area had actually been used to shoot the original *Dracula* with Bela Lugosi, *The Wolf Man* and most famously *The Hunchback of Notre Dame* and the original *Frankenstein*. This section of the park proved popular with horror filmmakers as the area was compact with many small streets representing vague areas of continental Europe; these were all put to good use when passing trams would be confronted by hordes of village folk chasing down the monster of choice for that hour.

The event was humble in its beginnings. The aim was to allow the famous studio tram tour to be run at night for the first time ever, with a new tour guide script focused on horror and sci-fi sights of the backlot combined with costumed characters jumping out at every turn. Local posters and newspaper adverts promised that:
"They're here. Lurking in the shadows. Hiding behind corners. Stalking dark alleys. Those terrifying monsters who haunted our streets for 60 years have come back... to get you!"
Whilst running the popular tram tour (or *Terror Tram*) and a few select attractions in the main theme park, the park also put on a concert to keep the event relevant and young in audience. Michigan based R&B band *Ready for the World* would perform especially for the event each night on stage at the park, performing such hits as *Oh Shelia* and *Love You Down* to delighted park guests. *Ready for the World* were signed to MCA, the parent company of Universal Studios and were only too happy to play to local audiences.

Using a *MCA*-signed musical act, costumes from their own huge costume department, and actors from their own talent agency with park operational staff kept costs down in what would be a water test to the local economy to see if such an event would be successful. After the first night, the studio knew they had created a hit.

The event was a huge success. Quickly, the event sold out, due in part to the advent of the ability to call the park and pay over the phone with a credit card. Universal's excellent marketing department quickly distributed posters and radio commercials informing the local communities that the event was sold out but had decided to run one extra day on Sunday November 2nd with a slightly earlier start of 6.30pm. Posters of Jack-o-Lanterns were printed showing the popular holiday icon being destroyed from above via a chainsaw, a symbol that would be reused again years later. The posters advised to book now to avoid disappointment as if you don't it "will haunt you forever!"

However, despite the sell-out of tickets and orderly manner of the guests, the event was soon marred by a very unfortunate tragedy. It was reported in *The Los Angeles Times* that late in the evening of November 1st, Paul Rebalde aged 20 of Woodland Hills, who was stationed along the *Terror Tram* route in full zombie makeup, had sadly been killed. He was tasked with sitting within a parked tram along the route with scores of mannequins which all had similar makeup applied, allowing the guests the ability to believe they were all dummies. Rebalde's role was to jump from the parked tram to scare guests passing by in another tram.

Rebalde, along with other actors, had been a theme park attendant who had been asked to work as one of the *Terror Tram's* new cast of over 70 costumed characters that lined the route of the tram. Rebalde had been described in a *LA Times* article as "a thin, rusty-haired youth who was quick with a smile". They said he had worked in the theme park at several jobs. "He was one of the sweetest kids that worked up here," one fellow employee said. "He was the kind of guy that always walked around with a smile on his face. Everybody liked him." Rebalde was believed to have jumped from his stationary tram at around 8.30pm to scare one of the passing trams when he became trapped between the third and fourth sections of the moving four-part tram. He was likely crushed to death and then sadly dragged some 100 feet. He was pronounced dead by local medics at around 9pm.

An investigation was quickly set up by investigators from the Los Angeles County district attorney's environmental crimes and occupational safety division headed up by John F. Lynch. Joan Bullard, marketing and publicity director for Universal Studios, said "There was no indication that the tram had a problem or anything like that. The sheriff has told us that it was an unfortunate accident." She continued, "The tour's safety record is exemplary and that we (Universal) have never had an incident like this in our 22-year history. We're all very sad."

The Terror Tram was abandoned for the rest of the night and additional safety measures for the final extra night were put into place to protect both actors and guests; this mostly included the omission of any actors being allowed to 'jump or attack' any moving trams and that only stationary trams would be allowed for scaring purposes.

Rebalde had worked in the merchandising department for the Studios since the beginning of May of 1986. His role was defined by a spokesman for the park as being "very broad," but several studio workers interviewed at the time said that Rebalde's job included selling various merchandise to park guests and serving as an assistant manager of a stall that sold film near the famous front gates of the park.

A combination of expenditure required for park refurbishments and backlot availability due to feature film and television requirements, married with the tragic consequences that occurred on November 1st, led to the event being discontinued for the foreseeable future. The recent addition of *King Kong* to the *Tram Tour* required further expenditure for maintenance purposes and various popular stage shows were being overhauled. *The A-Team stunt show* was swopped out for a *Miami Vice* themed show; this coincided with a huge increase in shooting space required for TV shows such as *Murder She Wrote* and *Matlock*. *MCA* was keen for Universal Studios to be the new home of televisual serials, particularly in the niche genre of 'afternoon murder mystery', something that could be readily and repetitively syndicated (still to this day even).

Soon on the horizon *MCA* had a planned expansion for more child-friendly areas of the park, including *Fievel's Playland*. Seeking to distance its image of a park that was built mostly for adults and teens, the park's image of horror was downplayed for some years in part due to the tragic events that had occurred but also in reply to an ever-growing Disneyland which was drawing ever larger crowds. Halloween Horror Nights or Horror Nights (as it was dubbed at the time) was not expected to return; indeed it simply did not fit with the park's revised family spirit but would return one day.

Chapter Two: A new player in town

Back in Florida, Disney pretty much owned the holiday seasons, particularly Christmas. Every festive period, the main park of the Magic Kingdom would put on their annual Disney Parks *Christmas Day Parade*. Airing on the *ABC show* would be a massive commercial for all things Disney in the Southern State and would highlight that Disney was the place to be for families. Starting in 1983 and continuing to this day, it has aired every Christmas with the exception of 1989 and 2000, where the latter year Disney chose to air a special on 'Tracking Santa' for Christmas Eve. Celebrities such as Regis Philbin and Joan Lunden were often on presenting duties during this time. Throughout this time the local buzz was all about coming to Disney and bringing your family.

In the late 1980s, the event at Disney was going from strength to strength. Disney Channel's extremely popular *Ducktales* had premiered in 1987 and by this time Scrooge McDuck himself was headlining the event. Scrooge McDuck would go on to star in *A Sparkling Christmas Spectacular*, a song-and-dance show that would premiere Dec 20th with daily performances through to Dec 30th. Completing the line-up with McDuck and his nephews would be the appearance of Santa Goofy and a cast of over 300. The show then alternated with the '15 Years of Magic' show on the Cinderella Castle stage which was also popular at the time.

Not only did Disney throw televised parades with national coverage bringing in characters from the new hit Disney Channel shows, it also started to test the market with special evening hard ticketed events.

Mickey's Very Merry Christmas Party, as it was then and still to this day, premiered in 1983 as a single one-time-only hard ticketed event. It sold out and the park reached capacity. The event was a huge hit but Disney being Disney, and not wanting to run before they could walk, ran the event again the next year for one night and then again the following year for exactly one night, with each year selling out. It wasn't until 1989 that Disney plumped for two nights, when again they sold out. Then in 1990 three nights were offered and again all sold out. The Party offered a mixture of caroling, hot chocolate, cookies, a giant Christmas tree and sing-a-longs. Disney was bringing the big guns out.

It was also around the late 1980s and early 1990s that Disney started to experiment with the success of these Christmas parties as to what else they might be able to offer. Senior management quickly happened on the idea of filling the slower months of park attendances with specially ticketed events. It was at this time the first *Flower & Garden Festival* premiered at EPCOT during the early spring downtime and the first *Holidays Around the World* was held at the World Showcase in Epcot in the late Autumn. *Mardi Gras* celebrations were ramped up at Downtown Disney's Pleasure Island in the slow month of February, with a weeklong St Valentine's special appearing too. The popular *International Food and Wine Festival* at Epcot and *Mickey's-Not-So-Scary-Halloween Party* didn't start until the mid-1990s, when Halloween Horror Nights at the Studios was in full swing.

Meanwhile, during this time Universal was having problems. Right at the beginning of the park's existence in 1990, they were having huge issues with their star performers. The biggest star and the most problematic was Big Bruce himself: *Jaws*. The sharks within the newly-constructed ride just didn't work and the press liked to report this often. *Jaws* updates on the local media outlets were becoming a regular topic of discussion and a mighty embarrassment for the company. From day one there were the tell-tale signs. Rumors were abounding that Steven Spielberg, the director of the original smash-hit summer blockbuster got stuck along with his family on the actual opening day. Rumors aside, we do know from press reports that the ride was forcibly shut down on the actual opening day. Other attractions such as *Earthquake* and *Kongfrontation* were not faring much better either, though their stories are less important when it comes to the development of Halloween Horror Nights.

Chapter Three: Jump-starting the Shark

Though the Universal Studios park had opened June 7th, 1990 including the *Jaws* ride, the ride was forcibly shut down by park management on the afternoon of the 7th and did not reopen until the 10th. Testing during this time found that the persistent breakdowns were a direct result of the range of special effects that were required, combined with the state of the sharks submersed under the water for 90% of the day, every day. It was quickly becoming a logistical nightmare and a daily occurrence for disgruntled families to be-rescued from the ever-halting tour boats. General Manager of the Studios at this time was Tom Williams who was providing the best disaster limitation he could, and was providing free tickets for extra days at the parks to complaining guests and any that had been caught on the broken-down ride. Celebrities such as Beau Bridges and Anthony Perkins were rumored to have been deployed by the park's management to save face. Bridges himself was documented to have greeted and spoken with guests about their experiences at the fledgling park during this first week.

Despite the handouts and celebrities, queues were forming quicker some days at the park's customer services than at some of the rides during this short period. Sadly, from the June 10th, even though the boats could physically move around the lake they couldn't get the special effects to work consistently. Some of the Amity Island skippers quipped to customers, "look over there, that's where explosions should be happening", much to senior management's reprimands and annoyance.

By June 9th one thousand people had demanded a full refund for their tickets. Engineers from both the ride developer and the park were instructed to work around the clock on the problem. This was combined with a park attendance high, reaching near-capacity on day one that was quickly cooling off as the passing days came. A park guest that week, 50-year-old George Lowke, of Laytonsville, Maryland was quoted as saying, "They weren't quite ready for us, I don't think, but we are having a good time. And we have a ticket to come back," though not all guests were quite that positive.

Finally the news came on Aug 23th, 1990 that the ride would shut down temporarily whilst adjustments were made. In fact, it would be a major overhaul and the closure would last well over two years. The press took delight in letting their readers know that the park was at this time starting to struggle. The summer of 1990 was a worrying time for the new park. The initial few days of reaching full park capacity (rumored to be between 40,000 to 50,000 people) was past and the summer returned no such visitor numbers. The park reported that this was just a blip and where they had fixed the *Earthquake* and *King Kong* attractions, which were both running reasonably well, a quick fix for the toothy shark would be addressed. They thought it likely that by the New Year the ride would probably be opened again; though in real terms it would be longer and the Park's management were seething at the developer of the ride for this.

The park president Steven Lew quickly announced to the media that a lawsuit was imminently being filed by Universal in Orange County Circuit Court against the ride's developer for the issues suffered by the park because of the *Jaws* ride. The developer had also built the *Earthquake* attraction for the park but the faults with this ride were deemed minor enough for technical adjustments to be made pro bono by the developer. These were sufficient long-term fixes, though this was not the case for *Jaws*. By the end of August 1990 with struggling attendance figures and a headliner E-Ticket attraction beyond repair, the park issued its
40-page suit which described at length the woes of the new ride but it did not specify the amount of damages the company was seeking to obtain from the developer. Naming both attractions respectively, it made the case that the fact that these rides were not working directly attributed to the park's profits being directly below even the most modest of expectations. Namely the two rides were victims of poor workmanship, defective design, bad planning with no eye on program whatsoever. When both the park's engineers and those of the developers could no longer fix the issues, the park hired external consultants to appraise the sheer scale of the faults that lay at the bottom of Amity Island's lagoon.

"We are angry. We are disappointed," Lew Wasserman of the park's parent company *MCA* said at the time. "There are numerous design flaws in *Jaws*. The ride works for a few hours and then must be taken down for repairs."

A lot of the local staff knew that as this issue had hit Lew's desk then the problem was a huge one for the company.

Attendance was diving and Universal had to make cutbacks. Very quickly many of the originally employed staff were let go and the law suit for the attraction was issued. The park then had to readdress all of the extensive marketing that had been produced that featured the headlining *Jaws* ride. It was an embarrassing time for the company as 3D bill boards along the Interstate 4 were taken down, TV commercials were re-edited and recalls to vacation brochures quickly began. During this time the ride's developers responded, off the record in the first instance, by informing the press that a lot of their company's issues were as a direct result of the company losing their president during the ride's planning stage. A spokesman for the developer was reportedly said to have remarked that the issues were due to the complexity of mixing live special effects that were timed to meet large mechanical maneuvers in a body of water. This had led to the project over-running in the design stage, which ultimately affected the construction phase of the project. He was also reported to have said that the concept was very optimistic from day one and this led to issues from the minute it was conceived right up to the second it was handed over to the park's management. The lawsuit eventually alleged that the developer breached its mutually agreed contract terms, violated all collateral warranties and failed to properly get the ride into working order for park guests. The list of faults compiled by the third-party consultants was extremely lengthy.

By early 1990 the scale of the problem was finally realized and park president Tom Williams announced to the press that the ride would now be closed at least until 1992. "We are undergoing a comprehensive engineering effort that will translate into an opening that has yet to be determined," Williams officially said. It was at this time that the park had let slip via the lawsuit, that the ride had cost *MCA* $630 million to build and that whereas *Kong* and *Earthquake* could be repaired, the mechanical shark was beyond any such repair. Despite this, the company was not discouraged and once the third-party consultants had finished their investigation, the park started to explore the possibility of refurbishing the ride in-house with their own engineers. It was rumored that throughout 1991 and early 1992, Universal tried to get the special effect (namely the explosive section of the ride) to work again, but with no success. Rumors spread that the electronics used in the sharks' deployment mechanisms were badly damaged due to insufficient waterproofing which led to the sharks seizing-up 'mid-bite' with no means of releasing them. Universal quickly realized that the ride was not salvageable in its current state, so a new approach was required.

Since the closing of *Jaws* the two companies continued to investigate and talk over the matter; the dialogue was reputed to be almost daily. Discussions continued until April 4th 1991 when finally a deal was struck and Universal settled out-of-court with the ride's developer. Ron Sikes the park's vice president announced to the local media:
"In the settlement agreement, we have both agreed that we would have no further comment beyond the fact that the matter has been amicably resolved."
Even the developer was reported to have said the matter was resolved amicably and that no further comment could be made, other than the fact that their services to redesign the ride would not be undertaken and that they hoped that they could work with the theme park once again in the future. The developer had been started in 1984 by former Disney Imagineers and is still trading to this day (in fact the company actually worked on the original *Monorail* at Disneyland).

After the out-of-court settlement, the park got on board *Totally Fun Company* (who had worked on other opening day attractions such as *E.T.*), *ITEC Entertainment* (which would go on to make the park's *Mummy ride*), *Intamin* and *Oceaneering International* in a collaboration of efforts to refurbish and enhance the ride. Top of the list of requirements were the re-engineering of the ride system and installing an entirely new track, with new special effects being devised to create an almost entirely new version of the ride. The redesign also included the replacement of two major ride scenes. While the others worked on the ride systems, it was *Oceaneering* who had the task of providing lifelike animatronic sharks for the re-engineered ride, which was their first ever theme park project. The ride was then officially re-opened by original cast members Roy Scheider (who had been at the park shooting *Seaquest DSV*), Lorraine Gary, the park's creative consultant, and the movie's director, Steven Spielberg in the spring of 1993.

Winding the clock back to the spring of 1992, the ride's refurbishment was well underway. Construction crews would access the ride from the parking lot behind, so as not to further impede the guests' experiences. The famous sign appointed to the ride's entrance of *Captain Jake's Amity Boat Tours* and all *Jaws* signage were removed. Construction walls went up around the lagoon, which left a very large empty piece of real-estate adjacent to the south side of the ride: that of the queue building and the extended queue building. Taking up almost a fifth of the Amity area, the queue building and extended queue building (both linked at the entrance) could be temporary repurposed, which was an idea that was initially thrown around at the time. What else could they fill this space with? Could it be a temporary attraction? Perhaps a walk-through museum? Jay Stein, Universal's then President had an idea and he knew exactly who could pull it off…

HHN usually auditions in June and July every year…

Chapter Four: From ravenous rats to actual ravenous rats

Julie Zimmerman had worked at Universal when the Orlando Park was just a thought in Jay Stein's mind in the 1970s. She recalls,

"I was working on the Orlando Project before they even pulled the gators out of the swamps there!"

Working with a large variety of creatives in the 70s and 80s (including Steven Spielberg no less), Julie was best placed at Universal to head to the East Coast to work on creating the new theme park. After the park's opening, Julie had put down roots and decided to stay on to help create ongoing future attractions and entertainment, along with managing any special events and activities. It was Jay Stein who came to her during the spring of 1991 with an idea he had about creating a party for the park that could outdo their mousey neighbor but also bring in the crowds during the characteristically slow season of Fall. Julie, who had been between projects at the time, was asked by Stein "Julie, if we could do a Halloween party at the park, what could we physically do and how would we entertain people? It would need to be in a new way but also in a way that gets the word out that Universal was throwing a party."

Julie had been stationed in a small static trailer at the very edge of the new park; she had a mere fold-up card table and an *Apple* computer that she had borrowed from another department. Julie set about working on Universal's first Halloween party.

In the space of a few weeks Julie had created a full rundown of the entertainment that could be provided using existing performers and current stages. A haunted maze could be built in the empty *Jaws* queue, local specialist performers could be brought in to perform in the streets, and music, dance, lighting, costs, etc, were all typed out. Eventually, the proposal was sent back to Hollywood for Jay's approval. For months Julie heard no news and thought that the project was likely dead in the water. It was then, almost of the blue, that notice came down from Jay's office that "project Halloween was a go". With full approval, everything that had been planned on the small fold-out card table in the trailer at the far end of the property was suddenly going to take center stage.

"Universal Studios Plans 'Fright Nights' For Halloween" ran the article in the local newspaper. "Capitalizing on a library of horror-movie classics, the park is planning three 'Fright Nights,' said Randy Garfield, executive vice president of marketing." Disney was the biggest player in town, and Universal, who had at the time suffered from lower than expected attendance levels and general negative headlines, needed something to draw the crowds. It is said that at many times in the history of the resort even before it was built, it was in a constant power struggle with its mousey neighbors to the north. Disney pretty much owned the holiday season and most family-orientated activities, particularly those focused on younger children. Universal needed to find its niche and it did that in these early days by focusing on Halloween and on the young adult and teenager demographic. Disney at the time was pulling no punches, as during the planning stages of the first *Fright Nights* Disney just happened to be announcing their own 'special celebrations' to mark the resort's 20th anniversary. Garfield continued, "This isn't a response to Disney's 20th. It's an attempt to establish our franchise on Halloween and to take advantage of the legacy of monster movies we've had for 60 years. And it's strictly to take advantage of people's desire to party on Halloween." And the key word was "party"; this would be a hard ticketed, ticket holders-only affair that would be held after the park closed each day for three select nights. It would contain a cacophony of freaks, side-shows and monsters all made up to scare, delight and entertain guests in a laid-back party (almost *Mardi Gras*-like) fashion, where having a good time was as important as the scares.

The papers were awash with notices from Universal that
"From 6 p.m. until midnight Oct. 25, 26 and 31, the park will open at a special price for ghouls and gals." Garfield continued,
"We've had a classic movie monster franchise for 60 years," referring to movies in the Universal library. "Included in its archives are Frankenstein, Dracula and modern creatures, such as Chucky, the doll with the attitude."
Whereas Disney had years of animation legacy, Universal had years of horror legacy. Garfield and others hammered home to the media that this would include your classic favorites such as *Dracula* and *The Mummy*

but also modern favorites such as *Beetlejuice* and *Ghostbusters* (though they were used under license as not strictly Universal properties but were present during the day hours). Other adverts in local shopping malls had pictures of Jeff Goldblum's portrayal of *The Fly*, Hitchcock's *Psycho* and even a character wearing a hockey mask (ahem!); though some of these more modern franchises did not appear at the event.

Tickets to each of the Fright Nights events would cost $12.95 per person plus tax, with a small service charge if purchased in advance, or $15.95 on the day of admission. On Oct. 25, 26 and 31, the Studios would close early at 5pm instead of the usual 7pm and the event would go on until midnight.

Before tickets could be sold, the park had a lot of work to do in preparation for their fledgling event. Julie Zimmerman, who was mostly in charge of park entertainment and events, called on Geurts to help build the event that she had planned. Geurts, who had worked on the Universal Orlando project from day one, had actually worked on the design and build of many of the opening day attractions.

"One of my favorite projects was the Hitchcock attraction and show. I worked with a team who were as dedicated as myself to making a true memorial to honor the work of Hitch." Geurts said. "We tried a number of concepts before the final attraction was designed. We had for many months wanted to build a bar on the first-floor, so guests could ascend the famous 'Vertigo' steps before stepping into a cocktail bar with Hitchcock-themed drinks. Unfortunately, the City required that any such bar would require restrooms to be located up there too and we simply couldn't do that due to space requirements."

Shortly after the park opened Geurts tried to see if it was still possible but to no avail.

"It was around that time that I was asked to sit down with Julie (Zimmerman) and explore the event that management wanted to stage." He continued, "Ideas were thrown around that we should do a Christmas event or a spring event, though it became noticeable to us both during these brain-storming sessions that we really couldn't compete with Disney, and at the time Disney seemed to own the spring and Christmas sections of the calendar. Fresh from my Hitchcock meeting, I made the idea of utilizing his brand in some way, this was quickly followed by Julie with a concept to expand that idea to a larger degree by utilizing other Universal brands of the same nature to create a Halloween themed event."

The idea was set, it was pitched to senior management, and they immediately asked the pair to go away and draw up a full concept. The idea had been reinforced thanks in part to swift pulling together of

Dynamite Nights Stunt Spectacular which was dreamt up, actioned and planned just 2 weeks away from the grand opening of the park. Knowing that the team at "Project Florida" could deliver to tight timeframes and budgets almost spear headed the confidence in a Halloween themed event at the Studios. Michael Rives then Universal Orlando producer remembers:

"It enabled the whole event in the same sense that *Jaws* did. The *Jaws* failure and the *Kong* and *Earthquake* troubles put management under stress. So, too, the *Jaws* queue building being available was a needed part of HHN. *Dynamite Nights* was the opposite pole. It was a huge hit. It was also thrown together in the last few weeks before opening, and it was never supposed to be a show in the first place. It gave management some confidence and bragging rights. It was edgy... and it worked. I doubt management would have green-lighted *Fright Nights* but for *Dynamite Nights*."

It was around late 1990 that Geurts, who by this time was employed as an outside contractor, sat down with Julie to design the 'nuts and bolts' of the event which by this time would be run on a very tight budget (as the park had only just opened). He said,

"Julie acted as producer for the event and was key to finding the Universal-owned concepts that we could play with and finding the talent to fill the streets. Whereas I took on the other areas of the event, such as the design, the lighting, the music and the general park atmosphere. So we didn't have to compete with Disney we really wanted to aim at the local young people and adults to make an event that was adult orientated but played out more like a party, where everybody could attend and have a good time. This was going to be a no kid-centric operation."

Planning continued into the summer months ready for staging the event that fall. He continued,

"As we worked on the details, the park's senior management referred the event to the central marketing department of the company – who absolutely loved the concept. They had a lot of fun utilizing the classic Universal monsters and Julie's idea of placing a woman inside a glass casket filled with rats idea, which they used to great effect in an effort to drum up trade for our new event. Selling a new theme park for a second time took a lot of thought and using the classic monsters (who hadn't featured in the original marketing) and the rat lady idea, was a great way to tap into the different demographic we were aiming for." Marketing also devised the name of 'Fright Nights' which seemed to sum up what the producers of the event were going for. Unfortunately, after the first event, Universal received a firm letter from the copyright holders of that name, something that everyone had not been aware of.

"Nobody thought it might be copyrighted, so when the project was greenlit for a second time, we changed the name ensuring to check all possible variations with the US Copyright people, before finally opting for 'Halloween Horror Nights' – which is a better name anyway".

Marketing loved the idea of the lady covered in rats. "It's not something you see every day!" said Zimmerman. Once the idea had been formed and the casket built, Julie set about creating a 'rat-sanctuary'. The rats would be properly cared for and looked after at the park prior and during the event (as they always have been at the event). A space was made for the rats behind the scenes in the then Earthquake attraction. Julie herself would go along every day feeding, caring for and cleaning out the rats. "In those early days we kind of just all messed in together to the job done."

The event's key performance goals were: to create a party environment, to ensure the whole park is utilized so every guest knew wherever they were that they were in the party and to ensure every guest had a good time by staging a huge variety of entertainment. These were no easy tasks, as Geurts recalls.
"Our budget was very limited but we wanted everyone who entered the park to know that this wasn't business as usual. We did this in a number of ways, which I guess most of which was myself just out there after park closing testing and experimenting with different light effects. We probably had more light effects utilizing technology that was built but not used often from within the façades to create the illusion of horror. Swopping out lenses with different colors to spots and putting in projectors really helped create the spooky environment. A lot of the projections were just drawings or patterns projected onto areas where their lights had been switched-off, this combined with a moving light enabled the backlot to look very different from the daytime with very minimal physical changes. This was long before the video projections they have now, we were just experimenting with simple patterns and effects but to great results."
The lighting effects combined with the music and dry-ice machines to create environments unlike anything at any East coast park, and he continued
"We started using the term 'street-mos-phere' back then to define what we were doing. I don't know if we invented that word or not, but we definitely used that terminology back then."

The idea soon came about to build a haunted maze within the event, something that could be built relatively cheaply inside a redundant building that wouldn't affect the park's day-to-day operations.

Management decided that the *Jaws* queue building was to be used, owed to the fact that the ride was now closed and would be so for quite some time.

"We initially didn't want to utilize the *Jaws* queue for the house. It has a great atmosphere there which when combined with the lake can be utilized to great effect, however for building of sets we wanted to use one of the soundstages. We were told that they were being used for TV and Film production at the time, so we couldn't use any of them," said Geurts. "We set about using what we had and by the end of the construction I was really happy with what we had created. The queue building, despite its limitations, actually added to the claustrophobic vibe we were going for. We wanted guests to feel trapped inside this house, and that's why Universal have always called them 'mazes' for the simple factor that from day-one with our house design we wanted guests to not be so sure of where exits are – its more frightening that way. Unfortunately, over time due to the massive popularity of the event and certain building codes, we can't build them like that anymore."

"We worked around the clock to get everything in place before the event," said Geurts. "We had a team that were so dedicated to staging this event that we had created from nothing, so absolutely nothing was left to chance, we ensured we checked everything twice before opening."

Zimmerman and Geurts' efforts paid off when news came that the event was selling extremely well, with visitor numbers expected to be into the thousands. "It was great news and a great time to be working in theme parks," Geurts said. "We wanted it to be the most interactive and thrilling experience we could, something new and fresh unlike anything that had ever been seen before in Central Florida," said Zimmerman.

Fright Nights

"Dying for a good Halloween party?" asked the theme park publicity.

Posters in stores, leaflets at every tourist spot, radio commercials, magazine placements and even a brief TV spot on the local *Fox network* highlighted the "huge" event that was coming that Fall at Universal Studios Orlando. *Pepsi Cola*, who was the official supplier of beverages at the time, paired up with the resort to market the event across the local TV networks.

"If you want to come party down with your favorite monsters."

Savings of a 'devilish' $16 could be made if you bought special Halloween-themed 2 liters of *Pepsi* and presented the coupon on the back. Locals were also encouraged by offers of buy-one-get-the-second-half-price. On opening night the car park was full (admittedly the car park back then was not as large as the multi-stories they have now), and queues formed quickly around the block and onto the I4. The main draw of the evening would not be a lavishly detailed house or packed streets of scareactors but the chance to party (and they meant party!) with others in a creepy and cool Halloween environment; a sort of lock-in

after hours party with those who were on the guest list only. "Come see the park after dark and experience it like never before" commented several of the Universal management. This was surely to be a unique experience and totally unlike anything Disney was doing down the road.

The streets were packed like never before or since, with performers of every type. A snake handler with a boa constrictor wrapped around his neck walked along the sidewalks, freaks and clowns stormed around the main gates, side shows from every carnival you've ever been to lined the streets, fire eaters performed near Hollywood Boulevard, a sword swallower astounded guests near Exposition Boulevard, and men hammered nails into noses. Even street magicians performing card tricks and pulling coins out from people's ears were spotted deep in the park and these were just the random street performers!

Specially pre-selected schools of Central Florida were asked if their students and their families would attend the event for free on different nights of the three nights offered.
The catch?
They had to come in costume. In all the press releases costumes were banned, because park management did not want members of the park confused with park performers. But a special nightly costume contest was performed with winners selected by the guests cheering for the best costumed kid or by those who brought the most family and friends with them. Named *The Monster Mardi Gras Costume Concert* (maybe that's where the idea for *Mardi Gras* spawned from?) it was held nightly at 7.30pm at the top of Hollywood Boulevard. Guests were asked to view a ménage of misfits and maniacs where 'intellectual properties' (or IPs) were discouraged. Parents had to ensure their kid(s) who were taking part were in full makeup and at the park before the park had closed for the day (5pm), ready to be inducted and prepared for the Halloween party (as some at Universal were referring to it). The gates opened at 6pm but all the 400 costumed kids were kept backstage until show time at 7.30pm where they were held in a pen during the show. It was the Ghostbusters team and old Beetlejuice himself who congratulated the winner, James Glore, 11, of Southwest Middle School in Orange County on winning the very first contest. After the short show and awarding ceremony, the kids were all sent back stage to de-frock from their costumes and remove their makeup before being released back to their families so that they could enjoy the rest of the park for the evening.

A massive hit for the park - and the one aspect that increased the guest numbers - was the event's only haunted house. Named *The Dungeon of Terror* the haunt was located in the *Jaws* additional queue building (as described earlier) and was unlike any temporary haunt that had been seen before. It took ten weeks to design and a further six weeks to build, as Universal wanted to bring everything it knew about movie-set building to a whole new level. Randy Garfield, executive vice president of marketing, promised before the event that this house would be "a murderous assortment of mazes, along with monsters and nightmarish images." The facade was a stony entry port to a terrifying dungeon of mixed horrors. Fog machines bellowed out smog to knee level, strobes lights cut the scene and a real eerie anticipation filled the air. This was to be a very special experience like nothing you had seen before. Rapidly-formed queues quickly appeared with three-hour waits being the norm for each evening. After night one, it was seen that locals, who had been the night before, were rushing to this attraction first on each of the two remaining nights before the queues built up.

Passing the stone façade, the public travelled into a world of torture and misfortune. Poor unfortunate souls were left dangling above spiked pits or being stretched on various apparatuses, all done with the skill and good humor that only Universal Creative can produce. The layout was a series of prison cells in a maniacal dungeon where the freaks ruled and guests just like you (well, cast members made to look like guests!), were being tortured for your viewing pleasure. In fact it was a series of ingenious but elaborate props made to look like implements of torture when in fact they were completely harmless. The creative team had made sure the experience was exactly 12 minutes in duration from the moment you passed the façade to the second your feet walked you under the final exit sign. "A lot of times it takes much less because people are literally running to get away from these monsters," Tim Sepielli of Universal Creative said.

There was one problem though: no air-conditioning in the claustrophobic and confined house. The guests sweated and the performers' makeup melted, and it was reported that as the night wore on, the makeup became more and more terrifying as the heat made the latex sag and the grease paint drip. The house experience was also incredibly short and many people tried to queue again to get another experience. People were proclaiming to those in the queue, "you'll want to queue again when you finish, it's different every time!" And people did, and the queue grew longer and people shuffled through like vastly slow moving conga lines. The house was also incredibly intense compared to what we now accept as the norm. One performer from the *Nickelodeon Studios* got so overenthusiastic that he brought buckets of slime from the attractions there and used them in his performance. Unfortunately he managed to dump a vast quantity onto some un-suspecting guests who were shuffling along in that particular scene. But there was one scene that would later go on to become a Halloween Horror Nights tradition. Towards the end of the house one cell had a particularly lackluster victim contained within. However the scare was not in front of you, it was below you. As quickly as the flick of a light, the misdirected guests' attention was quickly turned from the room beyond to the floor below, where, encased in a glass walkway, was a lady being eaten alive by ravenous rats. The lady would scream loudly, scratch and bang the glass when illuminated by the light to make people jump. Scores of the rats would run and creep all over her. The glass walkway was specially built for this scare and would go on to be used many times in events of the future becoming a tradition – 'The Rat Lady' was born.

"When you walk down one corridor, you're walking on plexiglass," Sepielli said. "It lights up and there's a crypt under your feet with a girl banging and clawing at the plexiglass. It's filled with live rats that crawl all over her body. Of course, the trick is that we smear peanut butter on her so the rats really nibble on her. That's a lot of fun!"

Beetlejuice from the popular 1988 Michael Keaton movie made the rounds and actually starred in two of the night's shows. It was perfectly choreographed to ensure no cross-over was seen for the made-up actor who played as the park's official Beetlejuice. The movie, which was a massive hit drawing in a reported $73million at the box-office, starred Michael Keaton in the titular role as the mad yet comical ghost who tries to aid the recently deceased Alec Baldwin and Geena Davis in scaring away the incumbents of their former home. Beetlejuice, who at the time was a part player in a day-time show with the Ghostbusters and occasional roaming character, would have two shows per nights with eight respective performances. He was a big draw for the event, so much so that the following year, the lackluster show *An American Tail Theatre* was completely repurposed and refurbished into Beetlejuice's own *Rock and Roll Graveyard Revue*, which continued in its original format right up until to 2002.

The first show of the night for 'Old Betelgeuse' was *Beetlejuice's Graveyard Tours*. The setting was the *Bates Motel* set from the movie *Psycho IV*, which had been dressed to represent a ghostly motel from the movie's netherworld, had regular performers "Joliet" Jake and Elwood Blues, aka *The Blues Brothers*. The show had been written by Ron Schneider who was now employed by the park as a show director, he had moved over from Disney where he had worked many roles, though most fans would remember him fondly as The Dreamfinder from Epcot's *Imagination Pavilion*. As the show begins, the Brothers, eager to get a room for the night, see a sign off the old highway for available rooms. They pull up in the Bluesmobile (1974 Dodge Monaco sedan in police stripes), where Mr. Psycho himself, Norman Bates, greets them. Norman instructs them that they must meet his host for the evening and with that Beetlejuice would appear from the grave, leaping from an actual open trench. Together they performed a number of song and dance routines.

Next up for the "ghost with the most" was *Beetlejuice LIVE (dead) in concert* which ran every night for two performances backed by the cast of the daytime park show, *Ghostbusters Spooktacular*. *Ghostbusters*, which had been a runaway hit in the 1980s with two fantastic movies and a cartoon TV series, was the perfect outlet for the park. The nightly show was similar to a seasonal show held on the steps of the New York Public Library within the park called *Streetbusters*. *Streetbusters* would later be replaced in 2002 by *Extreme Ghostbusters: The Great Fright Way* which itself would be replaced altogether in 2005.

The Beetlejuice LIVE (dead) in concert however would be a beefed-up version of the former show extended with more tongue-in-cheek bad humor and less kid-friendly gags. An unsightly cabaret performance from our Ghost Host would begin the show. He would open by singing (or screaming?) *My Favorite Things* from the movie *The Sound of Music*, with the lyrics changed in best Beetlejuice fashion to

"frogs in your oatmeal, dung in your sneakers, blackheads and whiteheads, squirts and leaches with moustaches, roaches with wings - these are a few of my favorite things."

Long gone were the raindrops on roses and whiskers on kittens! After *The Sound of Mucus* (sorry!), he then went on to perform *I got (you) Mildew* where he was disrupted by our heroes, the Ghostbusters. Arriving in their classic ECTO-1 vehicle, the Ectomobile was a 1959 Cadillac Miller-Meteor limo-style (with ambulance conversion) used in the first 1984 film *Ghostbusters*. Arriving on the scene, the team would stop Beetlejuice in his tracks, interrupt his rendition and then perform their songs. They would start with their own version of Gaye Marvin's – *Aint No Mountain High Enough*, along with a medley of *C & C Music factory's Everybody Dance Now*, Madonna*'s Vogue* and then the 1990 chart topper MC Hammer's *U Can't Touch This aka Hammer time*. It was then during the final number that Beetlejuice would join in and depart with the gang in the Ecto-1, played out to their Ray Parker Jnr signature theme song. "Who ya gonna call?" they asked; "Beetlejuice!" he shouted over the cheering crowd as the team majestically departed.

Just over the street from this show - situated on the corner near Finnegan's Bar and Grill - was another show that was much more grotesque. *The Chainsaw Massacre* debuted there for what would, over the coming years, evolve into another Halloween Horror Nights tradition. The show was based around a number of chainsaw-wielding maniacs who had taken to the stage to sacrifice supposedly unfortunate guests (in fact they were perfectly situated members of the crew). As the ad hoc victims were carefully selected and pulled unwillingly onto the stage, the chief of the chainsaw maniacs would begin their induction by describing the things that were about to happen to them. Then as quickly as it had begun various body parts of the "guests" were cut off live on stage and then tossed into the audience. Plastic body parts were thrown into the crowd along with sprays of fake blood (water) to ensure ultimate horror compliance for the gasping audience members. Such was the success of this humble show, that those chainsaw-wielding maniacs would eventually evolve into the chainsaw Drill Team and variations of that team would be seen in the years to come at the event.

Also in this area were *Dr. Death's Show*, *The Human Pincushion*, *Magical Mania*, *Madam Kuszel – The Gypsy Fortune Teller*, *Cobra Woman* and *Dragon Breath*. Whereas the other shows used fixed stages, these performers and their assistants mingled with the crowd and acted as great mini-attractions. There weren't any official scarezones at this first Halloween event but if there was anything that resembled a scarezone it had to be the New York area. It was like a travelling circus had taken over downtown New York and was putting on an impromptu show for anyone and everyone present. From magicians doing close-up magic tricks to a man eating fire, these were the days when activities like these could be performed at close quarters and everyone stood back and gasped in sheer delight and amazement. The level of detail here was definitely different as performers here were mostly independent and provided their own makeup and props, some of which were truly terrifying!

Between the newly opened *Back to the Future: The Ride* and *The Swamp Thing* sets, a newly-installed stage was erected. The park map declared that *The Gravediggers* would be performing and that the show would feature Laurel and Hardy. *The Gravediggers* were a rock-come-punk band of the 1980/90s who had reasonable success throughout the States. As they performed some of their songs and covers, two Universal staff members dressed as Laurel and Hardy would entertain the crowds. As the band performed *Monsters At Play* Laurel was spotted crying due to being scared by this perfectly suited horror-based band. Also in this area, another stage was set for the *Universal Science Band* right behind the *Animal Actors' stage*. A troupe of park employees with musical talents, playing various instruments, bellowed out *The Monster Mash* and *My Skin Crawls* to the gathering audience. Behind them, inside the *Animal Actors' stage,* was a magicians' act from the group *The Pendragons*, performing five times per night. *The Pendragons* were a husband-and-wife team based in California that called their magical act the 'physical grand illusion'. Numerous set pieces and props were used, including a scene where Jonathan caught a bullet in his teeth. They later collaborated again with Universal at Hollywood where their show, *Cinemystique: Illusions of the Night* ran in the *Castle Theatre* in the Upper Lot for three months between June and September of 1994. It was later crowned the winner of the "Best Magic Show of the Year".

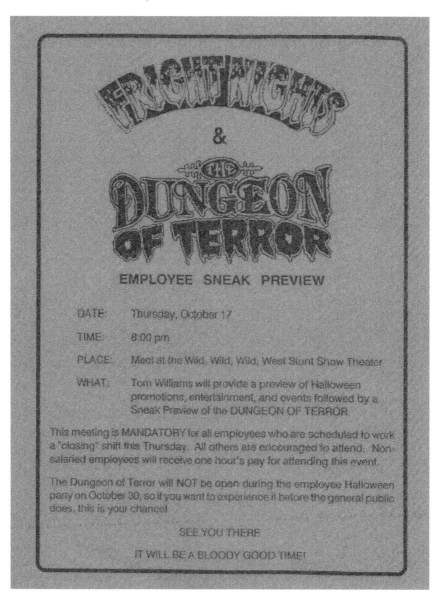

A copy of the flyer handed to Universal staff for their first ever preview!

Over the lagoon at Amity, *Prince Dragon* performed between the now-closed Jaws lake and Lombard's Seafood Grille, which was primarily a sword and stunt demonstration. Further down the street in the San Francisco area we had *Iron Belly*, who performed right outside Lombard's. *Iron Belly* was primarily a tattooed man with assistant, who ate fire and ice in front of a gathering crowd. It is quite foreboding that immediately behind where this small stage was temporarily situated in the lagoon, a timed fire canon would be installed for subsequent Halloween Horror Nights events, almost like homage (though probably and completely coincidental)! Up the road from *Iron Belly* was *Dr. Frankenstein's Theater*, featuring *Mistress of the Night*, *Frankenstein* and *Dracula*. The show was a horror-comedy style show taking place in the then-*American Tail Theatre*, and featured characters such as Victor Frankenstein, Count Dracula and Frankenstein's Monster. It shows the power of this event that this opening day attraction was then completely re-themed to become *Beetlejuice's Rock and Roll Graveyard Revue show*, which borrowed the costumes, songs and story from this temporary Halloween show to be played out daily to day guests. The main difference was that the host for each performance would rotate. Most nights, Frankenstein (well, his monster) would be the host at the 8pm show and then Dracula would take over at the 10pm show. Also in this area, just over to the side of Richter's Burger place, was the *Human Impaler* who had five nightly shows to perform. The classic Universal monsters also prowled the park from start to finish popping up in different locations.

Over in the Hollywood area of the park, *Starshower* performed as the warm-up for *Paul Revere & the Raiders*. *Starshower* had performed locally for many years. *Paul Revere & the Raiders* had been formed way back in 1958 but had come to prominence in the 1960s with their first official release in 1961. Their classic tracks such as *Kicks*, which was ranked number 400 on *Rolling Stone* magazine's list of The 500 Greatest Songs of All Time, was performed high on the temporary stage erected across from Mel's Drive-In, along with *Hungry, Him Or Me - What's It Gonna Be?* and their platinum-selling number one hit *Indian Reservation* (The Lament of the Cherokee Reservation Indian), which got park guests in the groove nightly at 9.45pm.

Along with all these great temporary shows and attractions, some of the regular day attractions were open. These included: *The Funtastic World of Hanna-Barbera* (Production Central), the *Murder, She Wrote Mystery Theatre* (Production Central), *Ghostbusters Spooktacular* (New York), *Kongfrontation* (New York), *Earthquake: The Big One* (San Francisco), *The Wild Wild Wild West Stunt Show* (Amity), *Back to the*

Future: The Ride (World Expo), *E.T. Adventure* (World Expo), *The Gory Gruesome and Grotesque Horror Make-Up Show* (Hollywood) and *Alfred Hitchcock: The Art of Making Movies* (Production Central) which even had an actor posing as Norman Bates at the exit just to give an extra scare or two. There was also for special guests of the event's main sponsor *Pepsi*, a special VIP party which was held on select nights by invitation only.

As the park closed a little after midnight on 31st October 1991, the clean-up began and the I4 was once again filled with worn-out party goers. Park Management knew they had a hit on their hands and so did Disney. Reports quickly spread of the first ever mention of Universal within the Disney World departmental newsletter. "Universal Studios Florida and Walt Disney World are tough competitors. So it was surprising to see Universal's *Fright Nights* event for Halloween praised in a Disney departmental newsletter", ran the article at the time, written by a Disney cast member who had attended one of the nights at the *Fright Nights* event. They described how successful the park was in turning itself into a Halloween attraction for weekend. The article read "While it is true that Universal Studios is the competition, they do have a great product (although *E.T.* leaves something to be desired) and can put on a great show." Suddenly, if only for a moment, Disney was starting to notice what their smaller competitor could achieve.

Icon Issues

Ok, now you've read the chapter about the actual *Fright Nights* event, I want you to look at the above "Fright Nights 1991 Universal Logo". The icon or icons of each Halloween Horror Nights would grow to become an important tradition and for this initial event the park opted for the ultimate horror icons, that of the Universal Monsters. So look carefully now at this logo. From left to right it features The Wolfman, The Bride of Frankenstein, Frankenstein's Monster, Dracula, The Creature From The Black Lagoon and The Mummy. However, one of them does not look as he should. The Wolfman looks perfectly like Lon Chaney Jnr's classic version, Boris Karloff's The Mummy and Frankenstein's Monster all look spot on, Both the Creature and the Bride, the latter made famous by Elsa Lanchester look exactly as they did in their classic movies, but Dracula does not look anywhere near as he should. Dracula was played most famously for Universal Studios by Hungarian born actor Bela Lugosi.

Lugosi had been starring in silent movies since 1917 (that year alone he made 12 films!) starting in Hungary and then in Germany. Germany at the time was experiencing a boom in its film industry where masterpieces such as the first sci-fi Franz Lang's *Metropolis* was created and a young Alfred Hitchcock first cut his teeth learning the craft of early German expressionist style. Soon after, the debonair and enthusiastic actor hopped on a ferry and travelled to America where their film industry was starting to emerge. Working initially as a laborer, the actor soon found his feet and appeared in a number of films in smaller roles. It wasn't until 1927 that he was signed to star in a Broadway production of *Bram Stoker's Dracula* adapted by Hamilton Deane and John L. Balderston. The production was very successful. It ran for exactly 261 performances before touring the States for just over two years, but soon after, Lugosi relocated to Hollywood to star in more character parts in early talkies.

In 1931 he was signed to portray his stage version of *Dracula* in film. Universal produced the film, directed by Tod Browning. The film was a colossal hit with audiences around the world and forever immortalized Lugosi as Dracula. This was a type-casting he would later learn to love and build a brand around. Lugosi went on to play the vampire on numerous occasions and was a crucial part of the franchise of monster movies produced by Universal during this time, playing not just the vampire himself but a collection of other creepy characters, most notably Ygor in *Son of Frankenstein*.

Towards the end of his career in the 1950s he starred in scores of low-budget movies. It wasn't until after his death that the image he had struggled to shift and that he later he capitalized into a personal franchise for himself started to cause problems for his descendants. He passed away peacefully on his couch in 1956, however by the 1960s the brand was now in high demand. New monster movies were being made in vast quantities in both the States but also (most notably) in Britain (with Hammer films) and in Italy. Renewed interest in the classic Universal Monsters was starting to peak again.

At the height of this renewed popularity in 1971 his descendants, Hope Linninger Lugosi and Bela George Lugosi (his fifth wife and his son), took Universal to court over their use of their late father's image which was widely used with the other Classic Universal Monsters during this time. Such was the advent of television, syndication, mass production of merchandise and pop culture that the Universal Monsters were in demand all over the world, and Lugosi's heirs felt his constant use and popularity should not just benefit the Universal corporation. Initially discussions were held informally before a court action was processed at California Supreme Court firstly around 1974 and then reviewed in 1977. The case rumbled on until a decision was made formally in December 1979.

Headlines in the national newspapers quickly capitalized on the story, citing that "Dracula rises from the dead to haunt previous employers". The question the court considered was whether Bela Lugosi's film contracts with Universal included granting of merchandising rights for his portrayal of the character Dracula from his original 1931 movie, and whether these rights could be adopted by his descendants. The hotly debated case was initially ruled in favor of Universal as personal likenesses could not be transferred, however the case was appealed.

Justice Roth for the Court of Appeal, Second Appellate District, upheld that the right to exploit one's name and likeness is personal to the said artist. The Supreme Court of California awarded the heirs $72,000 and ordered Universal not to enter into any more licensing agreements with the actor's likeness for the purposes of marketing or merchandising, however the ruling stopped short of losing all rights and licenses to the original 1931 Universal movie. The decision was later appealed citing that Lugosi himself made little commercial gain for exploiting his image as the classical Dracula. The State Court of Appeal overturned the original trial court and then two years later (prior to 1979) the State Supreme Court decided the appeal court was actually right. This left the whole issue much more conflicting but left Universal in no doubt that they had lost their use of Bela Lugosi's likeness of their famous movie character.

California's descendibility statute, which was the right enacted in the final court case for their decision, which covers the rights of publicity and their entitlements (named Civil Code Section 990), was later brought about at court again in 1988. Lugosi's descendants now have the rights to license for any commercial use of Lugosi's name and image from any of the movies he was portrayed in. Depending on the suit filed, the right of publicity in some states remains for 50, 70, 75, up to a maximum of 100 years past the date of the death of the performer. Therefore by the 1991 *Fright Nights* event, Universal would have had to pay for his image to be in the logo and that is why he, unlike the others, is not present. It is not known if it was a monetary issue for the fledgling event, as the budget was likely strict for an event where it was not known how successful it would be or whether the courts' recent decisions about using the character as portrayed by Lugosi was far more problematic.

This is a nice little unknown fact that is easily missed by the public and fans of the event but is equally important to know and forms part of the legacy of this great event.

Halloween Horror Nights: 2nd Annual

The event in 1991 called *Fright Nights* had been such a success for the new park that this year would be bigger and bolder with some five nights of Halloween entertainment. This year the event would have a larger budget (reportedly $1million) and would aim to reach out to all fans of not just horror but anyone looking to have a truly unique experience and good time. Planning for the 2nd event started January 8th that year when a full management meeting was held to discuss and plan all the options for the coming year. Everything that worked from the previous year would return, everything that failed would be dropped and the lessons learned would be implemented. Extensive minutes were taken at this meeting, which I shall refer to later.

The previous event had surpassed even the highest expectations for the park's management.
"We [at Universal Studios] see Halloween growing into a 10-day observance," it was said proudly by Universal Studios Florida PR Manager Joseph Curley. The park now had the confidence to pull off what could be a world staging event. Articles in the local newspapers ran rumors and speculation that Universal was starting to think bigger for the next event but also long-term. *The Orlando Sentinel* wrote: "All Hallow's Eve: Do people actually pack up and take Halloween vacations? And, if so, can Orlando become the destination of choice? Universal Studios Florida is betting on it". Such is the commitment of Universal that they knew from these very early days just what their small dedicated team of production technicians, artisans and craftsmen and women could seek to achieve.

Marketing was stepped up a gear for 1992, and they needed to as the name was about to change. *Fright Nights* of 1991 was about to become the name that is used to this day. It is not known officially why the name changed, however there are two main theories. The first is that the name may have been changed due to the film rights to this name being used in 1985. *Fright Night* (not Nights) was a 1985 American horror-comedy-fantasy movie written and directed by Tom Holland (a former assistant and student of Alfred Hitchcock). It starred William Ragsdale, Roddy McDowall and Amanda Bearse. The film's plot follows young Charley who discovers that his next-door neighbor, Jerry Dandrige, is actually a vampire. When no one believes him, Charley decides to get Peter Vincent, a famous vampire hunter and local cable TV presenter, to stop Jerry from starting a local killing spree. The film also spawned various sequels, comics and a remake some years later. Did Universal feel their newly formed brand might get confused with this movie? Nobody is sure.

The other formative theory is more complex but boils down to trademark usages. At the time in 1980/90s America there seemed to be a number of events across the country using the same or similar name to *Frights Nights*. First up was the country-wide Six Flags theme park corporation which held select 'Six Flags Fright Fest' or 'Fright Fest', and had done so since the late 1980s. Smaller events had been held going back to the late 1970s with no official naming of the event. They also trademarked the use of the name *Fright Nights* on December 20, 1988 for their first official 1989 event at their Texas park, though seemingly changed their minds and actually stuck with 'Six Flags Fright Fest' instead. Around the same time, the Anheuser-Busch corporation who also operated a small number of theme parks were starting to think about getting into the Halloween business. They even trademarked the name 'Fright Nights' in September 11, 1987 for use at their brewery in St. Louis, Missouri but nothing came of this and the Busch Gardens, we know today, only started offering their response to Halloween Horror Nights in a bigger way in 2000. There were also smaller events dotted across the country with fairs and travelling circuses that had used the name in the last 30 years. So was it due to some possible confusion with other operators that Universal changed the name? Though we are not certain about either of

the theories, Universal was certain about this event and billed it the 'Second Annual Halloween Horror Nights'. We do know, though, that a decision must have been made on or before September 2, 1992 as that was the day Universal applied for a trademark for the use of the name 'Halloween Horror Nights' and it was officially trademarked on September 2, 1992. The name had been borrowed from the smaller event of 1986 held at the Hollywood Studios Park, along with the use of the pumpkin receiving a blow from above as a ripping chainsaw was cutting into it; both of which soon became synonymous with the event.

"[This year] it would be like *Mardi Gras* in New Orleans. People would say, 'It's Halloween, let's head for Orlando.'" Joseph Curley was reported as saying (though his words were like a strange premonition for their own *Mardi Gras* event that would one day start at Universal in Orlando). The aim would be to bring everything that worked well in the first year back for the second year, add some new attractions, enhance some of their own attractions and really tailor the event to the people who were buying the tickets. Those buying them were adults and teenagers. Due to this shift in direction, the park actively made the classic Universal monsters take a side step. No longer would they be the main draw of the event, though they were featured on the streets and in some of the marketing. The classic monsters were definitely kept by the *Pepsi Cola* Company's marketing of the event, as they preferred their more wholesome appearance whilst plastering their images over their bottles across the aisles at the supermarkets and gas stations of Central Florida. In their place would be a more dedicated emphasis on popular culture that Universal would try to weave into every attraction on offer. Their aim was to keep festivities relevant, contemporary and wholly unlike anything their Mousey neighbor could possible put on. Joseph Curley said, "One way you can tell Halloween Horror Nights takes place at Universal and not Disney: There's a show featuring a Madonna impersonator, complete with the cones!"

You couldn't get more contemporary than that.

As the previous year's event held over three nights sold out, this event was held over five nights on Oct. 23, 24, 29, 30 and 31. The park closed again daily at 5.30pm, reopening at 6pm for guests of the hard ticketed event. A separate admission for the event of $22.95 was charged with the park closing at 1 am. Day visitors to the park could "stay and scream all night" paying just $12.95 to stay that same evening.

But it wasn't just the pop culture that would be ramped up, Universal was also aiming to ramp up the scares too. "We get the gears going inside your head by slowly building the suspense," said Tony Peugh, who helped design Universal's Halloween haunted studio sets. Starting with scary music and the sense of frightening people nearby, Universal's studio gradually works to a crescendo. "The idea is to keep the customer off-balance," he said.

Returning to the *Jaws* queue building, due mostly in part to the attraction still being under construction but also due to the fact that the location and size of the building was perfect for the creation of a haunted maze, was the exceedingly popular original house, the *Dungeon of Terror*. The original house had been dismantled carefully after park bosses immediately noted that the first event was such a success. This time the house would be re-used but it would not be exactly the same. Criticisms of the 1991 house was that it was too short.

"We'd waited in the humidity with no air-conditioning for 3 hours and the house was less than 5 minutes to walk through!" one annoyed guest had noted. This time the house would be longer with more set pieces and a few alterations to the original layout.

"At one point, those walking through are threatened by monsters on one side. On the other side is a mirror. The effect is to have customers bouncing back and forth between each side, recoiling from the monsters on one side, only to face them in the mirror on the other," said Tony Peugh about the new house. The result of the changes lead to the three hour waits of the previous year being extended to an average of four.

The other house at this event was based on a recent Universal Studios-released picture called *The People Under the Stairs*. The movie had been released the previous year in November of 1991 and was an American horror film written and directed by Wes Craven and starring Brandon Adams, Everett McGill, Wendy Robie, A. J. Langer, Ving Rhames and Sean Whalen. Craven had famously been the creator of the ever-popular *A Nightmare on Elm Street* franchise featuring the hideous Freddy Krueger character. *The People Under the Stairs* however was a Universal picture and had been reasonably successful. Filming of the movie had taken place the year before at Universal Studios Hollywood in one of the soundstages, and fortunately, due to Universal's investment in extending their prop warehouse to be one of the largest in the world, all of the sets and props from the movie were put into storage. Universal executives had hoped that a sequel would be in the pipeline, hence the use of the storage, and once the hopes of this were dashed the Studios in Florida came calling. Around the summer of 1992 the sets and props were all boxed up in Hollywood and carefully shipped down to Florida where they were assembled again, but this time into a house format inside Soundstage 23. Soundstage 23 had been used occasionally by all parties on the lot over the first few years, but had been used mostly in the early days by *Nickelodeon Studios* who often used the soundstage when their own soundstages were already engaged in filming. Nick's popular show *GUTS* had used the soundstage as rehearsal space and they were given other space for this to make way for the building of the house.

The construction was reported as being difficult from the outset within the massive 16,000-square-foot space. Workers were piecing together sets that had been used from a movie and were wholly temporary for each shot. This time round, they had to be more robust to cope with the thousands of party goers that would no doubt cause damage to the sets if they had not been shored up thoroughly, which took time. So much time, that although the sets were already constructed when delivered, the putting together, installing walkways and shoring them up actually took longer than the initial build of *Dungeon of Terror* the year previously.

"We also experimented a little in this house due to the fact we had more space because it had been located in one of the soundstages," said John Paul Geurts, producer of the event. He continued, "We had tried claustrophobic environments before to great effect, which were used throughout the house anyway, so we decided near the end that we would open up the house and put in a night's sky that would be beautifully dressed with stars and a moon etc., to make guests feel like they were outside but really inside. Unfortunately, it came apparent very early on during 'night one' that this scene was causing a backlog. Instead of people remarking on the scene and then moving out of the house, people were actively taking minutes to pause which caused not only a back-up along the route so guests were getting stuck in some of the scary scenes but also the queue to move really slow. We then tried to pulse guests through rather than allow a continuous flow through the house, but that didn't work either. It was then we came up with the idea of 'scare-moving', whereby when guests would arrive at this final scene we would put scareactors lurking inside near where the guests entered, who would then jump-out at select times to literally scare the guests out the door. It became such an effective technique to keep the queue moving, that they still use that technique to this very day!"

Lifted directly from the motion picture, the house featured themes such as cannibalism, incest, home invasion, sadism and poverty - a mixed bunch of adult themes that proved the house to be as horrific as the movie it was based on. This was a modern event for a modern audience in a claustrophobic setting (like the movie) which snaked around the large soundstage to great effect. Simulated mutilations were played out in one room, human taxidermy in another and dangling body parts decorated the corridors with the gore setting set to maximum! One overly enthusiastic scareactor within the cryptic set actually took it upon himself to add more fake blood within his scene. With such realism, he added to his performance the actual fake blood (red dyed corn syrup), which was reportedly sprayed over several guests while they enjoyed the house. Reportedly, one angry park guest with a now stained white T-shirt headed right for Guest Services to demand something was done. Universal reportedly responded by ensuring no future occurrences of staff members improvising with their own props was to ever happen again. But despite this minor setback, the house was a massive draw and lines quickly grew around the soundstage to be immersed straight into the hit movie. Before, you could ride the movies. Now you could physically be a part of, and interact within, a movie!

The People Under the Stairs wasn't the only film franchise to be utilized at the event. For one of the first and only times in the event's history, different rides were repurposed into temporary Halloween-themed attractions. Seeing the ride like never before was a true highlight, and this process took the pressure off of the two official houses. *Darkman* was immediately put into *Kongrontation* to become *Tramway of Doom*. *Darkman* was released in 1990, an American superhero action film directed and co-written by Sam Raimi (of *Spider-Man* and *Evil Dead* franchises). Raimi supposedly flew to Orlando to see his creation being applied at the event. The movie was originally based on a short story Raimi wrote that paid homage to Universal's classic early horror films of the 1930s. The film starred Liam Neeson as Peyton Westlake, a scientist who is attacked and left for dead by a mobster. Raimi was unable to secure the rights to either *The Shadow* or *Batman* franchises, so decided to create his own superhero and struck a deal with the motion pictures arm of Universal Studios to make his very first major motion picture.

The general theme of the ride was now changed. Yes, King Kong was on the loose and attacking your tram but you also had Darkman lurking behind every corner. Inevitably the staff members dressed as the popular movie character would be lurking within the expansive queue, but also at the end of the attraction, when to exit the attraction guests would then walk on the ground of the ride through the streets of New York that had been temporary repurposed as a short haunted house. Many guests remarked on the detail of the sets in New York, thinking that this level of detail had been added specifically for the event but it hadn't. The detail had always been there, such was the testament to the excellent quality to detail that Universal put into all their rides. Guests were also permitted to walk one final time on the ground of the attraction during Halloween Horror Nights XI, for the show *The Oozone Fright Club*, where guests entered a staff members' only area of the queue line, and then had to exit to the ground where another haunted house had been constructed. It was also noted by many attendees at the event that some of the Darkmen(?) actually rode in the trams with guests, which totally unnerved some people. One guest was overheard to say, "he looks like an evil cross between The Invisible Man and The Mummy, totally freaky!" What a premonition that a Mummy might occupy the building...

And *Kong* wasn't the only attraction to have the creepiness beefed up for the event either. *ET's* popular ride had the queue temporary reimagined. The tranquil Southern California redwood forest of the snaking queue was pumped with bellows of dry ice and ghoulish scareactors awaited on every turn. Some guests were so terrified they ran through the queue to escape to the relative tameness of the popular family ride! The newly opened and extremely popular *Back to the Future ride* was also given a similar makeover. This time ghouls and fog machines made way for mad scientists and strobe lighting. A crazy disco theme played out and crazy longhaired mad scientists with blood splattered white coats lurked behind every corner of the expansive queue area. Some guests even reported being chased out to the gift shop such was the lengthy and twisting layout of the exit path from some of the attraction's higher load areas. And Universal wasn't finished there with their ride makeovers or 'horror-fying'; *Earthquake*, which had recently been tweaked due to on-going maintenance issues, also got in on the act. At points, mostly during the queue section of the ride and the pre-show, various scareactors would be on the scene to scare up some frights and entertain guests before loading onto their ride vehicle.

Other rides and attractions that were open on these nights included: *The Funtastic World of Hanna-Barbera*, *Hitchcock's 3-D Theater*, *The Horror Make-Up Show*, (the recently installed-) *Beetlejuice's Graveyard Review* and the popular day-time *Ghostbusters' show*. *The Bates Motel* became an official photospot to take your picture with various Universal monsters and even characters from the popular syndicated show *The Munsters*. The popular *Pendragons Magic Show* from the previous year was back with fresh new tricks to amaze a waiting audience and the *Carnival of Horror* costume contest was also put on, with similar rules and restrictions as the previous year but it was only held on October 24 at 7pm.

Thunderdome debuted this year, based loosely from the motion picture *Mad Max Beyond Thunderdome* (as it was not a Universal property), with the stage mounted half way down the Hollywood Boulevard area of the park. It starred the Queen of Darkness and her evil Thunderdome henchmen, who seized guests from the crowd (well, cast members made to look like guests) to be tortured live (well maybe dead) on stage. Soon they would be locked in cages and lowered into a boiling vat of acid, reducing them to mere skeletons; which was neat addition that combined both horror and magic to great effect.

"Wanted - Person to share small, dark coffin with 100 live rats", ran on various ads in the local newspapers. Help-wanted ads ran over the weekend in eight Florida newspapers.

"The park has three Rat People but wants two more," said Universal spokeswoman Linda Buckley. The local ad would go on to make national headlines and for the first time in the event's history it would start to get national attention. "Those who get the job will wear Victorian garb and play possum in a coffin while dozens of rats crawl over them," she said.

Several applications were received with a general mix of both genders applying for the part. The Rat Lady had been so popular as one of the main scares in the *Dungeon* house that bringing her (or him) back would be a must-do for Universal Creative.

She continued, "These are the real McCoys - living, breathing critters with long tails and whiskers. And yes, sometimes they nip." It was a tough job and not for the faint-hearted but the remuneration for the role was more vocational than financial. The pay, you ask? "More than minimum wage, but not as much as (park president) Tom Williams," she said. However this time, she wouldn't be a fixed scare in that house, she would be mobile. Wheeled through the streets in a glass coffin (something that would later become her signature) the handler of the coffin would shout "come see a woman encased alive in a glass coffin filled with sewer dwelling rodents!"

As with the previous year, no official scarezones were set up, so instead assorted scareactors dressed as ghouls, vampires and monsters (including the Classic Universal Monsters) were deployed to roam the park. 300 scareactors were employed that year to roam nightly in the park, something that was a real challenge for Universal's 40 employed makeup artists headed-up by Hollywood makeup artist extraordinaire Joe Blasco. He said, "This is the biggest event of its kind ever. I was an apprentice to Ben Nye on the original 'Planet of the Apes', and we never did even close to this many apes at a time, maybe 80 at once at the most".

The scareactors each night seemed to congregate mostly around the New York, San Francisco and Amity areas of the park. Amity was also home to a district loosely titled 'Midway of the Bizarre', where scareactors named Blade Walker, Bone Bender and The Hex Maniac terrified guests as they left the signature house of the event from the *Jaws* queue building.

The event had many nationally famous acts attend for the festivities and none was larger (well physically at least) than the very popular *Robosaurus* who made his official debut at the event that year. *Robosaurus* was a transforming dinosaur robot (like a real-life transformer but not) created by engineer Doug Malewicki in 1989 but later sold to new owner

Monster Robots, Inc.

Robosaurus is operated by a driver sitting in the head of the robot, and was built with the ability to transform from a 48-foot semi-trailer into a mobile, mechanical Tyrannosaurus Rex. It had hydraulically activated arms, large grasping claws and jaws, and a flame thrower mounted in the head to give the effect of breathing fire out of its metal nostrils. It is still used today at motorsport and football events (particularly monster truck events) and even air shows to 'eat' and burn vehicles such as cars and small airplanes for various audiences. Jay Stein had originally seen *Robosaurus* on the West Coast, happening upon a show that the metal giant was doing while he was on a business meeting. After the show he called Julie Zimmerman and said "we need to bring this sensation to the Halloween event!" Zimmerman made enquiries of the owners and found that the small budget she had left over would not cover the fees to bring the monster to the Orlando event. She called Stein and told him that they wanted $150,000 (she had budget left over that was less than a fifth of that figure); Stein reportedly said, "I'll find the cash, you make the arrangements." Zimmerman recalls, "I couldn't believe it, but if Jay wanted it, we did it!"

The car-eating dinosaur was booked and proved extremely popular.

Mounted in the New York area of the park between the *Ghostbusters show* and the New York Public Library steps, the mechanical maniac acted as a giant weenie for entering park guests. Riding along the streets from the *Boneyard* area and then into position, the giant robot transformed into his trademark dinosaur appearance, standing at a height of 40 feet when fully extended, with a weight of 31 tons. Picking up car props that were provided, guests stood in astonishment as the beast picked up and then proceeded to eat the vehicles. Then just as park guests were reconciling what they were watching, the transforming mechanical reptilian spat vast lengths of fire from its nostrils and let fireworks off from its body. This surely was unlike anything that had been witnessed before, and indeed the first day saw the owners of the car-eating dino witness something they had never seen before!

It was on the first night of the event at the last show that the fire-spewing dinosaur was munching his way through his last car of the night. The cars were nearly always provided by the host of the event. The host (Universal) had to ensure that the vehicles used were all drained of gas, oil, batteries and combustible materials, which to Universal's credit they had paid to arrange. The problem was, that unbeknown to all, the final car had not been fully drained of gas. *Robosaurus* brought the car to its jaws and crushed down on the frame.

This punctured the tank, thus allowing gas to pour out of the car and into the mouth of the beast. A HUGE explosion was seen! The crowds, who were safely behind the barriers cheered in awe at the massive detonation. However, Universal and the dinosaur's controllers knew there was a problem. Within seconds the now burning gas had poured onto the street (far within the boundary) and was alight around the beast. Universal called the Fire Department (who were already on standby). Literally within minutes, the fire trucks pulled up and started to tackle the blaze and within a short while the fire was contained and put out. The crowds cheered and applauded the fire officers, still thinking it was all part of the show! Feedback from leaving guests that night said a mixture of how great the party was in general, but that the show with the *Robosaurus* was unmissable! Little did they know what they had in fact witnessed had been a robust and prompt response from Universal to actually save the day. Everyone thought it was the greatest show ever!

Also making their debut that year were a small, humble show duo of dudes who would go on to define the event but had started that year with very modest intentions. They were Bill S. Preston, Esq. and Ted "Theodore" Logan, the wild stallions themselves: Bill and Ted in the ever-popular *Bill and Ted's Excellent Halloween Adventure*. There were four shows each night, with two different casts alternating through the event. One half of the first's duo was cast member Toby Miller who played the part of Bill, who at the time was a ride attendant at *Kongrontation,* picked for the part for his uncanny resemblance to Alex Winter from the original movies. The other half, who played Ted, was *Back to the Future ride* attendant Joel Buntin who had a great ability to mimic Keanu Reeves.

Buntin said, "I've seen the movie 26 times . . . definitely know it pretty well. We each have friends that look like the other characters, so we've been doing it with them for about . . . well, I've been doing it for about three years."

"I've only been doing it for about a year and two months," Miller went on to say. "I saw *Excellent Adventure* and *Bogus Journey* like back to back in the same week, and I've never seen it before, ever. And I totally fell in love with the dudes!"

The other respective duo were John Gallagher, who was working as a studio tour guide at the time and Robert Ramos, a cast member from the daytime show of the *Ghostbusters*. Ramos was reported as saying at the time that he got into character by watching the original movie "about 550,000 times".

The main actors, along with the supporting cast, had been carefully selected some months prior, with full rehearsals starting exactly one month before opening night. The show, which was held at the *Wild, Wild, Wild West Stunt Show* building, would feature singing, dancing, comedy and event stunts. The show was set in an old western cowboy town, the lights dimmed and *Queen's We Will Rock You* was blasted out of the speakers prompting the audience to sing along (a song that would return almost every year with the show).

The show began with a stand-off between the town's Sheriff and a plucky bank robber. Just as the guns are drawn, Bill and Ted arrive on the set in their iconic phone booth, apparently lost from their mission to go trick or treating through time. The evil bank robber decides to corner the boys and steal their time-travelling booth to round up a new bank-robbing gang from history. After he leaves in a cloud of smoke in the booth, Bill finds that he has a portable telephone for emergencies which he can use to remote control the booth and bring it back to the town. But after he dials the number, instead of their booth appearing a DeLorian appears in a blaze of *Huey Lewis'* rock ballad *The Power of Love* driven by none other than Doc Brown (from *Back to the Future*)...

The Doc explains that they must bring back the devilish bank robber, but with the aid of famous musicians from past and present to help out. Just as the travelling booth re-appears with the robber, it contains an evil assortment of villains to aid in the robber's attempt to rob the town's bank (no less than Freddy Krueger, the Terminator and Jason). Fighting breaks out between the two groups and various stunts are undertaken. These include falls from various buildings (this and others lifted right from the *Western Show* which the temporary show had replaced), a fall down a supposed well, explosions and various props being smashed over each other's' heads. The fighting climaxes as the town's Sheriff gun downs the bank robber.

When the bank robber is no more and the villains have dispersed, Bill and Ted decide to hold a "most excellent" musical concert with their favorite performers, including: *MC Hammer, The Blues Brothers, Madonna* and an extremely portly Elvis! As they collectively sing and dance various contemporary musical numbers, including guitar solos (ex-cel-lent), they end with a version of Elvis' *Shout!* where the audience is encouraged to sing along. As the number finishes the house is literally brought down when the classic house façade in the middle comes tumbling down right to the actor playing Doc Brown's surprise. The audience immediately stand, cheering and clapping, and so a Halloween Horror Night's mainstay is born.

The performances didn't go without issues though as various special effects did not work in some performances. Both duos were reported to be extremely professional, even adlibbing lines to make-up for the minor setbacks that were seen. The audience didn't care though; they loved the show! The park stationed merchandise carts at the exits, selling t-shirts depicting Bill and Ted sitting on their phone booths with the Universal classic monsters cramped inside, along with baseball caps featuring the classic Bill and Ted logo. The carts were reported as being sold out nearly every night, such was the demand for this very early example of event merchandise. The 'Wyld Stallyns' had arrived and they were here to stay!

Other attractions at the event which were more party-like and musical included a mini-rock concert that was held at the *Mel's Drive-In Theater area* (with the lights first turned off at this event to read 'Mel's Die-In'). The radio presenter and personality Wolfman Jack DJ-ed this attraction and compered the show with three nightly performances. Performers included Roni G and Joe Savage, 'The Madman of Rock n' Roll'. The latter, a leather-wearing, larger-than-life character bolted out covers (but in his own particular style) of *Neil Diamond's America* and *Queen's We Are The Champions.*

Referring to the minutes of the initial planning meeting in January of that year, the ideas that were floated but never implemented included:

- A roaming tribute to Alfred Hitchcock and the *MCA* Monsters Universe was planned to create a walking photo opportunity (this would be the bare bones of what later would be called a scarezone).
- A musical revue band to play and dance near the entrance.
- A *Mardi Gras* style parade (that would come later in the event's run).
- "Halloween Hayride to Hell" stunt show to be penned by Ron Schneider, which would feature a *Ghost Town* for guests to explore.
- An 'Elvira' type show featuring a vamp like presenter doing a comedy and music number on a temporary stage.
- Public execution within the *Boneyard* area of the park that would feature an assortment of "hated" celebrities begging the grim reaper for their life and career back. A "It's a Wonderful Life" meets "Celebrity Roasts" styled comedy show on a temporary stage in the area now directly outside Jimmy Fallon.
- Good quality sideshow acts that engage with the public – good quality was underlined in the minutes!

Many of these ideas would be implemented in later years but it didn't stop the 2nd year running from a rip roaring success.

"You have to keep saying in your head, 'It's fake, it's fake,' but it's hard to believe it because it looks so real!" said park guest Michelle Martin.

"Gross" others said. "Scary! Really scary!" said Nicole Porter, from Levittown, N.Y., who said she had seen the movie and was more frightened by the live production. Ronnie Bach, aged 49, of Palm Harbor said, "That was the scariest experience I've ever had in my life. Better than Disney." Phrases like, "this is completely unique, like nothing we have seen before," and "last year was ground-breaking and this this year is even better," were all common responses from guests who had attended. Universal's expectations had been smashed, the bar had been lifted and now the quest was on to plan for the next year. Universal knew they were on a roll.

Halloween Horror Nights: 3rd Annual

The Shark Bites Back!

Halloween Horror Nights in the late September press of 1993 were dubbed as "The 3rd Annual Universal Studios Florida Halloween Horror Nights", though this year there would be some changes and none more so than the return of Jaws. Charting back to the summer of that year and rumors were spreading amongst the local residents and Universal fans that their beloved Halloween event would be toast. The thought was that now the shark is back and it needs its massive queue buildings for, well queuing, where could the dungeon house be sited? And would Universal even bother to take it down and then try to rebuild it again? Things were starting to look bleak for the event, in the fans' eyes at least, as many had perceived that the shark returning would make way for the event to go for that year; after all it had come and gone in Hollywood a couple of times. Fans were concerned.

"Biting Back" the national headlines read in February 1993. Linda Buckley, a park spokeswoman, said, "Universal Studios Florida plans to reopen its *Jaws* ride in June [sic]. The water-based attraction will be the key offering in the park's 1993 season and will be the cornerstone of new advertising." The June deadline was missed due to further testing required as there had been some issues with the new pyrotechnics. The new ride was, from concept to closure (in 2012), the largest ride of its kind to utilize the most amount of pyrotechnics (particularly gasoline for the finale) and things just couldn't get fixed right. Technicians and engineers worked around the clock throughout July and by August, on select days only, it was tested with park guests. By August 12th of that year Leslie Doolittle of the Orlando Sentinel had heard from hundreds of park guests that the new ride was amazing and unlike anything anyone had ever experienced before. In fact Universal were quoted as saying that just over 500,000 park guests had been selected on specific days to ride

65

the attraction in August to get all the bugs with the attraction sorted in time for the grand opening.

As she wrote, "Judging by the screams, shrieks and cheers from tourists lucky enough to catch a test run of the new *Jaws* ride, Universal Studios Florida in Orlando is about to open an immensely popular attraction. [sic] People who venture out on an *Amityville harbor cruise* are terrorized, drenched, rocked by explosions and seared by heat. The ride is a life-and-death, hide-and-seek game with a massive killer shark."

The park's marketing executive Randy Garfield was quoted as saying "You really think you are going to get your arm bitten off!"

They had missed the summer season, but Universal were not about to repeat the mistakes of the past and open a ride that was not perfect. The date was set for the official opening of 1st October 1993 ready for the celebrities of opening day to return and cut the ribbon once more. After all, Steve Spielberg allegedly got caught mid-shark attack when the ride broke down on opening day, so Universal was not prepared for that to happen again when the main man himself was due to have the inaugural voyage.

"Bringing *Jaws* on at this point really closes a chapter for us, and allows us to move forward," said Bob Ward, senior vice president for design and planning at *MCA Recreation*, Universal's parent company. "Obviously, we are all very excited that *Jaws* is becoming part of the family."

The ride was then ceremoniously opened by original cast and crew members Roy Scheider, Lorraine Gary and Steven Spielberg, who all enjoyed the attraction completely problem-free. In fact, the attraction ran all day without a single fault at all. But there was a problem for the fans. The ride had reopened just when Halloween was fast approaching. Now that it was problem-free and running daily from October, all hope was surely lost wasn't it, with no chance that the event was coming back? But then there was a glimmer of hope on the horizon...

The hope came in an advertisement placed in the local press for "roach wranglers" and "rat ladies" to apply immediately to Universal Studios.

"Send us your resumes," the peculiar ad wrote. The advertisement was placed the very day after the grand opening of the *Jaws* ride, and finally central Floridian fans could air a sigh of relief. So unless Universal had a massive vermin problem (hugely unlikely!), then Halloween Horror Nights would be back!

The roach and rat advertisement again started to make national headlines across the country. This really was the first time that Universal and fans alike started to see more attention from the event in other parts of the country than had been seen previously. By October 8th Bubba Smith had been hired as Universal's official roach wrangler, and four women had been hired as Rat Ladies for the event. Smith, who was a large man with a long, natural, scraggly beard debuted with his collection of real roaches in the *People Under the Stairs* house, which returned that year. Universal used the appointments to further fan the attention of the national presses. The Orlando Sentinel wrote: "Baker was one of 300 hearty souls who fired off resumes to Universal last week after the company advertised for "roach wranglers" and "rat ladies." Wranglers are a new addition to the grisly lineup of characters to be used in a haunted house Universal opens for Halloween. Two bug handlers were hired. The men will play deranged people caught inside the wall of a house. Their only friends are the roaches - so there's lots of nuzzling and cuddling going on. Some of the bugs are the hissing Madagascar variety, while others are the smaller, and equally vile, American cockroach."

So it was by October 15th that all fears could be laid to rest (then other fears renewed when the event started!) when Universal officially announced that the popular Halloween event would be back for the third time to run for five nights on October 23, 24, 29, 30, & 31. In fact Universal had no intention to not stage the event. They had, unknown to most people (outside of park management), been planning the 1993 event since as early as February 1993. Various members of the Park's creative had gone on specific fact-finding missions to Los Angeles and New Orleans to aid with idea development. The news quickly came when around March of that year permits were filed to show 'careful dismantlement and application of screeding' in an area known only as Nazarman's. Nazarman's Pawn Shop and nearby facades in the New York area of the park were mostly used for storage. Nazarman's had been constructed as part of the robust facades that the original park designers wanted installed before the park opened to attract filmmakers to Orlando, but also for guests to wander around and explore, in a way that they couldn't at Universal's Hollywood backlot. Nazarman's Pawn Shop actually comes from an *Allied Artists* movie called *The Pawnbroker*, made in 1964 and starring Rod Steiger. The areas behind the shop and immediately around were worked on all summer to create a space where future Halloween attractions and houses could be temporarily installed. The construction created various back alleys that regular day guests could not venture onto, and large spaces within the mighty steel frame ready for rooms to be set up, along with rigs and discreet towers to control the lights and atmosphere of any future attractions. This wasn't the first time that the park had undertaken real construction specifically for the event, but this level of construction went on to show that Universal from 1993 had true long-term ambitions as to the quality and frequency of the beloved event.

"In terms of our haunted houses," said John Paul Guertz, the event's artistic director, "we've created some really dramatic situations that people can find themselves walking into and our haunted houses are definitely more upscale than your neighborhood haunted house. People come to see our haunted house attractions, but we try to make the most out of our streets with roaming characters," said Guertz. "People feel very comfortable out on the streets and then suddenly one of the characters leaps out and scares the heck out of them. There's something lurking for guests around every corner." And every corner was true! Where the 1993 summer season had seen a slowdown in park attendances, which was likely attributed to the promised *Jaws* ride that only opened shortly before the event was held, some park employees were repurposed to work the streets to become scareactors with more actors than had ever been at the event before plunged onto roads to chase and delight the guests in equal abundance. However, this year a more concerted effort would be made to better organize the streets with hordes of roaming scareactors characterized into loose fitting groups rather than appearing at random (though still no scarezones were officially set-up yet). These included: a sword swallower, a fire-eating contortionist, the *Chain Saw Drill Team* and the *Dead High School Cheerleading Squad*. This marked the first outing of a Halloween Horror Nights tradition, that of the *Chainsaw Drill Team*. The team consisted of five males dressed in faux-marine combat attires and were particularly robust on the streets of New York where frightened guests queuing to get-in could hear bizarre roars of chainsaws in the distance followed by blood curdling screams thereafter. A new tradition was born. The original five actors included an ex-marine, a firefighter and a trainee cop. "The idea of maniacs with chainsaws throughout the park had been there since day one", remarked John Paul Geurts, the event's co-producer. "Julie Zimmerman my co-producer can be directly accredited with creating the idea. She researched the concept of using chainsaws with no chains and then using them to scare guests with. It's such a neat idea that had really stood the test of time, as them guys and girls who are employed to be in the *Drill Team* really are as popular and iconic back then as they are to this day."

There would be an increase this year in the number of houses; such was the popularity of the two previous houses where waits of over three hours were exceedingly common nearly every night. First up was a return of a house that had been present for the first time last year, *The*

People Under the Stairs which would be located in the expansive 16,000-square foot Soundstage 23. The house was intended to be dismantled after the event in late 1992 and put out back into storage or sent back to Hollywood (as the house was a mixture of additions and real sets used from the movie). Operations department intended waiting until Studio Operations called for the house to go, to make-way for a new studio production before it would be dismantled. However no such call was given. It was around this time that Universal, much like its neighbor Disney, was starting to see that Orlando was not going to become the next Hollywood. Production demand decreased and the productions that did need space such as *SeaQuest DSV*, *Hulk Hogan's Thunder in Paradise* and various *Nickelodeon* shows could easily be made in the other expansive soundstages that surrounded Soundstage 23. So in the Spring of 1993 the decision was made to leave the house where it was, to fix it up and repair it from the previous year's use and then re-open it for 1993 with pretty much the exact same layout and numbers of scares. Though minor alterations had been made, the house was incredibly scary.

"Each room is familiar yet spooky - a bare light bulb illuminates the ghostly attic, creatures lurk underneath the stairs and roaches scurry through the kitchen.

We like to tap into subtle, familiar fears," said Jerry Abercrombie, Universal's props manager. "The attics, the basements, the closets . . . the things you know you shouldn't be afraid of, but you are."

As previously mentioned, the *Roach Man* was located somewhere in the house, which brought a different almost creepier dynamic that had not previously been seen for this house.

As in the previous house where actual sets from the hit movie were used, the next house was the actual sets from a TV movie, that of *Psycho IV – The Beginning*. The direct-to-TV movie had been the final official sequel to the original 1960 hit movie of the same name and the last to star leading man Anthony Perkins. The horror-drama movie was both the third sequel and a prequel to the original movie, as it includes both events after *Psycho III* while focusing on flashbacks of events that took place prior to the original film. It was first broadcast on the Showtime cable network on November 10, 1990.

"I couldn't wait to build a 'Psycho' house", said John Paul Geurts. Geurts who had worked previously on the original Hitchcock attraction was a great fan of Hitchcock and wanted to bring all the best set pieces from the famous movies into one house. "For my time working on Halloween Horror Nights it was possibly the hardest house to physically create. We knew we were going to use the sets from *Psycho IV* but the problem lay that the motel especially had been built solely for the purposes of filmmaking, they just assumed that it would be torn down after production wrapped and then trashed. We went in to see where we could run lighting equipment, where we could make enough space to put 'boo-doors' in etc. but we just couldn't do it, there was no space and no actual floors built. I was quite upset about this, as I had really wanted to use the original sets from this movie," he said.

The movie which had been the first movie to be shot entirely at Universal Orlando (filmed on set during the initial weeks of park operation), had built sets using forced perspective that were entirely for the temporary use of film production, with no regard whatsoever for future uses. "Unperturbed we went back to the drawing board, and one evening I was out the back just surveying the area and I thought to myself, 'you know, between the motel and the *Hard Rock Building*, there's plenty of space', so the idea hit me of building an extension to the back to accommodate a maze," he said.

FUN FEAR FACT

The Monster Makeup Show hasn't just run during the day, it has actually run on select nights for past HHN events. Often, the shows were changed up and made gorier. Supposedly one night a guest even fainted when the show presented was so scary.

It had been noted that during filming the production crew had asked the nearby *Hard Rock Café* to extinguish all lights and turn their music off due to the proximity of the restaurant, though just enough space could be provided to fit an extension to the motel. Geurts continued, "So what we did was we propped up the front façade which was fully retained, we removed the side walls and replaced them with large wrap-around walls (all in the similar materials), we then built-out the back area and demarked it on the ground and poured a concrete slab. The roof we raise up slightly and put in additional supports (as we had removed the rear walling) and then to infill the rear area we approached a company that built a kind of tent over the back of it that would be obscured by the front façade."

Installing a tent for the purposes of building a house for the event was the first time the technology had been used, prior to the 'sprung tents' being installed years later, though as Geurts remarked, "our tent was far more simple in design than the technology they now have in the Sprung tents." He continued, "We were actually given free rein to do what we wanted with the *Bates* set as it had been earmarked from early 1993 to be demolished in or around 1995 to make way for an extension to the 'Fievel's Playland' [which would be *A Day in the Park with Barney* that opened in 1995]. So they let us do what we wanted as long as it was

70

within budget."

The house and motel for the shoot had been the first official production at the Universal Resort. Where the house and motel had been moved in Hollywood was now a part of their popular tram tour. The decision was made to move the production to the newly opened park and to construct a complete new outdoor set for the filming, with the set construction to occur shortly after the main construction of the attractions had been completed. Therefore, site contractors were utilized for this run-on work. Bill Nassal of *The Nassal Co.* (which is still trading to this day) was an external contractor who built many of the early attractions at the park, including: the interior and external train for the *Back to the Future ride*, the interior for the *Earthquake* attraction, the swamp for the set of *The Swamp Thing* television show, the sets for *American Tail* and *American Tail II*, attractions based on the movie; and the Lagoon Boathouse and restaurant, which was then a part of the set for the lagoon stunt show. In fact the company would continue to grow when in 2006 it was handed the contract to work again with Universal to help bring to reality the *Wizarding World of Harry Potter* at *Islands of Adventure* and then again at *Diagon Alley* at the Studios.

Bill and his excellent company of engineers and technicians soon got to work to create the house and motel for the production. Most of the construction and then the subsequent filming was all undertaken with guests watching, with it becoming its own unique attraction. Not since the 1910s at Universal's Hollywood Studios could you come to a working studio and see actual movies being shot in front of you.

Bill said at the time, "For instance, Nassal has cabinet makers who can undertake complex jobs, such as the intricate woodwork of the *Psycho House*, and artists capable of painting just about anything." And intricate it was. Using plans from the original construction they were amended to build all four flanks, whereas in 1959 only two sides were built. Filming in those days didn't require the camera to see the other sides, so they weren't built. In Orlando, like all the sets that had been built for actual and potential filming they had to be strong and withstand tropical conditions. Whereas concrete padded reinforced steel structures had been built in Orlando for the soundstages and outdoor sets, in Hollywood everything had been built and framed in timber, including the outdoor sets. The original *Bates* house in Hollywood had been a composition of other sets knitted together to save money, as Hitchcock had famously wanted to make this classic movie for a very tight budget. The *Psycho* house was built from a number of Universal's stock units to save money. In fact, Hitchcock staked his reputation on the fact that the movie could be made for less than $1million, in the end its final budget was close to $800,000. The front elevation of the house and the distinctive tower facade was removed from a house on what is now *Wisteria Lane* (then *Colonial Street*) and had been used in the 1950 Jimmy Stewart classic movie *Harvey*. Therefore, Nassal and his team had very high expectations to not only build an exact replica of the 1960 movie but to also make sure it passed various building codes for outside buildings in terms of bracing for severe weather conditions. It was therefore around the first week that construction of the sets was completed and the delayed production began shooting. The production of *Psycho IV* was delayed in order for the opening of the studios to occur, as park bosses were keen for park guests to get a taste of seeing actual motion picture (well, made for TV) productions being shot at the studios.

Skipping forward to 1993, and Studios creative had a new idea. The sets from the 1991 event were used as a show for Beetlejuice and co, and then underutilized for just a photo-spot in the previous year. But what if the sets built for the movie could be used to put the park guests through the actual movie? Quietly over the summer of that year the house and motel were converted into an ambitious house for the event. Guests would enter in in via their nightmare via the main Bates family mansion's looming porch and into the main house that had been dressed to look like a combination of the actual house from the movie and a weird composite of old-time movies from Norman Bates' mind. From there, guests would venture down the famous path and into the actual motel. Norman and his mother were the main antagonists and they were everywhere! In the house's living room a cozy fire is roaring and a large oil painting of a scenic view is hung above the fireplace. But wait! just as you are lured into a false sense of security, the painting would be flipped and Norman in full mother's garb would start plunging his kitchen knife right in front of your face from above; it was said to be one of the most popular scares from the house. Later a recreation of the famous kitchen scene from *Psycho 2* would see Norman appear from inside kitchen cupboards. There were Normans everywhere in this attraction! A corridor from one room in the motel to the next would be a closet filled with old lady's clothes when suddenly a scareactor dressed in a Mrs. Bates special would pop out and scare guests from behind the clothes rail. But it wasn't all just from the mind of Norman - there was one scene in the motel that was lifted straight from the original movie, and it was one of the most famous too, that of the shower scene. Bernard Herrman's eerie score would play as guests passed a bathtub with shower screen pulled around. Inside a puppet controlled mannequin would be showering (including shower cap), whilst a Norman Bates look-a-like would creep up and plunge his knife repeatedly into the back of the dummy just as the musical crescendo would occur. This scene, located near the end of the attraction, would send guests running into the streets!

Next up was the Slaughterhouse located in the *Nazarman's* area, as detailed earlier. It was hands down the goriest the park's creative had made thus far in the event's short history. Guests would enter near *Sting Alley* and into a packing and processing facility for meat. But this wasn't any old meat, this was human meat. Corpses were hanging from the ceilings like cattle in a butchery store, hairy brutes with blood splattered aprons would jump in front of you carrying large cleavers and proceed to start hacking to bits poor victims who had not been so lucky. The general idea was that a load of insane mutant cannibals had been left to run the local meat factory. With the ability to retro-fit and build a purpose-made haunt facility for this house, the Creatives at Universal used military precision in designing the attraction.

"Designing a haunted house turns into math, eventually," said John Paul Geurtz, the event's artistic director. "You have to calculate each step people will take and engineer their every move. There's nothing random about this."

It also marked the first house to have its tongue firmly pressed into the side of its mouth, where humor and light relief (if only for a second) were as important as the scares. "We do have bodies that hang or dunk or drape or spew, we also use a lot of humor and a lot of subtle scares," Geurtz said. Creative Director Julie Zimmerman said, "People love to be scared as much as they love to laugh. We all need to get that out, to scream and yell and do all the things we can't normally do."

A bumper crop of attractions were open that year including: *Kongfrontation, Ghostbusters, Funtastic World of Hanna-Barbera, Hitchcock's 3-D Theater, The Gory, Gruesome, Grotesque Horror Make-Up Show, ET, Earthquake, Back to the Future: The Ride, Beetlejuice's Graveyard Review* and the newly opened *Jaws*. It was the latter of these offerings that was ironically the most impressive. As described earlier, fans of the event had thought that the return of the shark would mean the end of their beloved event. But what actually happen was the creation of a new Halloween Horror Nights tradition and one that sadly now can never be repeated (least in Orlando) which was *Jaws at night*. *Jaws at night* took the attraction to a whole new level of terrifying. The Park's Creative department had not made any alterations to the ride; it just came into its own once the sun was down. The dark and sometimes foggy atmosphere made the experience more terrifying as the shark seemed to be coming out of the water at random locations, such was the dark foreboding ambiance that lead to regular park guests becoming temporary disorientated.

Other than the three house and roaming scareactor hoards, there were also a number of smaller shows. These included: *Hex Maniacs* (a magic act that featured a "live" cremation), the *Human Blockhead* (a gross-out sword swallowing and pinned head maniac), *Robosaurus* returned performing much the same act as last year, *Crossbows of Death* (as it says), *Burn and Bury* (an improvisation comedy act offering quick and easy burials) and *Rock Inferno* (a horrific rock concert) with *Herb Williams* and *Gibraltar* headlining. *Herb* and his band were a popular performer and rock band that performed extensively in the south of the country during the 80s and 90s. A mixture of classic rock, old school funk, Motown covers, smooth ballads, jive, swing songs and even dance classics, *Herb* played a plethora of hits that were popular with all age ranges in attendance. His silky-smooth vocals, combined with his natural showmanship, were a welcome, lively addition to Hollywood Boulevard. Playing four times per night, the final show of the night featured more slow dances and ballads. Other acts performing on the same stage included: Country and Christian band *Diamond Rio*, who had recently won the Country Music Association vocal group of the year award and who are still performing to this day, and R&B trio *Jade* who had released various singles to mixed success in the early 90s. The event was keen to retain the party atmosphere, which it did in spades during the performances.

Also appearing four times per night was the returning and increasingly popular Bill & Ted in *Bill & Ted's Excellent Halloween Adventure II*. The show was as popular as the previous and only minor tweaks had been given to the script, as everyone at Universal's creative team had decided that the original show was such a hit then perhaps the original script should be used. The guests didn't mind as every single performance played out to packed crowds.

The new national media darling of the tabloids was back too - the ever-popular Rat Lady. "Our Rat Ladies have really taken a liking to their job," said John Paul Guertz. "Rat Madames" Stacey L. Virta and Catherine Greenlief, he added, "have even put together a Rat Lady Manual" to help others play the role. Some of the four-page manual's tips include: Before the show: "You are encouraged to get to know the rats on a daily basis - (by) arriving early before the show, or stopping by during the week. The only way you can get to know your rats better is to show you care." (For the record, 500 applicants applied for this job.) In the coffin: "Aussie Scrunch hair spray works best. . .this brand keeps the rats coming back." Also, "it's a good idea to keep rat food or treats handy during performances in case the rats get the munchies." Suddenly the popularity of the role and press attention had led to the role becoming more like a vocation than a temporary regional haunt.

The event was a hit and Universal had achieved the impossible: they'd raised the bar yet again to create an 'institution'. There were nights that had sold out of pre-sales tickets and people were starting to come from afar.

The Orlando Sentinel wrote: "Three years ago Universal Studios experimented with a new idea, Halloween Horror Nights. It has quickly become an institution, particularly with teenagers who love to tour the specially themed haunted houses and can also ride on *Earthquake, Jaws* or the other attractions too. Be forewarned, however. Buy tickets in advance at *Ticketmaster* outlets because they sell out quickly."

And sell out they did. Nearly every night queues at the ticket windows would form and stay long well into the event. The ticket prices were $24.95 (plus tax) in advance for Florida residents, $35 (plus tax) for the general public, $28 (plus tax) and surprising even kids(!!) had their own ticket for ages 3-9(!!!) which cost slightly less at $29.95 (plus tax).

Halloween Horror Nights: 4th Annual

"The Scareactor is born!"

The event this year in 1994 marked the first occasion of the infamous Ghoul School. Universal wanted to take everything it had learned from the last three years of being in the fright business and now take the scares to the next level. Starting in late August of that year everyone who had previously worked the event as a scareactor was invited back to attend the classes before the new and willing participants were inducted. *The Ghoul School* opened to much media attention at the time and made headlines in some of the local newspapers. The classes consisted of how to apply one's makeup correctly so as to create your character but to not use too much of the products; costuming and how proper attire should be worn for maximum effect and techniques of terror and etiquette; the latter being everyone's favorite part of the day. Rob Anderson was the main coach of the training and had the task of making the zombies zombified and the mutants mad and maniacal.

A demonstration of how the auditions and training were being undertaken was held at the *Monster Make-up Show Theatre* on October 6th that year. A fake zombie training class was quickly performed to the press to highlight the exacting art of walking, groaning, moving and even speaking like an actual zombie. Jim and Debbie Klingensmith were in attendance that day. This was the third year the Kissimmee based married couple had worked at the event as scareactors. "It's become a tradition," said Jim, to which his wife added, "Each year gets better." By day the Klingensmiths worked together selling time shares, but by night the corporate suits were off and the make-up was donned. Debbie went on to recount a fateful night the previous year (1993) when working inside one of the houses she scared a couple so bad she had beer accidentally poured right over her! "It's a fright reaction; it's never bothered me. I'd do it for free!"

Also in attendance were Andy Campanaro and Mick Pless, a retired journalist and postal worker respectively, who were being trained for this year to become the gruesome 'Roach Men' of the event. And these weren't just normal cockroaches. Again, like last year, the use of 2 to 3 inch big Madagascar roaches with their hard shells and ability to hiss like rattle snakes were to be used. "They're like turtles with little personalities," added Campanaro. Universal Studios public relations representative Amy Moynihan said that hundreds of applications were received all year long now by their HR department, to work with the roaches and the rats. She explained that although they look disgusting, the rats and cockroaches were all actually bred by specialist companies for the event to ensure they were completely germ and disease free. She also went on to explain that during the event the animals are cared for on site but after the event they are re-homed. "The rats (of Rat Lady fame) go for pets (when Horror Nights is over). They're adopted by employees and their friends," she said.

During the Ghoul School, successful candidates were asked to pledge their allegiance to the event and promise to give the best scares they can. After which with a cheer and smile every successful participant had graduated and was given details of where they were to be working on the event. Some 400 actors were inducted on this course, such was the increased demand that year for scareactors.

Halloween Horror Nights 2 & 3 had started with just 5 nights. For this event this was increased to 8 nights: October 14, 15, 21, 22, 28, 29, 30, 31 (1994). This meant that the three weekends leading up to Halloween would all be 'owned' by Universal. Disney at this time had only arranged to decorate the water tower at Disney-MGM Studios with fangs and a small cape and then offer a smaller Halloween party at Pleasure Island named *Halloweird Bash*. The event would run only on October 31st and would see the plucky party island filled with lots of dry-ice and chances to do the Monster Mash. Universal, on the other hand, was offering more haunted houses than ever before, more musical acts than ever before and the set up of the very first scarezone.

The first ever scarezone was situated between the *Hollywood* area of the park and where the *Hitchcock 3D (Shrek)* attraction was situated. This large piece of real estate was then mined for scares by three roaming groups. The ever-popular *Chain Saw Drill Team* was back, complete with their chainless saws (shh!) plaid shirts and greased-up muscles. They shared the streets with the *Lizzie Borden's Band* and *Axe Corps*, who sang and danced with large axes in tow. The show finished off with the *Monks in the Hood*, a weird bunch of mad friars with painted white and black faces who hid behind corners and jumped out on unsuspecting members of the public. Along *Hollywood Blvd.* was a collection of sets and large fixed props to complement the actors. The placing of such items had never been done before. Cages, podiums, pedestals and prisons were all installed for the duration, and leather-clad muscle men and sexy animal furred bikini clad go-go dancers with fangs danced up. The sexiness of the event had definitely been increased.

Julie Zimmerman had championed the idea of the Scarezone from the very beginning. It wasn't until this year that the idea would come to fruition, initially starting off as a mixture of various murderous villains roaming at will for the formative years. It would see the concept develop and grow to encompass full narrative and set designs. By the late 90s the treatments for the scarezones would effectively begin to be as long and as detailed as the ones for the houses were.

Lizzie, who was acting Queen of the first scarezone, was modelled after the famous case of a woman who was tried and then acquitted for the 1892 axe murders of her father and mother in Fall River, Massachusetts. As the actress strode the streets with a powdery white face glaring at the masses of public she held up high her axe, and her assembled cast of weird period dressed singers would chant
"Lizzie Borden took an axe, gave her mother forty whacks, then she hid behind the door, and gave her father forty more."
Then just as the final word of the chant was over, Lizzie would point out into the crowds to indicate to the chanters to go out and round-up a willing victim. The showmanship of this first scarezone was a fantastic foundation and although not perfect, mostly due to the large area it was held in, it would serve the event well and ensure that scarezones would quickly become a tradition for the event in the years to come.

Though four houses were advertised there were technically five, though there has been some argument about this over the years. Officially there were four, and first up this year was a return for 'Psycho' Norman Bates. The house which debuted the year before inside the house and motel from the movie *Psycho IV* was a huge hit with the public. The house was re-dressed and where many of the popular scenes were retained, some new ones had been added. A graveyard scene was added just outside the motel, which had been used during the original *Fright Nights* for the show with the *Blues Brothers* and *Beetlejuice*. Having the gravestones and graves already dug was a no-brainer for repurposing into a scene for the house. They also added a horrific attic scene after using production stills of the attic from *Psycho 2*. This mostly contained stuffed animals, dust, and the ever-present Norman with mother's garb. Returning was the kitchen set with pop-out Normans in nearly every kitchen unit, the creepy closet walkthrough scene and the infamous bathroom scene.

FUN FEAR FACT

In the earlier years of the *Bill and Ted Show* the cast was assembled from entirely the day crew working on the then *Wild West Show*

The *Psycho* house was not the only house to return that year. *The Dungeon of Terror*, which wasn't present at the previous year (thanks to *Jaws* reopening), was for HHN4, having moved from one queue building to another. The *Earthquake* attraction's extended queue building would be the home of the new house. This marked the first time the queue building had been used for a house; it would go on to be a popular venue for staging houses. The house was very similar to the one that had been seen before where 'faux-guests' and other victims had been imprisoned and tortured in the inaugural maze. It featured the Rat Lady, again incased in her trademark glass coffin, along with a new character, the *Snake Master*. A man covered by two boas greeted guests halfway round the house. Reviews were positive, but the house lacked the hot, claustrophobic atmosphere of the previous incarnations.

Although if you wanted heat in your houses, you needed look no further than the house that was built over in *Nazarman's*. The brand new original idea house was *Hell's Kitchen*. *Nazarman's* had been used in the previous year as a slaughterhouse-type maze and although some of the props were left to be repurposed the rest of the house was entirely different. *Hell's Kitchen* was an industrial kitchen, complete with chefs with blood-stained aprons. Huge cleavers, pots and pans rattled on the stoves, bloody parts were scattered everywhere and blood 'n' sweat dripped from the ceilings etc. This house purposefully had the air-conditioning switched right off to create a steamy (thanks to the Floridian humidity) and hot atmosphere. Makeup melted on the performers and extended breaks were given to the scareactors with the most energetic roles. Head Cook of the house was a 6ft tall hunchback covered in blood and swinging knives at guests. He was played by John

McVay. "It's right up my alley," said McVay, a resident of Winter Park who by day was an employed carpenter and painter. *The Roach Man* was located back into this house in one of the smaller kitchen scenes, trapped inside a big glass case. Hissing roaches crawled over him, up his beard and into his mouth whilst crawling over rotten food and pots filled with slime; it was quite shocking. "I'm here to create hell and have fun!" remarked McVay of his time in the house.

The Boneyard, an area that has since disappeared at Universal, was an area of concrete located between where *Twister* stands today and the *Music Plaza Stage*. The area was an outdoor attraction which opened with the park in 1990. The attraction featured a variety of larger props and sets from past Universal Pictures films and TV shows, including *Jurassic Park* and its sequels, *Waterworld*, *Back to the Future*, *Jaws IV* and *Ben Hur*. Guests could get the chance to walk around the large props and see how they were built – not a real tour but more an outdoor scattering of props for guests to look at. A replica of the swimming 'Bruce' (shark) prop from the movie *Jaws IV* pulled in most of the crowds, along with sets from *Jurassic Park* and its sequels.

The house that was located here was a combination of sets built with timber frames and then covered by a fabric roof. It appeared as though it was a giant tent but strictly speaking the buildings weren't a tent, they were just sets that needed protecting from the Floridian weather. Also, to add to the confusion there were technically two mazes inside as different entrances were used, however the park map billed the location as one single house. The first theme was an old, abandoned insane asylum that had recently been excavated. According to the story, it had been abandoned many years prior but had now been reopened. Bloated corpses half dissected, melting zombies and maniacs controlling large machinery such as a giant grinder greeted guests throughout its winding corridors of doom (such was the space the house filled). Props from the actual Boneyard were temporarily moved and not repurposed for the house. The other theme was science-fiction set up, with mad scientists and evil clowns tying down helpless victims to large tables to experiment on. Large lamps and hideous ghouls disorientated guests, which made for good scares in this labyrinth of a house.

Bill and Ted made a welcome return that year with a show that, although had many themes from the past shows, was entirely different and had been written by a new member of the team, Jason Surrell. Julie Zimmerman, who was still the creative lead of the event during this year, had taken a chance on the young Surrell, effectively acting as his mentor. Surrell eventually left to become a Disney Imagineer before returning to

Universal to work on some very exciting future projects.

The previous *Bill and Ted shows* had all followed almost the exact same script and the same format, mixing horror icons with Universal icons set within the confines of the *Wild West Show*. Surrell took an altogether different approach, incorporating popular cultural references, current music, dancing and he amplified the comedy aspect. The show would prove to be so popular, that it would largely stick to this revised format to this very day. It would also see a young James Keaton take over the role of Ted for the next few years. He would continue in the role until his skills were called upon to aid in the creation of a certain murderous and maniacal clown...

The show would be dubbed *Bill and Ted Meet Timecop* and was held at the regular *Wild West Show* building and was loosely tied into a recent Universal picture, *Timecop*. The film starred Jean-Claude Van Damme as a police officer in 1994 and a U.S. Federal agent in 2004, when time travel was possible. It also starred Ron Silver as a rogue politician and Mia Sara as the agent's wife. The story follows a special agent's life through time as he fights time-travel crime and investigates a politician's unusually successful career. As the movie had been released in September that year (to mixed audience responses), the idea was sprung to tie the movie into the popular *Bill and Ted show* in an effort to give the movie one final push at the box-office. "He was a time traveler and they were time travelers, it seemed the perfect fit" said Surrell. As soon as the show started, the title characters danced and sang covers of *AC/DC*, *Nirvana*, *Queen* and *Offspring*. They were followed by Bill and Ted traveling through time to make very comical and relevant pop culture references. These included: Nancy Kerrigan and Tonya Harding fighting, cracks at O.J. Simpson and then Arnie's Terminator coming to save the day. It would be the reference to 'the Juice' that would really bring the house down in laughter. And although the *Timecop* tie-in was a little dubious, the show was again a massive hit, drawing crowds at the increased five performances per evening.

Robosaurus was also back this year. This would mark the last time the metal giant would be at the event before returning for a one-off in 2006. The show was incredibly similar to previous years and had been located again in the New York area of the park. Changes this year included some stunt performers working alongside the giant to add to the action. Three shows were on Fridays with four on the busier Saturday nights. Though this was the first year not to have a magic act of some kind taking part, there were other shows and attractions this year. These included *The Price is Fright gameshow* with Beetlejuice and a Vegas-style act called *The Devil and His Showgirls*. The former was a spoof gameshow where guests of the park could compete for ghoulish prizes with *Wheel of Misfortune* and *Win, Lose or Draw Blood* with a red glittery clad Beetlejuice on hosting duties. The other show was a sadist musical revue which featured a fair number of scantily clad Vegas-like showgirls, in keeping with the sexy theme that the event had this year. *The Price is Fright* was also written by Surrell this year. He had originally pitched a show called *A Shadow in the Night* which would have been located at the *Animal Actors' Stage*. Using the Universal Picture from that year, the show would see the Alec Baldwin character perform a number of stunts and action pieces within the 25 minute-long show. "I liked the idea and pitched hard for it," said Surrell, however the show would not be made and instead he would write *The Price is Fright*, though the idea of using the creepy comic book character would mean we would not see the last of him...

These two shows were both pretty enjoyable; however, for one couple they would never be able to forget *The Price is Fright show*. Starting in 1994 from the solid foundation of the previous year led to the central Florida event affecting the culture of the local communities like it had never before. Soon a special type of fandom was starting to emerge that enjoyed not only the great scares that could be had but also the amazing craftsmanship that the park created. People were celebrating events onsite and couples were starting to use the event as date night; the event was becoming something very special. So special, in fact, that this year marked the first time that the event actually held real weddings. Two Orlando-based couples held small ceremonies and said their vows during the event. The first wedding held was for Heidi Danzig and Hank Miller, who tied on the first Friday of the event, right on the *Price is Fright stage* which was located inside the *Animal Actors' stage*. The second wedding was for Cynthia Lopez and Peter Nazario at the other Beetlejuice show, the permanent day show of *Beetlejuice's Graveyard Revue stage*. Lopez and Nazario got married on site on the final Sunday of the event with witnesses to the ceremony of no less than Herman, Lily and Grandpa Munster.

A special *Rock 'n' Roll Inferno stage* was erected for the event that included a good number of musical acts this year. These included: *Flash Flood*, a local band that performed covers of various rock groups, *Sass Jordan* a female singer from Canada who had at the time had a number of hits, and *Jerry Lee Lewis*, the rock legend who needs no introduction. Obtaining Lewis for just one night was a great means for advertising the park and was a huge deal at the time. But he wasn't the only big-named celebrity to be at the event that year. Some of the cast of hit TV show

90210, namely heartthrob Jamie Walters and Stacey Piersa performed songs at the *Beetlejuice stage*. It was reported that evening that others from the hit TV show were also present. And finally, *Fox TV* and *ABC* respectively taped special programs on site during the event on the Saturday. *Fox's* was for *Fox's Halloween Bash*, a live party report from the destination resort, Fox having flown a number of stars from various hit TV shows to star in the live broadcasted program. The show ran on more than 100 *Fox* stations across the country, and helped generate plenty of out-of-state interest in the resort. *ABC's* was more subdued and featured other haunt attractions from Central Florida in *ABC in Concert*, though both were taped at the same time on the same night. "It's a huge deal - it's very big for us. Halloween is becoming a mega-holiday," said Fred Lounsberry, Universal's marketing spokesman. Soon after the broadcast people were reportedly clamoring for tickets. "We've been slowly building the event to make Universal the place to go for Halloween. We get media calls from all over asking what's new in Florida for Halloween," said Gary Stogner, a tourism spokesman. It was quickly realized that Halloween was becoming big business for the park.

Halloween Horror Nights V

The Curse of the Crypt Keeper

The competition that had defined both Universal and Disney in the 1980s would return for Halloween Horror Nights V. Every year the event at Universal, which at the time was still a relative newcomer to the market and had only just fixed their centerpiece ride (*Jaws*), was growing and growing. Disney at the time had owned the Christmas holidays but they wanted more. Executives at Disney had become increasingly interested in trying to grab a piece of the Halloween festivities. Last year they had dipped their toe only gently into the water with the redressing of the *Earful Tower* and an adult-only Halloween party at their party island, Pleasure Island, but it wasn't enough. Quickly a decision was made by park executives that although what Universal was doing was very successful, it just wasn't Disney. Disney needed a way to bring adults and children alike to their parks but without scaring the life out of them. So *Mickey's Not-So-Scary Halloween Party* was born.

The event for Disney would be a special one-night hard ticketed event held after hours in the Magic Kingdom and would specifically be aimed at families and young children. "If it's successful, we'll do it again," said Disney spokesman Greg Albrecht. Attractions at the first *Not-So-Scary party* would include: Cinderella Castle being shrouded in fog and eerie lights, Frontierland becoming an old-fashioned ghost town, where guests would hear a stage coach approach and passing unseen. Weird aliens would roam Tomorrowland, Adventureland would become a dark, torch-lit jungle and the Headless Horseman would haunt guests around Liberty Square. Complaints had been received by Disney that guests staying during the Halloween season had nowhere to take their kids during the festivities if they wanted to trick or treat; they either had to venture off property or stay in their resort. So for $18.50 ($16.95 if bought in advance), guests could trick-or-treat from 7 p.m. to midnight along Main Street with Mickey and his pals, who were all decked out in their own Halloween costumes in this specially designed hard ticket event. "You can go several places around town and get scared to death," spokeswoman Sarona Soughers said at the time. "This is a place to go to have fun without too many nightmares." Disney, keen to keep the scares to a minimum, also chose not to decorate Fantasyland at all, so kids who didn't want the scares but wanted the candy could trick-or-treat without fright.

Universal's mantra for every event was about building on the previous year and making it bigger and better. So this year they decided that someone needed to headline the event, bring it all together and present the houses as though they are a collection of gruesome haunts that have been specially selected and approved for your enjoyment. Many ideas were put forward including Beetlejuice (whose star was starting to fade a little), Norman Bates (though he lacked the showmanship needed) and even characters from *Jaws* were considered. The debate rumbled on until a decision was made to go outside of Universal's own characters and licensed agreements to see who else could host the event. Quickly a decision was made to approach the licensing company that owned the right to the Crypt Keeper. The Crypt Keeper and his TV show *Tales from the Crypt* had been running successfully since 1989 on *HBO* and had in 1995 been made into a movie named *Demon Knight*, which had been released by Universal to much success. A deal was soon granted and the Crypt Keeper was officially licensed to host the event that year, making him the first official icon of the event.

The Crypt Keeper had been born out of the boom of superhero, sci-fi and horror comics of the 1950s, a boom which was triggered when the older, more family-orientated comics were starting to seem old fashioned. Originally made by *EC Comics* as an anthology comic containing moral stories that were presented in a gruesome way (a medium which really spoke to children and young adults of the time), the stories were full of poetic justice or eye-for-an-eye in their telling of stories. Gone were the bible stories and innocent family cartoons, and in were the likes of *Spider-Man* and *The Incredible Hulk*. Some of the illustrations were incredibly detailed in a horrific manner. It was thought that many of the artists were returning veterans who had served in World War Two, who were drawing off their own experiences of witnessing first hand the atrocities that had been seen in Europe and

Asia.

The comics came under serious attack in the mid-1950s from parents, church members, teachers and other commentators who believed the books were contributing to a sense of perceived illiteracy and juvenile delinquency of the 1950s. In June 1954, a highly publicized Congressional subcommittee held hearings on the effects of comic books upon children which left the industry reeling. The subcommittee put a highly restrictive Comics Code onto many companies that were in the same market. This led *EC Comics* publisher Bill Gaines to cancel his wildly popular *Tales from the Crypt* and its two companion horror titles, as they just could not tailor the comics to meet the code the subcommittee wanted. Skipping forward to the 1970s in Britain they were experiencing a huge boom in horror-related media, particularly in film, with the likes of *Amicus* and *Hammer* who had been turning out their own British versions of *Dracula* and *Frankenstein* since the 1950s. It was the former, *Amicus,* who acquired the rights from *EC Comics* to make their own movie version of the comic book and then a sequel *The Vault of Horror,* though the Crypt Keeper as we know him today was sadly missing from both.

In the 1980s, *EC Comics* and other providers of 'classic horror' went through a revival with a high demand for reprints of the 1950s comics being demanded (the subcommittee's code now being dropped in modern America). This led to the production of a TV series that ran from 1989 to until 1996 on the *HBO* network, a network that could get away with more horrific or explicit shows than mainstream TV. The series actually moved production to the UK towards the final episodes to get the benefit from the Government's tax breaks that were being offered to production companies at the time. The show would start and end just like the original comic books with the mysterious Crypt Keeper himself holed up in his own haunted mansion ready to tell a tale of foreboding or sorrow that inevitably would include a twist at the end or some kind of horrific set-piece. The show was introduced by a Beetlejuice-esque haunting yet catching theme tune that funnily enough had been written by composer Danny Elfman. In a way, the show was a modern version of the 1960s *Alfred Hitchcock Presents* or *The Twilight Zone* TV shows. This new show was a hit and led to three movies being produced, a kid's Saturday morning series, radio plays and even a computer game. One thing was for sure: the charismatic Crypt Keeper was a huge deal in the 1990s, so Universal obtaining the rights for the character to host their event was a massive victory for the park.

The event was unofficially titled *The Curse of the Crypt Keeper* and would run for an extended 12 nights for this year. Park creatives were quick to point out that preparations for the event had taken the longest to date:

"Imagine buying 4,000 pounds of dismembered body parts props. Or making blood, brain fluid and primordial ooze by boiling a brew of 600 gallons of methocyl cellulose -- a water-based gel. Boil it and stir it for three days in 64-quart cauldrons."

One of the creative team was quoted as saying, "More than 500 scareactors will star in *Curse* (of the Crypt Keeper), using 1,200 prosthetic pieces - protruding foreheads, extended chins, gaping wounds, disfiguring scars, gangrene-infected limbs." Production had been ramped up for the event, with more production crew, more scareactors, more houses and more nights to entertain. The production crew had started way back in the Spring when they began an extended tour of horror inspiration. They traveled to Cajun country, abandoned New York subways, New Orleans historic cemeteries and other nearby real haunts. They also went to Hollywood's famous *Haunted Soundstage*, which was located at Hollywood's Universal Studios on soundstage 28 on the backlot. Although sadly demolished in 2015, it had previous held the original theatre set from the 1924 version of the *Phantom of the Opera*. Armed with video and still cameras, the creative team sought to explore these settings and record scenes such as decay on tombstones, moonlit shadows, the howl of wind through trees and other iconic scary moments, all of which could be recycled for the event. "We specialize in complete sensory overload," said Universal creative member Jerry Abercrombie. "It's not enough to recreate the visuals - our guests must hear, smell and feel the experience in order to have a good scare." He went on, "We continually evaluate our product based on guest satisfaction, and in this case, the louder the scream, the better."

The first house, a nod to the house that had been there before, was the *Crypt Keeper's Dungeon of Terror*, named after the event's icon. Though it shared the name partly from the original *Dungeon* house, the actual house for this event had no other similarities to its predecessor. This house was a "heart-pounding, palm-sweating journey into an evil crypt of unthinkable horror," according to Universal creative at the time. Built in the *Earthquake* extended queue area the house would heavily feature the house from the TV series along with the theme song bellowing out into the crowds to act as a draw. Unsuspecting guests would pass through the mansion's dingy root cellars and a cemetery of the undead, a library full of ghost stories, a parlor, a trophy room (with human heads as trophies), and eventually meet Universal's legendary Rat Lady. Dressed in Victorian fashion, the Lady lies in a glass coffin, with rats crawling over, under and around her. More than 125 rats, hand-raised at

Universal, are used in the attraction. This was the scene before moving into the last room: the coffin room from the TV Show where your host is waiting for you. A life-sized puppet of the Crypt Keeper sitting upright in his coffin would greet guests for one final scare. "Goodbye foolish mortals!" the gravely high-pitched voice of original Crypt Keeper actor John Kassir would yell out as guests passed by.

Next up, built into the Nazarman's area of New York was *Terror Underground, Transit to Torment*, a house that had been devised during the creative team's recent trip to New York. Guests would enter the house by walking through decaying turnstiles into the New York subway underground. Soon they would be up against slime-covered walls, through tight, tiled maze-like corridors and would eventually enter into catacombs where all sense of direction was soon lost. The house was exceedingly dark which played on many of the guests' own phobias. The path would then twist, turn, and even double back on itself slightly before guests were brought face-to-face with the mole people, a crazy mutant race of creatures who inhabited this maze of tunnels.

"According to city historians, it's a whole other city down there - the `mole people' elect their own mayor, have their own doctors - they've completely abandoned modern life to live within this vast labyrinth of darkness," said Julie Zimmerman of Universal Creative. "Because it's a real-life legend, the mole people are just as frightening - perhaps more so - than traditional ghosts and goblins" she said.

The next house that was built was arguably another dual house. This was located on Soundstage 23 and was just as detailed as the other two houses. Whereas the Crypt Keeper's house had drawn heavily on the TV show, and the Nazarman's house had been based on urban legends from underground New York, this house would bring back the classic monsters from Universal's history but bring them back in a wholly new and terrifying way. As part of the Universal creative team's extensive research, members of the department visited Universal Studios Hollywood. It was there they were given full access to the huge prop storage department located on the backlot, a resource that had been storing and protecting props from Universal's productions from as far back as the 1920s. The creative team reportedly spent weeks trawling through the collection until they found relics from Universal classics such as *The Hunchback of Notre Dame, Frankenstein* and *Dr. Jekyll and Mr. Hyde.* The team sent back to Orlando two tractor-trailers full of props and set-pieces from the Hollywood Studios for use in this house. Sure, Universal had used previous sets and props from their modern movies but never had they actually used props from classic horror movies. This was a revelation! And though most of the general public would not notice or not recognize the classic props that were used in this house, it is nice to think that this house was probably the most authentic house that had ever been made for the event surrounding the classic monsters.

Universal would often create displays from current movies that had recently been released by Universal. The displays would feature costumes, props and sets from these movies. They would be displayed in various locations around the park before finally space was found for a regular fixture inside Soundstage 54 (where the meet and greet with Donkey is now located). Recent hits from *Jurassic Park* to *The Mummy* all featured. The Orlando resort would swop these out at expensive to the movie studio who was paying for the onsite display as a means of marketing, often props would be built specifically for the stage and weren't always genuine screen used props; likewise, a lot of the exhibits would be trashed rather than the expense of sending them back to Hollywood. Julie Zimmerman recalls, "I definitely raided both the *Casper* and *The Flintstones* props from 1995. With or without permission, we took those props and they were all repurposed inside various houses for that year!"

Universal's *House of Horrors* offered two different paths with two different queues. The house was so large and had such distinct scares that it was the first official dual house, even though a dual house had unofficially been offered the year before. The classic monsters from the golden era of Universal were offered on one side of the house with newer monsters on the other side of the house (Chucky had featured predominantly on this side of the house). Though they weren't officially at the event, the other house did contain non-Universal-like monsters which could have been reminiscent of other popular monsters of the time, though no licenses had been officially applied for by Universal. The house would prove so popular that it would be used again.

Hollywood Blvd would again become *Horrorwood Blvd* and be home to one of the two scarezones this year, and would include the ever-popular *Chainsaw Drill Team*, along with various mutants and freaks, and distracting guys and girls in not much clothing. The other scarezone this year would be located over in the Amity-named *Midway of the Bizarre*. 'A *Mardi Gras* gone wrong' could be a perfect description of the event. Evil clowns chased guests, whilst a carnival voodoo lord of the cemetery would seek to raise the dead and any evil spirits in the neighborhood. Like a Mexican day of the dead festival, the scarezone featured bright colors and skeletons in equal measure, along with jesters dancing to freakish music and cannibals-a-plenty. The scarezone was a sensory overload of smells, sounds, colors, dry-ice and scares. Recognizing for the first time that not everybody comes to the event to be scared witless, this scarezone was the first in the event's history to offer a 'chicken path' for anyone not quite brave enough to venture in, as a discreet path to the south of the *Jaws* attraction was offered. To compliment this 'chicken path', Universal also created unofficial 'safe areas', in *Central Park* and *Avenue of the Stars* where ghouls were not allowed to roam. They also marked on the park maps skull-and-crossbones symbols so guests could recognize the scary areas of the park. This was likely due to Universal wanting to attract more people to the park (a response from the *Not-So-Scary* starting that year?); people who perhaps didn't want to be scared and wanted to enjoy the party atmosphere without the fear of spilling their drinks or dropping their popcorn!

Again, as in previous years, various shows were offered to keep the party atmosphere alive. First up was *Rock of Ages*, a rock 'n' roll street party that featured various musical acts such as *Raven & the Nevermores* as well as a DJ for the event who played pop songs from the 1960s to 1980s. *Michael Jackson's Thriller* song was noted to have been played numerous times each night. Beetlejuice also returned that year to host his four-nightly interactive game-show spoof *The Price Is Fright* back in the *Animal Actors' Stage*. Bill and Ted were also back this year but minus the *Time Cop* from the previous year. Other attractions for this year included: *Kongfrontation, Funtastic World of Hanna-Barbera, Hitchcock's 3-D Theater, ET, Jaws, Earthquake, Back to the Future: The Ride* and *Beetlejuice's Rock n' Roll Graveyard Review*. The latter, the ghost with the most, was also presiding over *Beetlejuice's Plague Ground*, located outside the *Animal Actors' stage*, and the area became host to a number of carnival games. Such games had not been installed permanently at the park yet and were a welcome sideshow to the park's festivities.

The final show offered featured the park's icon for the evening, the Crypt Keeper. A lagoon show entitled *The Crypt Keeper's Revenge: Knights of Hell* was staged, with the Crypt Keeper this time played by an actual person and not a puppet like in his house of that year. The show, which was held three times per night and was the last show of the evening before closing, saw boats with demonic symbols duel with other boats, undertake stunts and jump through fire. Many guests commented that it was similar to the then-*Miami Vice* stunt show that was offered during the day, but being at night it took on a whole different vibe with additional pyrotechnics, lasers, fireworks and fire.

Halloween Horror Nights VI

Journey Into Fear

Halloween Horror Nights VI: Journey into Fear was held on October 11, 12, 17-19, 23-28, 30, 31, and November 1, & 2 (1996) for an unprecedented 15 nights, with the event starting earlier than before and now ending in November. The event was going from strength to strength. Not much was said all year regarding the event until around the beginning of September, when Universal ramped-up the marketing, choosing this year to make Frankenstein's monster the unofficial center of the marketing campaign. The monster was paraded on various TV spots including many on *Fox* which were seen around the country. During this time, *Fox* also partnered with the event, as did *Doritos*, to sponsor many TV shows to gain more advertising for the event. Popular teen orientated programs such as *Goosebumps* which aired at the time ran competitions with Frankenstein's Monster to attract people to call in to local radio stations (such as *Kiss FM*) to win the chance of all-expenses paid vacations to Universal just for Halloween Horror Nights. A buzz was growing around the country, and the event was starting to be the place to go if you wanted a truly unique Halloween experience. "Nobody does Halloween like we do," said Universal spokesman Fred Lounsberry. "October, traditionally a slack period for Florida theme parks, shows up on Universal charts as an attendance spike as a direct result of Halloween Horror Nights."

The dates for the event were leaked to the media around the 8th September when auditions for the event were taking place. For the first time in the event's history there were to be fewer parts for potential scareactors, with only 400 official parts to be cast. They did, however, have a good reason for this...

For the first time in the event's history Universal wanted to provide a parade. It had been this very year that earlier in the season in March that Universal had the first in another long-running annual event: their own version of *Mardi Gras*. This was a similar, party-like event which prominently featured a parade as the highlight of each night. The event's icon from last year was back - the Crypt Keeper - and he would be appointed the grand marshal of the parade activities. *The Chainsaw Drill Team* would sound their saws as the fireworks and flames would fire high into the sky to signal the start of the parade. The first float from the backstage area was the Crypt Keeper's own, with the maniacal zombie himself perched high above on a regal-looking throne. Next up was a float that showed a human sacrifice, followed by a float dedicated to snakes with a large serpent head mounted at the front. Along with the unofficial icon and drill team, there were skeletons dancing in the street with elongated arms, werewolves, horned demons, voodoo dancers, ladies with fake snake appendages, funky vampires playing pianos, exactly 75 trained stilt walkers and a stilt walker made-up to look like the Devil himself from the movie *Legend*. *Legend* was a 1985 British-American fantasy-horror adventure film directed by Ridley Scott and starring Tom Cruise, Mia Sara and Tim Curry; with Curry playing the devilish role as Beelzebub himself. At the very end of the parade we had an undertaker throwing ashes at the crowds (instead of beads). Though dressed similar to a character that would be born soon at the event, the character proved popular and provided a good deal of banter with parks guests. As the floats passed along the streets, ghouls and goblins of every type would throw beads into the assembled crowds, in true *Mardi Gras* style. There were five floats in total. All had been re-themed from the *Mardi Gras* event that had started earlier in the year at the park. The parade route started at the top of *Hollywood Blvd* by Mel's Diner, it then ran down *Hollywood* to *Production Central* where it would turn to go into the park and along the main path, through New York, exiting behind *Kongrontation*.

Universal had in the previous year formed a travel company to deal directly with customers wanting to book Universal packages to the resort. With low expectations, the fledgling subsidiary had done very well, so well in fact that the Halloween event this year was the first time that direct packages had been offered. The travel company had sought in the previous year to add cruises and beach trips to its current travel packages, and they then expanded the offering by adding packages including ground transportation especially for Halloween Horror Nights and *Mardi Gras*, respectively. Since September that year the company had offered both one and two night packages for the Halloween event, which included theme park tickets, Halloween tickets and accommodation. This would later go on to be called 'Stay and Scream' but the name had yet to be realized. It had been seen in the past year that attendances were growing significantly for guests coming from out of State. It had particularly been noticed that nearly 20% of the guests' attendance was coming from Georgia. So along with the usual adult and child prices (yes child tickets were still sold in 1996!), the discount for Florida residents was extended for this year to include Georgia residents too.

The Frankenstein's Monster used in the marketing.

The Crypt Keeper wasn't restrained to being part of the parade this year, as he again had his own house back in the *Earthquake* queue. The house was called *The Crypt Keeper's Studio Tour of Terror* and was not a copy of the previous year as it was an entirely new attraction. Instead of the tour of his old decrepit manor house this time guests would tour a haunted studio backlot, complete with a Norman Bates shower scene with mother, an electrifying room showing a studio worker getting shocked and various other dusty and cobwebbed props and sets.

The next house located in the *Nazarman's* area was *Toy Hell: Nightmare in the Scream Factory*. *Toy Hell* was a combination of toy factory and back alleys immediately around the factory where the insane toy makers had decided to use actual human body parts to make the toys seem more life-like. Think *Pinocchio* gone wrong, or the movie *Child's Play* (though Chuckie was not present in the house). The Franken-toys had all come to life and eventually killed the toy makers, and were now setting their sights on plucky park guests. The house was filled with great scares; one notable example was a huge pile of discarded stuffed-toy-animals in a heap on the floor. Actually, inside the pile was a scareactor ready to pounce on unsuspecting guests. Combined with the good scares were costumes unlike anything that had been seen before. With fur-like covers 'sewn' onto flesh and human arms 'stitched' onto teddy bears, it was an exceedingly creepy house.

As in the previous year, there was a final house located in Soundstage 23 that was again a dual house with separate entrances and queues, entitled *Universal's New House of Horrors*. One half of the house, featuring the classic Universal monsters was entirely similar to the house that had been seen the previous year, but the other side was altogether different. The other section was called *Reel Life Horrors* and featured a bizarre wax museum where a rogue lightning bolt had brought the horrors of the museum to life. If you thought the classic Frankenstein's monster and Dracula were scary then you would be terrified on this side, as you would soon be up against 'real monsters' with the likes of Jack the Ripper and the axe-owning Lizzie Borden. Rumor had it that the previous year's monsters had been swopped out to make way for real frightening monsters, so in their place true-life villains were presented, much to the guests' delight.

Due to the parade's route, the number of scarezones was reduced to just one, with *Midway of the Bizarre* in Amity being offered again. Although larger it was entirely the same as the one held the previous year. This time, the *Chainsaw Drill Team* was also not restricted to just the parade; they were allowed (after parade duties) to roam the park at will. With the solitary scarezone, the park brought back the magical offering and provided a magic show with a twist. *Tricks, Treats and Trances* would debut in the *Animal Actors' stage*, providing four shows per night. The show was hosted by Cindy Layn who combined traditional magic with hypnotism to great comedic effect. The rock 'n' roll party that had been seen in previous years was also back. It was called *Welcome to my Nightmare* and was located outside Mel's Diner and played to three shows per night. Various lookalikes were used to depict rock bands from the time including *Kiss, Alice Cooper* and *Black Sabbath*.

The Bill and Ted show was again back this year and was as popular as ever. This year would also mark the first time that *Bill and Ted* writer Jason Surrell would also receive the director's chair. The whole script was based around the hugely popular franchise at the time of *The X-Files.* The same TV series' main villain, the Smoking Man, was the head villain for the show and kicked off proceedings by kidnapping our plucky hosts leaving Agents Mulder and Scully to track them down. Along the way they meet fellow Agent Ethan Hunt (from the successful *Mission Impossible* movies), using every Tom Cruise gag in the book. This includes a scene from *Risky Business* where the actor dances on stage in just his underpants and sunglasses, just like Cruise had done in the movie. Gags abound for all agents of the large screen when James Bond was introduced to help out, as well as the Terminator, who had just seen his show open that year at the park (the *Terminator show* had opened on April 27, 1996). It was all topped off with a Will Smith lookalike rapping as his character from *Independence Day*, but in the style of his earlier character the *Fresh Prince*. At the very end of the show our heroes were reunited with the *X-Files* crew for a singalong with *Kiss* (the band) lookalikes, singing various hits including their 1975 hit *Rock and Roll All Nite* whilst the others all danced about. As *Bill and Ted shows* go, this was a very memorable show.

As the 1996 event came to an end, so too did the show for the lady that started it all, Julie Zimmerman. She was offered the chance to work on a different project away from Universal that would see her travel the world. The offer was just too good to miss so she tendered her resignation. She moved on, safe in the knowledge that the event she had started and project-managed for so many years was now safe in the hands of a new guard of inspiring creative talent: Jason Surrell, James-Michael Roddy and TJ Mannarino.

In the Monsters' Café: "I'll have the spare ribs please!"

Halloween Horror Nights VII

Frightmares (You'll never sleep again!)

The marketing for Halloween Horror Night's seventh event entitled *Frightmares* started in earnest around mid-September. This year a little fanged goblin (unofficially named Igor or "eye-gore" – get it?) floating above a terrified looking eyeball became the event's logo and was used in all marketing (Fun side fact: Universal's in-house horror awards given there each year are named after the little imp and the statuette is in his image). Universal employed a local animation studio to create the creature just when CGI technology inter-spliced with actual film footage was its early days of use. It may have been genius or pure chance that the little creature would bring so much publicity to the event, but not for the ghastly reasons intended but instead for copyright problems. A European heavy-metal band named *Krokus*, who had received some success in the States, had released a single called *Stayed Awake All Night* in 1989, and the artwork for the cover had featured an almost identical little goblin attached to a brow lifting an eye lid on an unsuspecting person. This was extremely similar to the one Universal was using for their marketing at the event; apart from the color of the eye ball, the actual image was almost exactly the same! Around early October, the image was rolled-out to billboards, TV commercials, magazine advertisements and supermarket points-of-sale. It was everywhere. And although *Krokus* had at the time disbanded (they have since reformed), the image was still unmistakably that from the original album sleeve from 1989. As quickly as the image had been rolled out, rock 'n' roll aficionados were quick to spot the similarities. Colin McCormick, editor of an online magazine about tourism to Orlando was one of the first to spot the similarities when browsing that month for CDs at a local music store. "The similarity is phenomenal," said McCormick, who noticed the album art in the store whilst looking across the street at a poster of that very image advertising Halloween Horror Nights. McCormick, like many others, voiced their concerns to the local Orlando Sentinel who were quick to point the matter out to Universal. The paper, thinking that Universal had made a grave error of judgement, was quick to extinguish all concerns when Universal's Vice-President Jim Canfield issued a note to the local media saying that Universal loved the artwork so much they actually bought the rights to use the image specifically for their event this year.

Frightmares, as the event's tagline would read, would be expanded again to another milestone, that of 18 nights. And once again it would contain a parade, one scarezone and 3 houses, with one being the dual house that had been seen in the past. The other key feature of the event this year would be the expansion and anticipation of the houses' facades. Though the facades had been prominent at the event from the very start, it was this year that more meticulous design and consideration was given to these house entrances. Creative believed that as the houses were attracting such long queues, the need to build anticipation through the house entrance would be essential to the overall enjoyment of each house.

Jason Surrell and James-Michael Roddy would both begin working on the houses from this year; by 1998 they would share the role of Co-Creative Directors following Julie Zimmerman's departure in 1996 to work on other projects within Universal. It was during this year that the idea of creating 'house bibles' would begin. The idea was that each house should contain a 'bible' on how the house should look, feel, smell, and scare. It would ultimately show how the story could be told.

"Ensuring a unity of time and place was essential, it would be this year that we started to treat the houses as full blown attractions, no detail was spared" said Surrell. Houses of the past had been too reliant on unconnected scenes from room to room with no overall theme or narrative. The treatments would contain an approximate three pages per room and would detail everything, including: the cast required, the stage hands required and their roles, any special effects, the music and sound effects, the flow of the public, and the 'art of the scare'. The scare would be defined as 'entry, awe, the distraction, followed by the final boo to propel the public into the next scene'. It was all designed to be flawlessly executed.

The first house up would be exceedingly detailed, located in the extended *Earthquake* queue area. *Tombs of Terror* would take guests on an extraordinary tour of New Orleans and the Bayou, which had been specifically designed to fit the parade and scarezone of that year where the horrific *Mardi Gras* theme had spread and rooted across the park. The house featured: pirates, ghosts, zombie soldiers and vampires, set in the area's many mansions and focusing mostly on a decrepit funeral home at first. After clearing the buildings, guests would be led into creepy, deserted cemeteries before being taken into the misty swamps where the swamp monsters and ferial vampires lurked. The famous streets of New Orleans and the Lafayette Cemetery had both been heavily surveyed by Universal's creative to ensure all the details of the area could be included to make the experience as authentic as possible. The Rat Lady was also present in the house during one of the graveyard scenes, encased in a tomb surrounded by her rats (which were really starting to become celebrities in their own right by this time!).

Next up was a return to Universal's *Museum of Horror* which had moved up the road to Soundstage 22, still retaining its dual house status. *The house of horrors* was given a slight name change, and became a more museum-like dual house. One side had the classic monsters, pretty much the same as in previous years, and the other side had modern day horror films, loosely based on recent horror movies such as *Scream* and *Candyman*. The soundstage had two large facades built that year to mirror what was being done elsewhere to build suspense in the queue. A gothic interior with stone vaulted ceilings and columns welcomed guests into what was billed as "the world's only museum where the guards have to warn the exhibits not to touch the visitors!"

Last up for the houses was a return back to the popular *Nazarman's* area with *Hotel Hell*. The house had a large fake hotel façade built in Sting Alley which had been made to look like a hotel that had gone out of business and had been boarded up. Once inside, guests would venture into the hotel's check-in lobby and its rooms (which was not all dissimilar to a certain ride in a certain theme park which may or may not include a hotel). Then guests would explore the kitchen, the dining room and some of the guests' rooms. Ghosts of the dead hotel guests and staff (including the bell boy and a sadistic chef) were all present, ready to jump out at unsuspecting guests. This also marked the first time that the Rat Lady would be located in more than one house, as here she was incased in a sewage pipe with glass around, located in the laundry scene.

Midway of the Bizarre was back and still located in the Amity area. No real changes were seen here other than the addition of carnival games, which had not before been added to the Amity area. Likewise the parade, *Festival of the Dead*, was a near-mirror of the previous year, following the same route and having nearly all the same floats. One large addition that was instead of the Devil from *Darkness* being on stilts, he had his own float towards the front of the parade. A magic show was also back this year, entitled *Abra Cadaver*. It was again held in the *Animal Actors' stage* for five performances a night. The show included the usual mix of thrills and guest participation where a plucky member of the audience was hauled out and cut in half. The show was presented with different magicians and did not feature any hypnotism as it had done in the previous year.

The Bill and Ted show was back again for an impressive sixth outing and was as popular as ever. The overall theme was based around the original *Star Trek* and the *Next Generation Star Trek* crews (as both franchises had been making movies and TV shows recently). Both Captains Kirk and Picard would do battle over who was the best with the audience cheering to decide. Various banter-like gags are batted to and fro amongst the two characters about wig wearing and being 'a true number two' instead of a number one (Picard's famous nickname for his second in command Riker) as they explore Gotham City. They are soon joined by the performance's villains who were the Borg Queen from the recent *Next Generation* movie *First Contact* and a Klingon to represent both franchises' respective villains-au-jour. Ripley from *Aliens* soon shows up, along with a lookalike Will Smith from the recent *Men in Black* movie, along with the Terminator (again), and Batman and Robin from their recent *Batman* movie *Batman & Robin*. Then the both the villains from that movie, Poison Ivy and Mr Freeze, show up. The Terminator and Mr Freeze on the big screen had both been played by Arnold Schwarzenegger, so two lookalikes of Schwarzenegger both square up with some funny back and forth gags about the two roles by the same actor. The cast of *Seinfeld* arrive to much comedic affect in a stolen DeLorean time machine followed by Darth Vader. The song *Greased Lightning* is performed from the movie *Grease* with Kramer on lead vocals. At the end of the song Bill's cell phone rings and it is the classic Ghostface voice from the *Scream* movies who soon appears on stage. He is then quickly defrocked to reveal his true identity - that of Austin Powers. The assembled cast dance to his signature theme before the Men in Black interrupt and start to perform their signature theme. Finally, Elaine from *Seinfeld* interrupts and a performance of the *Spice Girl's* number one hit *Wannabe* (which was still riding in the charts at the time) ensues. She is joined during the performance by the Borg Queen, Batgirl and Poison Ivy characters. As the song continues it blends into *Smells Like Teen Spirit* by *Nirvana* where the whole cast reunites on stage to sing and dance, with Bill and Ted taking center stage. At the very end of the song it is the lookalike of Kramer from *Seinfeld* who gets the signature chance to bring down the house as in previous years.

This year's *Bill and Ted show* would attract a lot of attention for just how great the Jason Surrell-written and directed show was (it would in fact be Surrell's last year for Universal before he left to work as an imagineer for Disney). Fans across the fledgling internet would report on how the show was a 'must-see' even if you didn't care for the scares in the rest of the park. The attention that it garnered would also find its way to the Burbank HQ of the *Warner Bros Company*. The studio allegedly sent a formal request to Universal asking as to why their characters of *Batman* and co were reported to be included in one of their 'new attractions'. By the time the studio had written to Universal the event had actually ended, so no further letters were recorded.

The final remarkable aspect of the event this year was the first occasion that Universal had expanded its travel company's operations abroad to offer packages for tourists from the UK. In the previous year packages for transport, hotel and tickets had been offered domestically to US guests, which continued to be rolled-out to great effect. It was this year, however, that the roll-out included UK guests. The reasoning behind the decision was that in the previous few years the company had witnessed a growing number of guests travelling especially for the event from the UK. To capitalize on this growing movement of fans from abroad, Universal were quick to offer complete packages just like they had done to domestic guests for the past couple of years.

Eyegore!

Halloween Horror Nights VIII

Primal Scream (The last scream you'll ever hear)

Originally starting as a humble three-night event back in 1991, the event this year grew to another milestone to span 19 nights for this year. It would also increase the house content to feature five haunted houses, three shows, one scarezone and a nightly parade. There was a great emphasis this year on the fact that the event had become a juggernaut, and that with every year that passed it had reached new boundaries and become even more successful than the previous. To match this demand Universal had to keep pace and ensure they were providing an upscale event that always built on the previous years. The event had grown so rapidly by this point that attendance had almost doubled every year, year-on-year. It was projected in 1998 that by 1999 it would finally become the most attended Halloween event in the entire world. Michael Gilligan, Universal's senior vice president of marketing said at the time, "Our goal is that by this year or next year, no one will be able to come near this (in terms of attendance figures)." The gauntlet was laid down by Universal, as the current owner of the title of 'most visited Halloween event' was over on the West coast in Southern California with Knott's Berry Farm. Knott's had been in the themed Halloween entertainment business far longer than Universal, starting their event back in 1972. Knott's were keen to retain their title, so after Universal's impressive announcement they went ahead and bumped their event out to 16 nights, a decision they made due to the fact that 'most of the nights had already sold out'. Knott's spokeswoman Dana Hammontree said at the time, "We are still the king of Halloween". Universal weren't daunted by the challenge. They countered Knott's offerings by providing stage shows featuring internationally acclaimed acts, using the best acting talent in the business and by providing some of the largest most ambitious houses it could manage; Universal did not disappoint...

The first house, which although billed separately, was a dual house with a shared theme and it was unlike anything the park's creative team had built before. *S.S. Frightanic* would be built into the whole *Earthquake* queue housing. It was a life-sized ship of epic proportions and would borrow heavily from the smash-hit movie *Titanic* which had been released the previous year and had smashed all box-office records. The house had been designed by Jason Surrell and had originally been entitled *The S. S. Satanic*. But when the name had been forwarded to the Marketing Department, a memo came back to Surrell's desk which read, "suggest name change to *S. S. Frightanic*".

"I initially didn't like that they had changed my idea, then I realized it was a whole better name, so I immediately changed it and the rest is history!" said Surrell.

The house would offer two unique and detailed entrances with separate queues that would provide guests with two very different experiences; these were *Carnage Crew* and *Fear in First Class*. The ship had taken all summer to construct, and when fully realized it was an impressive 520ft long. Nobody could surely take credit within the Halloween industry for creating such a large detailed set as this before; it was incredible to behold!

As the event had now by this year become a year-round venture to plan and construct, the creatives at Universal were keen to draw on all experiences of the 'fright-science' to create the world-class haunts that were constructed. It was having this time and space to create that led to this very ship being constructed. The backstory of the damned vessel was that the *Frightanic* ship (a luxury liner) had just docked in San Francisco after a mysterious voyage to Hawaii where the ship was sucked into a black hole and into another dimension. When it returned to dock, the crew had gone insane and the ship was in an awful state of dilapidation where ghosts and ghouls of every caliber lurked behind every corner. Surrell said at the time, "It's like the *Titanic* gone bad, if that could have gotten any worse." The idea for such a house had been kicked around for a while but the park's creative team struggled to bring the concept together. It wasn't until this year, when the trophy of 'most visited haunt event in the world' was within reach, that the button to proceed with the elaborate plans was pushed. "We've had the idea to do a death ship or ghost ship for three years without success," said T.J. Mannarino, Universal's then scenic designer. Now was the time to proceed!

Inside the ship, guests will find that lights flicker and water sprays over the deck, along with sounds of creaking metal as though the ship is starting to sink. Narrow corridors with exceedingly low ceilings direct guests into various scenes. These include the office of the ship's dentist where a zombie is sprawled in the operating chair, his teeth drilled so painfully that the smell of burned teeth is pumped into the air. Rotting corpses of former crew members lie in swing bunks along the ship's crew quarters. In the old-fashioned smoking room, the chandelier and furniture are installed with mechanical arms discreetly hidden to give the effect that the ship is moving with the tide, with the aim of evoking real feelings of seasickness. On the bow of the ship a pair of rotting skeletons made to represent the characters of the movie are seen with splayed out arms. All this is done firmly tongue-in-cheek, but as you pause to chuckle that's when the scareactors get you. In total across the two areas of the house there were a cast of 80 scareactors (a new record), all in costumes and makeup, playing the crew and dead passengers of this damned voyage. A luxury carpet moves underfoot to add to the disorientation. The level of the floor changes height to add to the claustrophobic nature of the house combined with multiple paths ahead. The acts of disorientation reach a crescendo when, as you try to gain your bearings, a scareactor will jump from behind that fake mirror or wall to get the best scare. "All it takes is one second of not paying attention and we get you," boasted Universal's J Michael Roddy, the show director.

Each room was designed to have at least one moving part to create the illusion that you had left Florida and were now on the open seas with the crew from hell. In the glitzy ballroom of the ship the team even installed fans and mechanical arms to propel human looking mannequins in a waltz around the dance floor while real dancers would twirl with the dummies before breaking the dance pattern and giving the best scare to unsuspecting and disorientated guests. "There are 'boo corridors' of quick jabs that prepare you for the big one up ahead," Surrell said. In fact due to the level of staffing within the house, you could be no more than a couple steps at a time from being got at with a perfect scare.

"People have got a three-second attention span in a room while they try to see what's safe," Mannarino said. "So if we can distract them for a second or give them a sense that an area is safe, then we can scare them. The thrills are choreographed and timed to catch the crowds of 10 to 15 guests just as they are halfway through a room. We scare from the side or behind so that they will run forward rather than backward and keep the line moving." There truly had never been such a large and detailed house built for what was just a temporary haunted attraction; Universal had upped their game big style.

The next house offered this year was *Hell's High… School's out forever!* Located in the purposely crafted *Nazarman's* area, the house was a combination of low-budget slasher movie (aka *Scream* or *I Know What You Did Last Summer* which were both popular at the time) and a teen comedy. It was the latter that was just starting to come back as a very popular cult comedy genre. The combination of the two made for scares and laughs in equal portions. The storyline was that a slasher movie was to be shot in a real high school but the unsuspecting film crew had inadvertently used real murderers. Add evil substitute teachers, zombified nerds and cruel gym coaches, and you have a recipe for a great house. Guests would enter into classrooms, a puke-filled cafeteria, science labs, the nurses office (complete with a needle-swinging deranged nurse), and even a disgusting kitchen. Also on ready to explore was a gymnasium with countless body bags hanging from the ceiling, moving along with the cries and screams of the nerds placed inside. The tradition of having a least one house that contained an element of comedy in equal measures to the horror was widely seen from this year onwards.

FUN FEAR FACT

A voodoo house has been proposed by Universal's Art and Design team more times than any other concept, yet has never been made.

The event also had a return of *Universal's Museum of Horrors* house that had been experienced in previous years. Once again it was a dual house; this marked the first time that Universal had held two dual houses in one year. Split in two with two queues, two entrances and two huge facades, the houses were very popular with the park's guests. Billed as *Chamber of Horrors*, with the original monsters from Universal's back catalogue coming out to scare there was then an *Unnatural History*, where modern horrors lurk. To charge up the classic monsters section of the house, the park's creative focused on creating elaborate sets and facades to ramp up the feeling of being in the actual movie. The Universal movie *Casper (the friendly ghost)* had wrapped filming a few years prior and when scouting for props on the west coast the park's creative spotted the pipe-organ from the film. They shipped it to Orlando to repurpose it as *The Phantom of the Opera's* organ for a loud spectacular scene half way through the house. Classic scenes that were reimaged that year include: *Frankenstein*, *Psycho* and *The Shining*.

Midway of the Bizarre was back, slightly bigger than previously. The ghoulish Mardi-Gras-gone-wrong scarezone was again held back in Amity, much to the event's fans' approval. Along with the scarezone, the parade was back. This year a couple of floats were tweaked but largely it was the same as previous years. Grand marshals for the parade were Chucky and Tiffany from the *Child's Play* franchise. The Universal movie *Bride of Chucky* opened to much success a mere week before the event started. The black comedy horror film was the fourth installment in the *Child's Play* film series. The film was written by Don Mancini and directed by Ronny Yu. It starred Jennifer Tilly (who plays and voices the titular character Tiffany) and Brad Dourif (who voices Chucky). Heading the parade in their matrimonial parade float the characters also starred in the first ever webcast for the event to have been streamed live on the main Universal Escape (the then name for the Orlando resort) website. The webcast featured a ghoulish-looking minister forming the marital bond between the two characters with Beetlejuice and others as witnesses – guess who caught the bouquet!

Along with these attractions, the park also built the largest set for any show they had put on before, for the *Inferno* event. A spectacular gymnast meets circus performing acts (similar in content to a *Cirque du Soleil* performance) the show combined acrobatics and daredevil acts against a huge, spectacular backdrop. Held in the *Animal Actors' stage*, there were three shows per night. Next up was the rock festival that was again held outside Mel's Drive In. Big-named actual bands were mixed with local sound-a-like bands to give a great atmosphere to the proceedings. *Horrorpalooza* was the name of the event, and such real acts as local Florida band done good, *Lynyrd Skynyrd* bolting out *Sweet Home Alabama* and *Free Bird* to cheering crowds. Peter Frampton, Tommy Shaw and sound-a-like band *Kiss Army* all performed during the event.

Bill & Ted were back again for a very similar show to the one seen in the previous year. *TJ Hooker, Lethal Weapon, Goodfellas, Zorro* and the characters from *Titanic* all starred in another comedy romp with the time travelling dudes. Like the previous year, songs from the movie *Grease* were added for the climax where the house literally comes down. This also marked the first time that James Michael Roddy (then Universal Creative) took the reins for the writing duties of the show, and it was an "excellent" addition that year.

Another first this year was the use of an outside contractor to help build the sets that were required, mostly because the success of the event led to the ever-increasing expansion of requirements. *Fake Productions*, a local specialist in this field, first helped out in 1998, and they would go on to be appointed again for future years to help with set construction.

Other notable firsts for the event this year include the opening of Universal Studios' *Classic Monsters Café*, which was heavily featured in the marketing. On some nights the queues were reportedly out the door! The use of interest marketing was really pushed this year to maximize the event's world-wide credentials; after all, if you wanted to be the biggest in the world you had to reach out in every way you could. The other big change for this year was the use of scents. Remember the burning teeth smell I mentioned earlier? Getting the right smell, working out how it was to be distributed and to what levels took a huge amount of planning. In preparation for the event Universal bought gallons of custom scents with titles such as 'Eau de Dead', 'open coffin', 'rotting corpse no.5' and 'Burning Flesh (general)' from a New York perfumer to add a sensory dynamic to the houses and one scarezone.

The Theme That Was Never Seen

Back in the mid-90s when the Crypt Keeper was the main icon for two of the events, the park's creatives came up with one of their first ideas for an icon. The icon would be designed in-house, rather than a property from outside of the company to which they had to pay royalties. Designing in-house would afford them the luxury of being able to do and design whatever they wanted, without the need to agree strict terms and designs for the use of any IPs.

Several themes were batted around the offices of Art and Design, before one theme started to fall together to fit a nice overall narrative. Inspiration had come from two sources. The first was the Universal-owned version of Lon Chaney's *The Phantom of the Opera*. The idea was to have a ghoulish phantom stalking the streets of the Studio after dark. The phantom would be an updated version of the classic character that would live and breathe Universal Studios Florida.

The second inspiration came completely by chance one night. One of the event's designers just happened to have fallen asleep in front of the TV one night over the weekend. He awoke in the early hours of the morning to find the TV still on. Flicking through the channels he happened upon an old 70s TV movie with the exact same context: a modern-day phantom running amok in a working film studio. The movie was the 1974 *The Phantom of Hollywood* starring Jack Cassidy, Broderick Crawford and Peter Lawford. *IMDB* lists the synopsis as "The internationally famous *Worldwide Studios* has hit hard times and is forced to sell its back lot to Hollywood property developers. The trouble is someone keeps killing off the site surveyors. The studio chiefs then learn of the legend of a masked man who lives on the lot and is sworn to protect it from harm."

The backstory to this little-known TV movie is actually quite fascinating, and when you know what it is about it makes the movie all the more melancholic. The *Worldwide Studios* backlot that the movie takes place on is in fact the famous *MGM Studios'* backlot. And all the demolition that takes place in the movie is in fact all the actual sets from some of the most iconic movies ever made being trashed. The premise of the movie used these real-world events to film the last ever movie on these hallowed movie set streets. Overall the piece borrows generously from Leroux's *The Phantom of the Opera* and the subsequent Universal release of the same name. Instead of a revenge-filled and deformed musician living underneath a grand opera house, the movie features a shunned (and still deformed) actor living underneath the ruins of famous film sets from the golden era of Hollywood. Hoping to prevent the demolition and punish the Studio Heads for allowing the wanton vandalism, the phantom strikes out by killing the workers of the Studio one by one.

The movie intercuts clips of old classic movies from the black and white days of cinema with color versions of what they looked like now, dilapidated and decrepit. Much of the action takes place in these actual sets with some quite elaborate deaths played throughout. It is true that the murderer of the piece, the phantom, is somewhat a heroic character in many regards as he battles bulldozers to end the carnage, which leaves the audience wanting to cheer on the bad guy much like many other classic thriller or horror movies (*Psycho* for example).

The designer in question was surprised to see the TV movie, having never seen it before. This, along with the classic iteration of the monster, came into play and the proposed idea finally fell into place. The idea would be to have a Phantom of the Studio, a guardian, a person that came over from Hollywood to build the Orlando Studios (as in a carpenter or director etc.) and then disappeared. Living in secret quarters between the rafters of an empty soundstage, the Phantom would protect and guard the Studios against any woe. The Phantom's biggest woe would be Halloween Horror Nights, he supposedly did not like the event and during the run of the new event would threaten that he would be unleashed onto the Studio should the event continue to be held. The idea would be seen to have some kind of faux media battle with the press (they would be in on it) that would see the Phantom as an anti-icon for the event. Mock phantoms would be placed in window and perched on soundstages. Actors playing the character would be seen through every soundstage, appearing in the shows or even taking over control of shows. He was even alleged to have his own house; a house that would have been similar to the *Silver Screams* house we had in 2009 (which was a composition of movies set out in an old movie theater). Weirdly enough, this house actually featured the Universal *Phantom of the Opera* in the first scene and then in the fifth too.

The idea was borrowed, in a way, by Universal Hollywood for their 2006 event. The premise was that Paulo Ravinski (aka the Orlando HHN created icon, the Director) had been hired by Universal Hollywood to create the most demonic horror movie of all time. The Director was supposedly sent to Hollywood to create a short film detailing his expectations for the project in a preview for executives. However, when viewed, the short film was supposed to contain real scenes of brutal torture and death. They immediately cancelled the project and the Director disappeared, in the wake of the Studios banning him from the lot. The Director had actually hidden out in an old disused soundstage on the backlot, the same soundstage where the original *Phantom of the Opera* set was still housed (now demolished, ironically enough). Working within this abandoned soundstage he continued his work of torturing lost members of the public on film. Universal, knowing of this vast evil unfolding on their premises, were unable to do anything about it by the time the Halloween event came about, so they warned people to not enter during the event. In reality, the Director did feature on the *Terror Tram* and in the shows that year. The ability to have his own soundstage to house a maze version of this backstory never happened due to filming commitments across the backlot, which was a huge disappointment.

Back at Orlando, the overall idea of a having a Studio Phantom was extremely meta for its day, and was perhaps a bit too early in conception. If it had been created today, much like the character of Fear, it perhaps would have been more viable. Nobody knows why the idea never came to be, but speculation has it that the concept was not strong enough and that using the press may have backfired. Whatever the reason, the Phantom of Universal Orlando will never be seen... or will he? Perhaps there is actually a Phantom...

To get a taste of what could have been, the movie is available on DVD or from streaming service *Warner Instant Archive*.

Halloween Horror Nights IX

Last Gasp (Sayonara!)

Halloween Horror Nights IX: Last Gasp would debut at the park in 1999 and this would be what some people call 'the last of the formative years' of the acclaimed Halloween event. The events from the following year onwards would still utilize everything that had worked before but with new twists, which I shall discuss further in the next chapter. It was August 8th of that year when auditions for the various park roles were being undertaken with the usual required mix of actors, actresses, performers, dancers, stilt-walkers and people who are "very comfortable with rats". It also marked the first occasion that people who auditioned were given jobs based purely on their looks, and no - not how you think. Show Director J Michael Roddy explained at the time, "There were auditions and some characters were added to the show based on their talent, at that audition. A prime example was the *American Pie* characters. I had toyed with the idea but couldn't figure how to include them. Two of the performers auditioning - June Lindle and Dave Tomasi came in and I knew I had a Jim and Michelle that would start the pre-show and be a thread throughout. Another example was Meghan Maroney as Heather Donahue from the *Blair Witch Project*." In fact, that day alone 500 people showed up to audition for the 25 parts for the show.

The announcement of the park's event actually happened exceedingly early by earlier years' standards when a press-release was issued on July 26th. The release mentioned that the event would run for 19 nights (the same as the previous year), a house based around a new concept using

3D technology would be added and that the popular dude duo Bill and Ted would return, but that was all. Anticipation was building as to what a 3D house could be and how it could be implemented. Eventually the wait was over and the opening night came, and fans flocked to the *Nazarman's* area to see for themselves. On that very night the queue for the house quickly exceeded 3 hours. "The 3-dimensional haunted maze was my favorite," said one guest. "After an hour-and-a-half wait, I was given my 3-D glasses and then realized it was worth the wait," another said. Neon strobe lights and luminous paint would combine, together with the guest's free 3D issued glasses, to deceive their very eyes into believing they were seeing things in front of their faces, which weren't in fact there until an actual scareactor jumped out. The house was receiving high praise from all guests.

The house was called *Universal's Creature Features in 3D*, and used many of the classic horror creatures but was presented using this interesting technology. The house like many this year included very detailed and elaborate facades again. This house had a whole New York theater frontage that had been boarded up to make guests feel as though they were entering a dilapidated old cinema. It also blended well with the Nazarman's New York setting. Frankenstein's monster, Dracula, and the Wolfman were all present for the technology's initial outing. A forest scene was seen, the Wolfman was on scare duties with little nods towards the recent hit the *Blair Witch Project*. There were monsters coming from below, from the sides and even from above on cords; any which way was utilized to confuse and disorientate guests using the glasses. It was something that had never been seen before.

Though the *Mummy ride* at Universal would not be open for a few years yet, this year did feature a *Mummy house* that was also wildly popular. The park had also re-imaged their popular *Stage 54* exhibit with props, sets and costumes from the summer blockbuster. On top of that, the event's logo for that year featured a ghoulish-looking mummy as the centerpiece for the marketing. Universal had gone Mummy mad! Some speculation based on the reaction from guests at this event (and the box-office success that the modern franchise was having) led directly to the *Mummy* becoming a permanent fixture at the theme park. The house, entitled only *The Mummy* was based on the popular movie that had been released in May of that year to much critical and financial success. The film totally refreshed the old Karloff version of the movie into a new, edgier, dynamic adventure movie that played well to all audiences. Located in the *Earthquake* queue building, the house tied directly into the movie where actual scenes were recreated putting guests right into the heart of the action. A scene showing a 'live' mummification was added, along with sounds and projections of beetles crawling everywhere, secret passages, ancient crypts, scenes of torture and lines of those dog-faced zombie soldiers queuing up to scare guests. The house was a massive hit for the park.

Norman Bates was back again this year and it was understandable why he was so furious, as Universal had at the time just demolished his old house, the *Bates Manor*, which had been used as the location for the fourth installment to the popular franchise. Not having his own actual home to be located in, Bates was moved to Soundstage 23 where the past *Psycho* house themes could be built on and expanded due to the larger size of Soundstage 23. *Psycho: Through the Mind of Norman Bates* would start off in familiar settings but would quickly take guests into the twisted mind of the man himself. A shower scene in a replica of one of the infamous motel bedrooms would soon see 'mother' jumping out around every corner with a further descent into his madness. Rooms full of wet, blood-drenched shower curtains were hung where guests had no option but to pull their way through. Then a dark path leads into a room full of huge, 6ft tall knives, with mirrored faces adding to the disorientation, before dumping guests onto a spinning runway (which would later be used very often in houses at the event). The house was loosely associated with the remake of the original *Psycho* which had been released by Universal Pictures in 1998.

Next up was a house called *Insanity* and it was, completely. The house is important, because many fans of the event will testify that this is the first house to start using the Shadybrook association with the event. However there was no direct tie at this time; that would come later. This house, though, was intense. Event staff were directed by Creative to slow the queue down to stop conga lines, so scene-by-scene could be presented more intensely. The fear of not seeing ahead or seeing where the exits are was prominent in this house. In the first room the lights would go out and it would be pitch black, then suddenly you'd hear doors open, creatures scratching at the walls and dogs growling. Some believe this house to be the first early test of an 'extreme house' where the scares were notched up a level to great effect. After the initial dark room scare, the house would lead guests into an insane asylum with padded cells and strait jackets. Then guests came face-to-face with an evil clown-come-jester, who would dance about and distract guests before other inmates would jump from around the corner for the ultimate scare. After this area, guests would walk down corridors filled with body bags hung up from the ceiling that twitched and moved to suggest the victims contained within. Meanwhile, a heavily tattooed inmate with a knife and another with an axe would prowl as guests looked for the exits. The house was intense!

The final house offered this year was also located in the *Earthquake* and was entitled *Doomsday*. Guests were led on a journey through the underground of New York City as the clock strikes midnight on the New Year's Eve 1999. The house played on an unfounded myth that the world would end in 2000. Those that will remember the time will say how some people believed this was a genuine threat to humanity at the time. Some people called it the Millennium Bug or Y2K, which supposed that as computers could not comprehend the 21st century within their databases they would stop working and would therefore cause the world to end. Some states and countries around the world actually issued advice to citizens about what to do if Armageddon was about to happen. Looking back in retrospect it was a crazy time, but this house was created to play on people's fears and present a scenario of 'what if'. Initially guests were taken down into the New York subway where trains had derailed (similar to the attraction that the house was near to), and hooded freaks from subterranean worlds were present to oversee the end of humanity. A more religious overtone of the *Book of Revelations* was presented where witches were being burnt and demons were present, as guests explored deeper into the house and closer to hell. Towards the end, the hooded freaks were revealed to be demons and the heating was cranked up, much to the guests' annoyance (as the *Earthquake* queue is technically outside).

The parade was back again this year and followed the same route as previous years. New additions this year included: a float filled with spiders of all sizes, a rat float, and a Mummy float featuring characters from the movie. The snakes float which had been vacant for a year was also back. There was another return for the accompanying *Midway of the Bizarre* scarezone located once again in Amity. Due to the parade every year, the park could not facilitate further scarezones, except for a few roaming gangs such as the *Chainsaw Drill Team* or the Rat Lady. The merchandise for this year was also increased substantially. Universal having noticed that past event merchandise was selling very well on online auction sites during the event, decided to sell more merchandise at the event to attract more dollars their way. It also marked the first time that the 'I Survived' t-shirt made an appearance, a tradition that follows to this day. *Trick or Treat – Deadman's Party* was present this year, a rock show featuring heavily made-up sound-a-likes singing monster rock and pop songs from the 80s and 90s. *Deadly D'illusions* located at the *Animal Actors' Stage* was billed as "You won't believe your eyes as you witness this spellbinding display of unbelievable effects, magic and shocking illusions." A magic show at heart, the show also featured death defying acts like fire eating and sword swallowing.

As announced back in July, the popular dudes were back again this year (though they would be back every year). Famous and popular movies of the time were given the Bill & Ted treatment, including: *Austin Powers 1 & 2, Mystery Men* and of course the very popular *American Pie*, plus appearances by Jerry Springer and Marilyn Manson lookalikes. J Michael Roddy, the show director, had taken the reins that year as script writer and producer for the show, an appointment that would see the show obtain the highest guest satisfaction level that had ever been seen.

Three other notable events happened this year. The first was that Universal had purchased a warehouse down near the Orlando International Airport, due to reaching capacity storing everything on site. The warehouse could be used to build props and sets all year round and would provide important storage for their collections of ever-growing props. The warehouse would go on to be featured in the marketing for a later event (Halloween Horror Nights XX), though to date no guests or fans have ever visited the now infamous warehouse. The next event that is significant to the timeline of the event happened on the West coast of Florida in Tampa at a competing park, Busch Gardens. *Spooky Safari* would debut this year at the park and would feature, for just two nights, *Dr. Livingsdoom's Haunted Jungle Trail* (their first ever house), a large pumpkin patch for families to explore, various children's activities and the ability to ride all your favorite rides during the night. The special after-hours hard ticketed event would be Busch Gardens' first ever foray into the Halloween business. These first two nights were such a success, the name would soon be changed and Universal would start to see some real local competition.

The final event, and possibly one of the most important in Halloween Horror Night's history, was taking place very quietly right at the park exit. Every night guests were asked about their experiences by Universal employees hoping to secure feedback from their visit to the event that year. After all of the questions on houses and shows had been answered the poll-takers would ask one final question, "what is your biggest phobia or what are you most scared of?" The answer to this would prove to be the catalyst in the creation of an icon that would go on to define the event.

Halloween Horror Nights X

Not afraid of the dark? You don't know Jack...

The next decade in Halloween Horror Night's history would focus more on originally-crafted content and less on obtaining external intellectual properties (IPs) for the event's many houses and attractions. This initial step change, many have speculated, could have been brought about as a result of the pressures of setting up a new park: Islands of Adventure. Time and/or money were naturally more constrained to help open this new park. Or possibly, as Universal Escape was no more and now Universal Resort was here to stay, this might have led to a change in direction? It's also possible that as a new generation of creatives had gradually taken the reins at the in-house creative team, they potentially wanted to take the event in a new and exciting direction; perhaps we'll never know. What we do know is that the event this year was going to be unlike anything we had previously seen.

Quietly, in late August of that year, near the area where people pose for photos with the newly-erected Universal globe, a small sign was deployed. It read:

"HOT SET! Beware of demented clown! He's been known to scare the socks off people! Universal Studios is conducting a test to determine the scare factor of a key Halloween Horror Nights character. Please avoid this area if you are not interested in entertainment of this nature."

And so Jack the Clown was first introduced to the public at large. Jack, who had been born out of the surveys from the previous year, was to be the event's first icon that had been wholly developed in-house. Created by then Universal Creative James-Michael Roddy, he said at the time of these tests,

"[He's the] Scariest clown every seen! What we've seen today shows

121

we're right on the mark, and this Halloween [Horror Nights] will be the most extreme and the most scary we have had up to this point." The survey information had been gathered and the A&D department looked at how the many phobias could be assembled into one character, that character would become Jack. The very first makeup tests with actor James Keaton in the role commenced in the *Hitchcock* trailer, located behind the former Hitchcock attraction (a very apt location for the birth of new horror icon). On completion of the makeup, the character was photographed in front of a curtain in the PR room, these were the very first photos of the character whilst the paint on his face was still drying.

Later that same day, the public tests were carried out on a dry sunny afternoon with no sets or props, just Jack in all his awfulness, and the park guests were terrified. Universal knew from these early tests that they had created something very special.

The very first concept sketch of Jack the Clown.

Jack Schmidt would have an elaborate back story to create his character that would measure up to any horror icon of the last 100 years. He would be bolder and more dynamic than any character that the park had used before. No longer would lengthy IP negotiations be needed where detailed analysis of what characters can and can't say, or can and cannot do. The park had free rein to deploy their new creation in any horrific manner they wanted. The first step was creating that very back story, and although it was added to and changed a little over time, the rough original outline was this:

"Jack Schmidt was a circus performer. He loved to entertain children with his practical pranks and prat-falls during his stint with *Dr. Oddfellow's Carnival of Thrills*. But underneath the greasepaint and clown nose, he held a hideously dark and sinister secret. Jack was a twisted murderer. He was wanted for the abduction and disappearance of several small children throughout the Southern states. Police officials soon caught on that the missing children followed a pattern that led them closer and closer to the travelling freakshow.

On Halloween 1920 the police were closing in on the Clown killer. Fearing capture, Jack revealed his sinister secret to Dr. Oddfellow in the hopes of possible concealment. The Good Doctor was himself wanted by the police for the accidental death of several patrons in a freak circus accident years earlier under a different name. The Doctor was not sympathetic to Jack's cause; in contrast he quickly admonished him for potentially bringing the police down upon the entire band of miscreants. He asked Jack to show him what he had done with the bodies of the children. Jack revealed the bodies of thirteen children hidden in the confines of three small trunks that were kept in his travelling coach.

Fearing the worst, Dr. Oddfellow had Jack murdered and his body hidden within the travelling carnival's *House of Horrors* as an exhibit, along with the bodies of the children. Years later the Carnival was sold by Dr. Oddfellow, and the various dark rides and exhibits were split and sent to various owners around the states, including the *House of Horrors* and its grisly secret.

Sixty years later, in the Fall of 1980, a television crew from the *BBC* was documenting the great *Dark Rides of America*. They journeyed throughout the eastern seaboard looking for forgotten carnival rides and attractions. They stumbled upon the *House of Horrors* as it sat abandoned in a Louisiana Junkyard. The crew asked permission to film the interior. Twenty dollars later, the film crew pried open the doors of the forgotten relic and stepped inside. The smell of decay was overpowering as the bright camera light illuminated the darkened corridors. Moving past the faded walls and hanging fabric, the smell began to increase. The cameraman wretched as he panned his camera towards a series of trunks. Behind the trunks was a large wooden box stenciled like a children's toy. One letter filled each side of the box: J-A-C-K.

The Cameraman steadied his camera as the Host of the show investigated the box. He found a large crank on the side of the box. He turned the crank with some resistance, but after a few twists, it freely moved in a clockwise rotation. A clanky musical melody played out as the Host smiled into the camera.
"It still works!" said the Host. Suddenly the Music stopped. The Host's smile turned to an embarrassed clench of teeth. He rotated the crank once more with no result. Suddenly the Light from the camera died. He turned to see the Cameraman move away. He heard the sound of something wet. He grabbed his flashlight and clicked it on. The Cameraman was standing a few feet further away. "Sorry - My light died." he grinned. Then, without warning the crank rotated a few spins. The top of the box flew open and a form sprung out. Affixed to a giant spring was the decomposing body of Jack Schmidt.

After a thorough police investigation, the bodies of the thirteen children as well as the body of Jack were shipped to the local Louisiana Coroner's office for further examination. The bodies of the children arrived later in the evening. At approximately Midnight on October 31st, the van carrying the body and box of Jack disappeared into the Louisiana swamp. A freak accident. Later that week the bodies of the *BBC* cameraman and Host were found, the result of a grisly and unsolved murder.

Throughout the following years there have been urban legend retellings of this tale, with a corresponding story about the decomposing body of Jack killing again. The legend states that Jack is searching for Dr. Oddfellow, in a thirst for vengeance. The legend also states that Jack will reward anyone who releases him from his toy tomb by turning the crank with a very special reward.
(This also tied into the emergence of the media gift which debuted this year. A small, detailed prop would be sent to select members of the press with the aim of inviting them to the press preview but to also shock them enough into writing about the gift. Impressive media gifts from over the years include: Bloody Mary's jewelry box with sound from 2009, 2010's popcorn box with 'real' werewolf hair and *SAW* recorder to this year's Jack-in-a-box prop).

The local press ran the story: "October 2000 - Universal Studios is bringing some of the original pieces of Dr. Oddfellow's carnival of thrills to highlight the popular Halloween Horror Nights event. The Publicity and Marketing Department have also decided to play on the urban legend of Jack. Designers of the event have been able to acquire what has been sold as the original box in which Jack was trapped. No word yet on the actual validity of the find."

With the backstory in place, the creative team decided to focus on the look of the monster. A mixture of real-life clowning killer John Wayne Gacy, a hint of the chaotic clown from *Stephen King's IT* ably played by Tim Curry, a splash of the Joker from the Tim Burton version of the original *Batman*, a dash of original Universal horror movie *The Man Who Laughs* (1928 film) and a spate of any urban legend from the many regional carnivals that had toured, were all possible ingredients in the 'DNA' that created the character. "As we start to get older, we realize that smile is nothing but paint. And there could be something dark and sinister behind it," said J Michael Roddy. And that was the point. Jack would be an amalgamation of all the urban legends that have been told, all the movies that used a terrifying clown and all the times you as a child saw a clown and wondered who was under the grease-paint; Universal played to all these sensibilities to great effect. Using Roddy's own face as a starting point, the look of the monster would use facial attributes of Roddy to exaggerated proportions, combined with the aged makeup, elaborate hair styling and sharp claw-like nails ensured that the character was made to scare anyone, including the non clown-fearing masses.

The next element of building the monster was to select an actor who could play the character in a terrifying form, who could really get under people's skin and who would add all the little nuances that were required to make a truly great monster icon. Park creatives looked no further than Central Orlando theme park veteran James Keaton. Keaton had played Beetlejuice for the park's daytime show and in commercials and other park events; in fact, up until 2015 he had played the part of Beetlejuice for just over 18 years. Keaton would be perfect for the role, as he could nail the part of Beetlejuice every single day without fail, so to bring the true character of maniacal clown to life would be an easy task for such a gifted acting talent.

The initial tests were all positive, and Universal knew they had created something special. The next step would be to unleash the character on the public at large. Universal took the bold step of marketing the character via every media outlet they possibly could, such was the confidence of the department. Jack would be everywhere, starting in September as just a jack-in-the-box on highway billboards that would open slowly through re-postering every couple weeks to reveal the character. The tag line of: "Not Afraid of the Dark? You don't know Jack!", a play on words with great post-modern emphasis to attach to the new era of Halloween Horror Nights was heavily used, along with appearances of the clown. Along with radio ads, they used a new commercial where unsuspecting teens get murdered at a Halloween Horror Nights, through to a heavily publicized outing at a *Fangoria* convention that was in Orlando at the time to actual interviews in the local press. Suddenly the lines between fact and fiction were starting to blur, a policy that would add weight to the character and increase the scares from members of the public who thought, maybe, just maybe this guy is real... In an early October interview with members of the press, the character said,

"[To scare guests] Completely, to the very core of their bones. In every manner. Everything is planned for Halloween. No matter what you come to see, I will be there to scare you. If you go to see *Terminator 2*, I'll be there. I will be everywhere. So complete is the frightful experience this year that not only will people be completely frightened in the houses, they'll be completely frightened in between and even during the parade - with my bloody playthings."

And he wasn't wrong. Not only would Jack be everywhere in every media outlet before and during the event but he would also be everywhere inside the park too, from rides to shows to just lurking in the streets. Such was the confidence of the park's creatives that they had created a solid event icon, he was deployed everywhere with everybody coming into direct contact with him at some point; a strategy that would really pay off.

October 6th soon came around with park guests clambering inside the newly built parking structure, creating queues from the park gates that extended almost as far as City Walk. 19 nights of horror were planned, with 5 houses and not just one scarezone any more, but an increased 4 zones, 2 shows, and 2 rides that had become specially 'haunted' for the event. They even had the parade back. The event was bigger and better than ever before. Guests were desperate to get into the event to see the horrors that awaited them, and they weren't going to be disappointed.

The first house that was offered was *Anxiety in 3D*, a house that used the very popular 3D technology from the previous year. Built inside Soundstage 22, the house would again deploy the disorientating technology to fox and confuse guests with a video game setting; this made it the first video game house seen at the event. The house had been 'designed' by Jack to play on all the main phobias that people held but in a video game environment. Fears such as confined spaces, spiders, rats and heights were played on to make guests terrified and disorientated in equal measures.

Sharing the same Soundstage as *Anxiety* was *Total Chaos*. It also shared the first mammoth-sized entrance canopy of temporary scaffolding and staging to highlight their entrances and queue areas, built in the Boneyard area of the park. The house would feature an alien on the run inside an Area 51-type setting with freakish mutant aliens from outer space running amuck inside a secret government facility. It was also one of the first houses to install a slide as part of the house's path. The following treatment had been written for the construction of this area, *Room 106 – The Attack Tunnel*: "As we are propelled downward, we come to an abrupt stop and find ourselves in a four foot wide room filled with small glowing orbs (ball pit), painted with wildfire paint application, stretching out before us. A blast of air causes our guests to quickly get to their feet, as they stand, a triggered nine-light blasts our retina with a powerful burst of light. Our eyes begin to fix, and we can make out the forms of decapitated heads that seem to float in space around us. We force ourselves forward through the thigh deep round and gooey objects. From behind and above us, a large hideous disfigured creature rushes forward and attacks, his attack cues a monstrous scream. We move quickly forward up and out to escape its tentacled clutches and find some solace in rejoining our group."
Universal built a pair of slides for guests to travel down that emptied onto a ball pit with scareactors lurking in the pit to frighten guests forward. In many ways, this was a genius addition to the normal mazes built which under current accessibility laws could never return.

Though being everywhere for the event, Jack did not have his own house this year, though this is a common misconception of fans. The house was actually the creation of Dr. Rich Oddfellow (Jack's nemesis) and was entitled *The Fearhouse*. Located again in the Nazarman's area, the house would have a beautiful highly detailed façade of a clown's face installed to whip up terror and anxiety in the awaiting queue line. Similar to Krusty's face on *The Simpsons ride* that would come much later in the Universal timeline, guests would enter on Sting Alley and walk up a red carpet installed like an elongated giant tongue that would wrap its way down the alley to the queue, like a showbiz carpet meeting a wet tongue. The mood for the house was set before guests took one step inside. Once inside guests would be attacked by clowns from above and below, big clowns, small clowns, old clowns, toy clowns, clowns everywhere, including the master of ceremonies himself at the very end. If you had coulrophobia (a fear of clowns) you shouldn't be at the event, let alone be inside this house!

Over the road was the house *Dark Torment*. Entering inside, the popular *Earthquake* ride, guests would be dumbfounded to find the pre-show was now a queue area for the same ride which ultimately would lead to the house. Entering onto the usual subway tram, guests would be attacked by the usual fire effects, road collapse, tram collision and rush of water. After the effects had ceased the ride vehicle would remain stationary before Jack would pop up to the tram and proclaim to the guests that "Congratulations, you didn't survive, you're now all dead! Welcome to hell my pretties!" Disappearing as quickly as he arrived, the tram doors would open and guests would disembark the ride on the set and into a side room where, before a short queue, guests would enter into a *Dante's Inferno*-like house. The first room would be a graveyard, and entering via "your grave" guests would appear to walk underground further to the second room where hooded creatures awaited. The following original treatment was written by Universal:
"We move forward into a chamber of seven tall and ominous robed figures, they stand four feet above us along a circular platform which we must follow. The faces of the figures are masks representing the seven deadly sins. Across the faces, scrawled in blood the words: lust, greed, sloth, anger, pride, gluttony and envy. One of the masked sins, with the mask that reads 'envy' suddenly springs forth sweeping at us with a sharp ceremonial dagger." Guests would move along from this entry port to various rooms depicting each of the seven deadly sins and the punishments laid out for each sinner per room with infill rooms in between. The house, including the pre-house ride, was quite lengthy.
Another Universal Creative treatment was written for the Hades room.
It read: "We exit the darkness and enter our next chamber through eight foot wrought iron gates that are slamming and askew, forcing us to wind through them. Beyond the steely entrance lies a chamber of ghastly and grotesque fear, a precursor to the horrific experience that awaits. A wall of tortured bodies surround us to our left and right. Strobes gives the walls the illusion of movement. Concealed amongst the bodies are two tortured souls. As our new arrivals make their way through the carnage, the souls break free from the wall. Their eyes are bone white and their mouths sewn shut to hold their tongues in their hands, thrusting them toward you."
The treatment went onto say, "4 scareactors required".

The *Earthquake* queue area also housed another maze, that of

Universal's Classic *Monster Mania*. The classic monsters were back but this time for a new generation. Gone was the classic-looking monster and instead were exaggerated monsters of pure evil. Frankenstein's monster looked like he had been assembled from former dead pro-wrestlers, Dracula had reportedly been twisted into a half-man-half-bat creature with razor like teeth, and the Wolfman had become more wolf than man. These mutated misfits were totally unlike any incarnation of the classic monsters that had been seen before.

The next house was an unofficial house but was similar to that of the *Earthquake* ride's house in that guests would queue in the same manner for the *Kongfrontation* ride. But instead of entering onto the ride, guests would be let loose to explore the highly-detailed sets of New York. Billed as *Nightmare Creatures 2* the house would return to original Halloween Horror Nights territory. Unlike a house where a strict path was used, this house/ride was more like an indoor scarezone that guests could explore at their own peril. The ride, along with *Kong*, were all switched off and the detailed sets were anyone's to explore. One of two 'haunted attractions', the sets held scareactors around every corner. Tall stilt walking scareactors were complemented by shorter scareactors and copious fog machines made for a mysterious foggy New York setting. Though the advertising didn't do the ride/house justice, the attraction would go on to be a fan favorite that can never be reproduced due to the fact that *Kong* (in this incarnation) is no more at Orlando.

Nobody knows why or how, but in the houses of this year an unknown person or persons would continuing drop or hide HHN coins within the houses. Universal collected the coins and gave them to the cast of each house after the event ended. To this day, this still happens and no one knows who did this and why.

FUN EAR FACT

The other haunted attraction this year was the *Jaws* ride. *Bloody Waters* was the ride's new name for the event. *Jaws* was a particular fan favorite for many years during the event, as the park map would advertise "see the shark in the dark". Now, the ride would have a whole new repurpose and theme. All of the then-current *Jaws* effects would be included. The change would be an addition to the boathouse scene where a haunted looking fisherman, complete with steel shark hook, would swing at unsuspecting guests. Then Jack would jump from behind a barrel, and just when you thought you had seen enough the ominous shark would make his giant splashing entrance. Like the *Kong* attraction, the ride was a huge hit for park guests.

Four official scarezones would be seen this year unlike the previous few years where just one large scarezone was always used. The scarezones this time would be sparsely decorated with little sets and props to make way for the twice nightly parade. In fact, the scarezones would simply disappear for the parade duration and reform after completion each time. *The Gauntlet,* located in the Bone Yard area and scaring guests directly into the queues of the two soundstage houses, was complemented by the *Chainsaw Drive Team* (who all seemed to have *KISS*-like black and white face paint this year) that patrolled between here and the park's entrance every night. They did this along with Jack, who had an official photo opportunity with a photo booth from the commercial installed to the side, near the Twister store. The area also housed another official photo opportunity of the Classic Universal Monsters just outside of the Monster Café, with Frankenstein's Monster, the Wolfman and a gothic-looking Dracula completing the line-up.

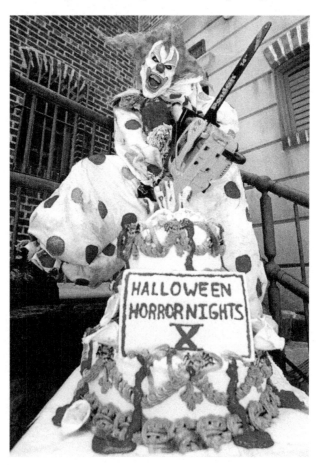

Midway of Dr Morose was held in the Amity area where again a band of freaks and clowns descended on the area to create a mini carnival of terror. *Apocalypse Island* was held in the Central Park area by the lagoon side. It featured lots of zombies and mutants running around and eating human flesh, with customary appearances by the icon at random times through the night. The final scarezone was *Clown Attack* located in Hollywood. The scarezone would again feature clowns of all sizes and ages that would terrify and delight guests in equal measures. The beginning of photo spot scarezones really began with this scarezone, as the clowns were only too happy to pose for a quick picture in return for a good scare. The parade was also back this year and it featured much the same as the previous years with the only extra addition of (yes you guessed it) a Jack-themed float. Otherwise it was the same, except they ran it the opposite direction to the way it had been run before, starting in New York and ending in Hollywood. But if you wanted even more Jack, he had his own show called *Jacked Up* located in the *Animal Actors' Stage*, which was a mixture of magic tricks gone wrong, edge-of-your-seat acrobatics and performers dancing to deranged musical numbers. A DJ played howling tunes at the top of Hollywood and Bill and Ted had their usual popular show at the *Wild West Stage*. Pop-culture items that were lampooned this year included: the then content sharing website *Napster, Mission Impossible*, the new *Charlie's Angels, Simpsons* characters Mr. Burns and his loyal sidekick Mr. Smithers along with Britney Spears and Lil Kim impersonators. The whole thing was finished off by a song-a-like Eminem singing *Slim Shady*, and then finally the whole cast assembled to dance and sing *Bye Bye Bye* by *N'Sync* ready for the house to once again come down. If partying with the time-travelling duo wasn't enough, guests of the park could gain free entry into City Walk's many clubs each night after the event, this being the first year that allowed this additional benefit.

When Jack was interviewed by the press he was reported as saying: "I'm hoping, personally, that they will be very afraid. I'm hoping that people will see me and say, "Ooohhhh, ooohhhhh, he's scary." And then boys will bring their girlfriends here to show how manly they are to not be afraid of such a big, spooky clown. Oh, look at the big spooky clown. Then more will show up, and then they will be afraid... That's the type of impact I'm hoping for. I'm hoping that people will see that clowns aren't so bad after all, and more people will show up here." He continued, "Oh, I'm not done. I will be here. Universal thinks that Halloween will be done at the end of the month, but I have another plan. I'm going to stay..."

And stay he did…

Halloween Horror Nights XI

I.C.U. / Jack's Back

Speculation for the event was growing as far back as August for this year's event in 2001. Billboards featuring a bizarre logo with the letters ICU were appearing along the Interstate 4 road, and slowly over the next few weeks ahead of the event the boards would be updated to show a creepy pair of eyes glaring out at you. They didn't go unnoticed by local members of the community, some of whom made complaints to Universal and the local media. One resident wrote to *The Sentinel* and complained, "In driving about town of late, I have been startled to discover the specter of sinister eyes peering down at me from the Universal Studio's current Halloween billboard advertisement. It's true that many older kids - high school and college - find it appealing and enticing. For them, after all, it's fun to be scared. As a grandmother and a former preschool teacher, I wonder if we might not have forgotten some of the little children who in their innocence do not have the ability to distinguish reality from make-believe. What responsibility do we have as a community in this regard?"

Universal knew that they needed to top their original character icon from last year (Jack) with someone who would be as equally mad and dreadful, if not more so. Universal again turned to surveys that had been undertaken by park guests to see what else made them anxious and frightened. At the time of the event there was much discussion about the ever-increasing power of computers within our daily lives, known as 'Moore's Law'. This says that computer power doubles every two years and was of much concern for some people. It tied into the fact that discussion was moving onto how much power the governments of the day should have when viewing our own personal computer usage. This combined with the spate of television networks putting out hidden camera shows and fly-on-the-wall documentaries at the time; *Big Brother* for example had just aired on *CBS* at the end of the previous year. So when Universal got around to asking the participants of the surveys what scared them the most, they said "clowns", and Universal covered this the previous year with Jack. They then looked at the second most popular fear of the surveys, and that was 'the fear of being watched'. Therefore Universal knew that the next horror icon for their event would have to have sinister eyes or at least a mysterious stare for the icon to be successful.

The original planning was for the event icon to be called Edgar Sawyer and there would be a twist that he was in fact Jack all along. 'Edgar' - because it sounded gothic like Edgar Allen Poe and 'Sawyer' because it sounded like 'saw you' - as the new icon would have a readily-available chainsaw as his main tool of dispatch. However, this brought problems... problems which only rose to the surface some months into the planning of character. *Vivendi* and *Canal+* had merged back in 2000 and that merger meant that the owner of Universal (then the Canadian company *Seagram*) would be bought by the merged companies. The ultimate shareholder of the new company was a Mr. Edgar Bronfman, and because of this the creatives at Universal decided to drop the name to respect the name of their boss. The other problem was the surname. The surname of 'Sawyer' was actually the surname of Leatherface and Co from the original *Texas Chainsaw Massacre* movies. And as Eddie had been designed for the purposes of scaring people with his stare but ultimately via his large chainsaw, Universal did not want any possible lawsuits filed, so they had to drop their surname and effectively re-design their character's backstory and name.

The new idea was for him to be Jack's own younger brother named Eddie. This meant they could share a surname, and thankfully no one called Eddie or Edward was on any of the parent companies of the then media conglomerate! The appearance of the character would largely remain the same. Eddie would be a composite of all the best scary horror icons from movie history. He would have the leather face muzzle of Hannibal Lecter, the glassy, expressionless stare of Michael Myers and the sheer violent rage, complete with chainsaw, of Leatherface. And to add a visual connection to his brother, some of the white and green face paint from Jack would be applied to his brow. Like Jack in the previous year, Universal were sure that this year they could increase the gore, increase the horror and bring the event to a new insane level of terror to scare guests like never before. There was however a tragic event about to unfold that not only changed the event completely but also changed the Western World.

We won't go into detail about what happened on September 11th, because we all know what happened that day and we all know of the tragic loss of life that was suffered across the States. The auditions for this year were actually September 11th and 12th, so they were postponed to respect what had unfolded over those days. As the auditions had been cancelled, speculation quickly grew that the event would be canceled altogether. "Despite last week's terrorism..." said Jim Canfield, a Universal spokesman, "...there aren't discussions at the attraction about canceling Horror Nights altogether, or at least postponing its start." Peter Stapp, a former operations executive at Universal and now a theme park consultant said at the time, "I'm sure they will examine the appropriateness of the plans and make any adjustments that are needed." News finally came just over a week after the tragic events of 9/11 that the show would go on and thus ended the speculation that the event like many others at the time would be cancelled (events at Disney, Pleasure Island and various local conventions were all cancelled during this week). Cranfield spelled out details of the event that would be coming: "19 spine-tingling nights during this spookiest of seasons when the park is overrun with ghouls, goblins, monsters and mayhem. Horror Nights is guaranteed to disorient and startle even the most fearless of thrill-seekers with gleeful gruesomeness." No mention of the blood and gore that had been planned was made. Obviously, in an effort to respect what had happened and to not allow the whole event to get cancelled (though it had been postponed somewhat), Universal decided to tone down the gore, blood and horror of the event. Names of attractions were changed, blood day (the annual day the park's creatives go around and splash the 'red corn syrup' over each house was cancelled), bloody props were swopped out, anything that resembled confetti or dust was removed and any horror that showed too much peril was cancelled. This included the *Opening Scareamonies*.

The *Opening Scareamonies*, a tradition of having a single, pre-opening show on the first night was a tradition that had loosely started in the previous decade, and was used as a media-type press preview event in the previous year. This was due to be held this year where Eddie the new event icon would largely dissemble Jack live on stage. The original treatment is presented here:

"On Hollywood Boulevard: Guests entering the gates of Universal will be corralled onto Hollywood Boulevard. Here we are treated to an opening ceremony in the grandest tradition. A Flatbed truck extends across the street. A makeshift hangman's noose hangs above. On the truck we also find a large box. It is a recreation of a children's toy block with the letters J-A-C-K all around. Fog pours from the box as we hear a rock version of "Pop Goes the Weasel". A low growl turns into a laugh as the maniacal clown Jack springs from the box. He bounds around the truck laughing at the audience. "Miss Me?" snorts Jack. The clown killer launches into the attractions and shows. He is immediately cut off by the sound of a rock guitar. We hear the Duane Eddy rock classic "Rebel Rouser" as EDGAR (Eddie – as mentioned earlier) our new master of scareamonies enters, Chainsaw in hand. "Who are you?" yells Jack. "Me?" glares Edgar. "I'm your replacement!" "You don't know the Saw! String him up Boys!" Two other Chainsaw Maniacs enter and grab the clown. They place the makeshift noose around his neck and lift. We hear the snap of bone as Jack's body goes lifeless. Then it springs back to life. "You'll need more than that to get rid of me, freak!" snarls the Clown. They lower the clown and place his head down on his box. Edgar revs up his trusty chainsaw and tears through the clown's neck. Blood sprays as Jack is beheaded right in front of us. His head drops down. The new reigning champion lifts the clown's severed head high for all the audience to see. The mouth still moves as we hear Jack scream out his objection. "I'll be back!" yells Jack's severed head. "Time to go back in the box!" smiles Edgar. The evil chainsaw-wielding madman drops the head into the box. Then proceeds to chainsaw it. Suddenly the *Chainsaw Drill Team* appears from behind our audience and attacks. They chase our guests into the park as the New Icon screams – "Open for Business!" A pyro hit signals the opening of our event."

Due to the perceived violence and gore of previous *Opening Scareamonies*, it would be cancelled for this year. In fact, as Eddie was already frightening people on the I4, the creepy monstrous and violent connoting character would at the very last minute be cancelled. The billboards were taken down and the commercial was redubbed. Months of planning on the part of both the resort's theme park creatives and marketing had to be either removed or re-designed. Some of the advertising couldn't be recalled, such a deal with *Taco Bell*, with *Walgreens* and with various local papers. Some fans of the event remember spotting both advertisements in the local papers for the event where one in the center had a photo of Eddie and another on the back had a drawing of Jack. Suddenly the pulled marketing of "I see you!" (I-C-U) was to be hurriedly replaced with "Jack's Back" and "There's no more clowning around." Eddie was rapidly scrubbed from history and the popular clown from last year was brought back to be the event's new icon.

Other changes include: *Bloodbath Underground* would become *Ooze Zone,* where the blood-splattered streets of New York inside the *Kong* attraction would now be covered in slime rather than blood, along with the planned foam. Foam parties were going through a fad at the time. *Deadly D'illusions* became *Dangerous D'illusions,* and the show remained largely the same. A slight tweak in the name of *The Festival of the Dead Parade* saw the popular parade become *Nightmares on Parade. Terror Land* would become *Scary Tales* (a name that would ultimately stick for this house's future use). And *Slasher Alley* became *Nightmare Alley.*

Scary Tales would be a successful house for this year and would ultimately ensure it would be brought back in various guises over the forthcoming years. Soundstage 22 would be used for the house, as large elaborate sets were required to present everyone's favorite fairy tales. The concept was that all the fairy-tale characters and stories we knew as children have been locked away in an abandoned carnival for 30 years. They've morphed and mutated during their imprisonment and now they want revenge. Large cute sets would be juxtaposed by hideous, large monsters hidden inside each room. The Snow White scene for example featured a large and terrifying wolf, complete with sharp teeth and claws. The Wizard of Oz scene would feature a room full of blood-hungry vampire-like Scarecrows. The Mad Hatter's Tea Party scene would feature a long table complete with bodies hanging from the ceiling and a mad demented zombie-looking Mad Hatter would scare guests forward into the next room, which was Alice's Toy Room complete with mad, Frankenstein-looking dolls. Another popular scene was towards the end of the house where guests were led into a darkened room where squishing and squelching noises could be heard, complemented by a foul smell, before the lights were lifted and much to the guests' surprise they were walking on top of rotten pieces of guts, though they were actually walking on a glass floor. "We have these smells in these houses that are just vile," J Michael Roddy of Universal Creative said at the time. "There's a company that provides them, a catalog you can order from. Soil and Rotting Flesh are especially popular this year." The house was wildly popular and there were long queues each night.

A house that was set up to be the former *Icon's* house had to be toned down. That house was *Run* and it was built inside the *Earthquake* queue. Original ideas from the park's creative minds were to build on the previous year and make this the most extreme house that had ever been built. Adrian LePeltier was tasked with the design of the house. He, along with others from the resort's Art and Design department, had holed themselves up in one of the Portofino Bay's suites for several weeks while the team brainstormed possible ideas for the event at large and the house. "Some ideas got thrown out because of safety or other issues," LePeltier said. "For example, we wanted to blindfold guests and have them feel their way along a gunky rope through a dark room to escape". He continued, "In the end, you're forced to acknowledge that some of these things can't or shouldn't be done. After all, it would take some people an eternity to find their way along a rope in the dark and we need to move our guests through quickly to keep the lines short."

Eventually the design of the house would evolve to become narrow, twisty and dark (but not pitch-black). He continued, "Guests are thrown into a diabolical game show where freaks and maniacs menace with chainsaws. To escape, guests must literally run through a series of dark, winding corridors of padded walls and chain-link fencing, with hardly a chance to catch their breath, let alone scream." The house was planned to be as intense as possible to afford the largest terror of any house ever created. And to crown the house with the most scares, the park's new icon would be the chieftain of the chainsaws.

The original treatment promised the most terror of all houses, ever: "Universal Studios Halloween Horror Nights presents the most extreme Haunted maze in its ten-year history. As our Guest Contestant, you will be thrown into an environment that has no rhyme or reason, only the most diabolical combination of unsettling imagery and dark, winding corridors. Your challenge is simple: Get out as quickly as you can. Through chain-link barricades and padded walls, you must make choices to survive. Think you know the way out? Good Luck. Remember to keep moving. Don't stop, not even to Scream!"

The treatment would go onto describe a gameshow host that would open proceedings from the façade. This would be followed by light tricks and sirens sounding, to allow the chainsaw maniacs free to come and select their guests. Caverns and junkyards were seen, as guests made their way through a twisted maze of confusion and terror, and it was the latter that was toned down. Gory scenes were removed, the number of maniacs with saws was reduced and Eddie was pulled altogether. The event's icon who was replaced would not even be present in his own house.

Next-door to this house was *The Mummy Returns: The Curse Continues* and would be directly tied into the then Mummy movie of the same name which had been released in May of that year. The park promised, "Venture through a maze of tomblike corridors and dark caverns in the Temple of the Scorpion King, where danger lurks around every corner." The house was not as detailed as the former house to bear this name, but it had many good scares. It came at a time when *The Mummy* franchise was at its most popular, with actual sets from the movies being showcased in the Stage 54 area of the park, along with wax models of the original Mummy and co who were on display in the foyer of the *Monster Makeup Show*. Made by *Madame Tussaud's*, the figures were on a tour of America before they were permanently installed in the creator's New York branch. The figures were a part of the 70th Anniversary celebrations of the classic monsters, as Universal was keen to highlight both the modern and classic Universal monster franchises. Guests could enter into the theater after inspecting the waxworks to see a continuous running of the film *Boogeymen* which played clips of older horror movies, such as those featuring the characters depicted in wax in the foyer.

Superstitions, a house that featured many of our popular-held superstitions, was built in the Nazarman's area of the park. The park map billed the house thus: "Explore a hidden warehouse filled with ancient relics and urban legends that will have you believing in the supernatural."

The house had been toned down a little from the original treatment but it still featured black cats and witches a-plenty.

Before Eddie had been settled upon for HHN 2001, the Art and Design team had thought about making the icon 'Jill'. She would be the female version of Jack though would be disgruntled and angry at recent divorce.

FUN EAR FACT!

The last house would be *Pitch Black* and would share the soundstage with *Scary Tales* as many houses had in previous years. The house was lined up to give guests a thrilling experience. Guests would be plunged into a world of darkness that to some was extremely disorientating, though strobe lights had been added. The house had been loosely and unofficially based on the 2000 movie of the same name. The park map said: "A mysterious zone of darkness has appeared causing weird disturbances. It's up to you to investigate... if you dare." As with many of the houses, the scares were reined in and the scareactors were asked to tone it down. What would have been a mysterious dark adventure into the unknown became a rather temporary, light-laden affair that unfortunately was not as good as it had been designed to be. The house had been designed fully by Skip Sherman working in the resort's Art and Design Department. Adrian LePeltier said, "...at the start of the event, that was the most intensely scary haunted house I had ever walked within in my whole life!"

One of the most exciting shows of the event had been *Dangerous D'illusions* with Franz Harary. Franz was a magician of international acclaim who had been made famous by television shows such as *NBC's The World's Greatest Magic*, during which Harary made a *NASA* Space Shuttle vanish live on television. He had also worked with the likes of Michael Jackson and Alice Cooper on their many respective tours. The show featured a mixture of mind bending illusions and feats of amazement. It was held four times per night in the *Animal Actors' Stage*.

Scarezones this year were all non-removable and located in areas that did not affect the parade. These were: *Midway of the Bizarre* which had been reduced in scope and size unlike previous years, held once again in Amity; *The Unknown* in Central Park which was a gothic setting with ghoulish gargoyle-like creatures hiding around every corner; and *Nightmare Alley* located between where the *Hitchcock show* had been down to where *Transformers* is now.

Both the parade (with slight name change) and Bill and Ted were both back in their respective attractions. The parade featured a return Mummy float, along with giving guests who had purchased 'Stay and Scream' tickets the chance to ride one of the floats and to distribute the colored beads to onlookers. *Bill and Ted's show* that year featured a lookalike of Christopher Walken dancing to the famous *Fatboy Slim* music video, *American Pie, Sex in the City* and a rendition of the *The Lady Marmalade* music video featuring sound-alikes of Pink, Mya, Christina Aguilera, and Lil' Kim. This was all topped off with an impromptu game of *The Weakest Link*, which had been shown on TV around the same time as the event.

In efforts to boost attendance at the event, the park bosses decided to use their links in Hollywood and attract celebrities to attend the event as members of the public (rather than performing or signing autographs). Universal would go on to do this most years in an effort to attract headlines in the local press and attract more guests. This year it was confirmed that Howie Dorough from the *Backstreet Boys*, and then the couple Britney Spears and Justin Timberlake of 'N Sync were all spotted at the event. And attract guests they did, but they needed to. This was the first year that metal detectors had been introduced, done so in response to the terrible events of that year. Though they were not popular and did create longer queues for entry, they would soon become a mainstay of the event as attendances grew. This year the attendance did fall, and though some people have estimated it still maintained between 10,000 to 20,000 guests, overall it was down a hard 10%. Park bosses were grateful for foreign tourists, particular British guests, who often pre-booked their vacations months (even years) in advance. These went a long way to make up for the reduction in domestic visitors (mostly out-of-state visitors) which had significantly reduced due to 9/11. The local community did respond by coming back more often for the event, and the fans, by way of the internet, did help publicize the event in an effort to try to attract more people to give it a try. And although the event was by no means a failure that year, Universal had to do their best to try to pull the event back from being cancelled and to provide the world-class event that guests had become accustomed to.

Rex: "My shift at IOA just finished, let me in!"

Halloween Horror Nights XII

Islands of Fear (Your time has come)

As early as late April in 2002, Universal was building anticipation of their forthcoming Halloween event. The event in the previous year had not been as successful due to the events of 9/11, and this, combined with issues of marketing the event, ensured that attendance was down for the first time in the event's history. But it wasn't just the event that was suffering; park-wide attendance was still down about 10% for the main Studio Park and 8% down for the still relatively new park, Islands of Adventure. The new park had failed to meet attendance expectations since it had been opened in 1999.

Universal, knowing that they had a mountain to climb, had to think bigger than ever before. This was a process that started by feeding information to the press as early as April that year. A small article in the local Sentinel provided the information required: "Universal Studios' top-drawing annual Halloween Horror Nights might get a new home this fall: Islands of Adventure. The proposed move being researched by Universal Orlando executives would be part of a major expansion and upgrading of the scare-fest."

Susan Lomax, a Universal spokeswoman, confirmed the information from the paper,

"We are looking at a variety of ways to dial up the fear factor. It's our signature event - the biggest thing we do all year."

Other commentators were less than impressed with the news. Peter Stapp, a former Universal executive and an attractions consultant in Orlando, said, "You know the old saying, 'If it ain't broke, don't fix it.' I wouldn't tinker with something so successful."

A local resident expressed similar concerns, "I don't see how the other park could be managed, it's huge!"

But not everyone shared these sentiments.

"Islands is a teen-oriented attraction, and the nature of Halloween Horror Nights really speaks to that demographic," said Dennis Speigel, president of International Theme Park Services, a tourism-attraction consulting company. "I think this could push Islands up a tick on the attendance barometer by bringing in new users who have never seen the park before."

And that was exactly what Universal was hoping for…

The decision had been made in May of that year by park executives before it was officially announced to the media in June.

"This is a scare-maker's dream come true," said Bob Gault, president of Universal Orlando.

The event would be bigger than ever before and be staged in the newer theme park of Islands of Adventure, where the latest rides and attractions would be complemented by houses, scarezones and shows. Gault teased, "…its narrow, winding walkways and many nooks and crannies, will be one giant haunted house. That tropical forest in the Jurassic Park area is really going to be frightening at night when we add weird music. Islands offers more places for monsters to jump out at people and plenty of theme-park story lines. In the Marvel Super Hero Island, evil super-villains will reign supreme."

Starting the speculation as far back as April and then confirming proceedings as early as June was exceedingly early for the park and showed the resort's determination to turn around the event's fortunes from the previous year.

Around September, billboards started appearing locally for the event, combined with posters and even a banner tied to the Pharos Lighthouse at Islands of Adventure. A sinister-looking gaunt man wearing a top hat and clutching a weird pair of metal scissors featured in all the advertising. The park's creatives had taken great care and consideration in choosing who should headline the event as park icon. Some believed that Jack should return again, other believed strongly that a new character could be created, others wanted to see Eddie return and be the actual icon rather than last year when he had to be dumped right before opening. The debate waged on before the selection of a completely new character was agreed; new location, new character, it just made sense. Initially the idea of creating an evil-child icon for the event was proposed. She would be called Cindy (SINdy) and the park would be her playhouse, where everything she has created would be brought forth for us to enjoy. She would then be tied to each house, each scarezone, each show, each area to create an overall themed story arch, something that was important to the creative team at Universal at the time. The event would be her thoughts, her will and her ideas from her evil little mind. Each Island would showcase the disturbed and frightening depths of her mind as we, the park guests, explore them.

The character was chosen and an elaborate back story was produced. The park's creative design manager, TJ Mannarino said at the time "We find that the story is as important to guests as the scare." Everything was set for the character to be the event's new icon and this was set right up until September that year when concerns were raised right at the top of the organization. A number of child abductions had occurred that summer on both the East and West coasts. Though not linked in any way, they did put this topic on the news agenda for many months. Fearing a media backlash for being unsympathetic, Universal quickly decided to revise their icon choice. Though only the minimum amount of park literature and marketing had been done with Cindy, it was relatively easy to swop her out for a new icon. The hard work would be deciding on a new event icon and then design this icon in time for the press deadlines.

Undaunted and fearing a repeat of last year, the park's creatives worked long and hard crafting the new icon. Looking at Cindy's backstory, they chose her parents as a starting point. Originally Cindy's obsession with the dead would come from her upbringing being in and around a mortician's office which had been owned by her father. The father's character morphed away from him being her father (though temporarily) and that the character would be an evil, demented mortician-come-funeral director. He would be using unsuspecting locals as vessels from which he could explore whether bodies have souls, obviously by mutilating them horribly. The inspiration had come from many years prior, where for some of the years when there was a parade, a character dressed like an undertaker would scatter ashes at the rear of the parade informing guests of their impending doom. The character had been played by park regular and local Orlando acting supremo Bryce Ward. Bryce's deep mid-Atlantic accent combined with his long, drawn face (with make-up applied, obviously) would be perfect for the role. Building on Bryce's former performance in the parade and the backstory that had been created, the park creatives used various sources as inspiration. These included the movie *Something Wicked This Way Comes* which featured a gaunt top-hat wearing Jonathan Pryce; the foreboding Jud Crandall character ably played by Fred Gwynne in the Stephen King *Pet Cemetery* movie; and the Reverend Henry Kane character, the main antagonist of the *Poltergeist* film series. Making a nod to the latter inspiration the character's name was changed from Dr. Paul Bearer to

Dr. Albert Caine (note the spelling), but who would also be known as the Caretaker. Luring victims to his Victorian manor, the Caretaker would seek to operate on them and find their soul. Finally, the park had their icon.

The character was approved by everyone at Universal and Marketing started the task of adding the character to all marketing. From billboards to posters, the character would be seen across the land. Back in the Art and Design department, they quickly set about adapting the event's plans to make way for the new icon. Two houses which had been planned were due to be re-imagined, but luckily these were the two that had not started construction at the time. They were a tropical voodoo doll house and a cannibal meat factory house. The latter was due to be built in Soundstage 20, a soundstage that had not been used at the event before due to filming requirements, particularly seasonably for gameshows and wrestling programs. The soundstage was so large that in coming years it would be used again to house two houses in the one soundstage. Luckily, due to a slowdown in production and filming requirements at the time, the soundstage would be the perfect venue for a haunted house, not least because of its size but also because of its proximity to the neighboring park. It was physically the closest, or the closest with ease of access and egress to Islands of Adventure. Having scrapped the idea of a cannibal house, the park creatives started the process of developing a house to fit the backstory of the Caretaker. Utilizing the space available in the soundstage, the park's creative minds could build one of the largest houses they had ever designed and fill it with all kinds of unimaginable horror.

The house would become *Scream House*, and would take guests on a tour of the Caretaker's actual home. A full house façade would be constructed to give guests the illusion that they were entering into an actual building (within a building), something that had never been done before. After designing and building the house, the team scoured all the thrift and antique shops locally to fill the house with peeling wallpaper, an organ, caskets, stuffed animals, vases, pianos, velvet curtains, fire places, glasses, and antique furniture; all dusted and distressed to give the appearance of age. "To have this level of detail is critical for us," said TJ Mannarino at the time. "Our goal is to take you out of reality and put you in this imaginary world and give you that second of disbelief, `Am I really in a funeral parlor?' Then you see something move in the corner and you think, for that second, maybe it really could be some strange, disfigured monster."
The scents of rotting flowers and dirt were added to ramp up the scares. Finally, a cast was needed to staff this significantly detailed

house. 26 scareactors would be deployed at any one time (allowing for breaks), which was a record at the time to fill this huge house. The cast would be a combination of unfortunate house guests who were dying from wounds half-way through their operations, to zombified former patients now inhabiting of the haunted house. The cast was topped-off with several Caretakers, complete with rusting metal shears.

The Caretaker also needed a show. It was too late to put him into a main show or create a special sit-down show for the event. The idea from previous years of having an *Opening Scaremonies* was brought back. The idea would be perfect for the character, as he could introduce the event, what the guests would expect to find beyond the gates and build anticipation. Brought to the event via a horse-drawn-carriage, the aloof character would appear on a small stage in front of the park gates. Selected guests (really actors) would be plucked from the gathered crowds before being tortured by snakes and scorpions inside a raised coffin before being gutted live. One victim's heart would be pulled out, still beating; the Caretaker would announce the opening of the event and then guests would go forth.

Inside the park, guests would enter into the first scare zone, *Port of Evil*. This scarezone featured tortured souls in various levels of distress. Guest flow could be better controlled here than in the Studio park, with most guests opting to go left entering into *Island Under Siege*. Anticipation for this island was extremely high. Universal promised an experience where, "The super heroes have all been defeated. Now you're trapped on a decaying, lawless island under siege by the minions of the most vicious super villain of all, Carnage." Carnage was a popular character at the time from the Spider-Man universe. The island was like nothing that had been seen before or since, with Thor's hammer laid on a crater in the ground. Spider-Man's webbing was seen applied to various walls, parts of Iron Man's armor had been stolen and strewn around, and Captain America's blood-splattered shield was nailed to the *Dr. Doom ride* walling. There was smoke, overturned cars, burnt out vehicles, police running around with blood-splattered uniforms and general destruction all about. Various villains from the *Marvel* universe prowled the streets with water pistols, along with Carnage who was positioned atop a tower of scaffolding flicking his long tentacle like fingers down to the shocked passing crowds. The whole island looked like we had all just missed one huge battle to the death which the heroes had lost spectacularly.

Carnage wasn't just situated on the streets; he also had his own house. Located behind *Dr. Doom's Fearfall* in building B285A that would later be named the Carnage Warehouse (the building had been erected specifically for the event, then used for storage ever since), the house would be entitled *Maximum Carnage*. Universal's park maps promised: "Venture into the labyrinth-like secret hideout of the malevolent Carnage, an insane criminal with incredible alien powers, who's bent on mindless destruction." The house would contain toxic waste-splattered walls, chemicals dripping, barbed wires hanging from the ceilings, laser beams and strobe lighting to disorientate guests, with villains and henchmen chasing everyone; the house was skillfully managed to give great scares. Skull-masked, leather-clad chainsaw henchmen, complete with gas mask-wearing scientists would chase guests into the classic turning tunnel (which Universal had used regularly), past waterfalls of toxic waste and through loads of scaffolding. Music would blast out of the speakers playing fast drum and bass, while guests would have seconds before the nuclear reactor would explode, with alarms going-off and hot aired pumped in for maximum effect. The house would end with our host Carnage on top of a podium waving his tentacle-like fingers down to unsuspecting guests.

The next island on would be *Toon Lagoon*, renamed *Treaks and Foon's* and would be a welcome respite from the intense devastation of the preceding island. Originally designed as a scarezone for Cindy to deploy her twisted imaged characters on guests, the area included scores of charming cartoon-like characters that worked the area in pairs. Combined with the largest foam machine that had ever been deployed by the park it made for a very weird experience. The pairs of grinning ghouls would dance with guests while their other half would lurk behind corners or within the foam, before jumping out on the guests lured into a false sense of security.

The Scary Tales 2 house was also based here, built into the *Popeye and Bluto's Bilge-Rat Barges* queue housing. The house had built on the reputation of the previous year and would mostly be about childhood fears. Little Red Riding Hood and Alice were back, along with the vampire-like Wizard of Oz scarecrows. The house also used the first attempt by the park's creatives to install black and white camouflage tactics into some of the rooms, complete with strobes and light effects. Scareactors would be dressed in black and white costumes before being posed directly in front of black and white walls to give the effect that the walls were literally moving and reaching out to the guests. A huge façade was constructed with a big blue goblin face on it, lots of nursery rhymes and child-like-chants playing throughout the house. One room had the famous rhyme of *Mary had a Little Lamb* which had been taken to the next level; she had slaughtered the poor animal, plus other lambs, and strewn them everywhere! Plus it wasn't the wolf that had killed grandma in the classic tale, it was grandma who had killed the wolf. Hiding behind her bed the grandma would push the decapitated, blood-dripping head in your face before scared guests would rush into the next room and be confronted by the Three Little Pigs, all complete with roaring chainsaws. This house had everything!

Next up would be the Jurassic Park Island that was as wildly anticipated as the Marvel Island transformation. Props and set pieces formerly stored off-site and in the Boneyard were repurposed to become JP Extinction. The concept was that the island's scientists had started to experiment with dino DNA to create human-dinosaur hybrids. The hybrids, along with the actual dinosaurs, have smashed their way out and roam free within the island. Actual props from the *Jurassic Park* sequel *The Lost World* were used in both the streets and the island's house. Raptor costumes were adapted to fit scareactors who hid in the bushes and jumped out on passing guests, along with a large life-sized Triceratops (though some speculate that this prop was from the original *Jurassic Park* movie) which was pulled to pieces, covered in fake blood and hung up in the house. The house would be dubbed *Eviloution* and be built in the then attraction of *Triceratops Trail*, with the original animatronic triceratops used at the start complete with strobe affects to make the animal look like it was in some distress. Further along the house, the same animal would be gutted and hung up by the hybrid men (as described above). Dr. Burton, the evil maniac scientist employed on the island, would at the start of the house warn guests not to enter as the hybrids he had created would be coming for you. By the end of the house, the hybrid-monsters had caught Burton and hung him from the neck on the ceiling. Half-dinosaur-half-human monsters complete with the traditional raptors and spitter dinos would fill this house with scares of every nature!

The popular TV show *Fear Factor* had a house this year within this island; it would eventually relocate to the studio park as a show full-time. Based loosely on the TV show it would feature all the main phobias and fears that the general public holds. The house would be very dark, slimy and sticky, with scareactors pretending to be sick, with fake roaches, snakes, spiders, and worms crawling about and all this in the pitch black! Scareactors trapped with creatures such as snakes in their glass helmets, a gooey hair room, a bridge dropping 2 inches but making it seem like you are falling far in the complete darkness were complemented by compressed air guns shooting at you.

The next island would house *Studio 666*, a dance party on the Lost

Continent complete with the fountain being used to step up the scares. Next, guests would reunite at the Port of Entry via Seuss Island which had been allowed to have a small amount of mist applied and nothing else, as per the strict instructions from the creator's widow, Audrey Geisel. Bill and Ted were also back this year, this time housed in the expansive and underused *Toon Lagoon Amphitheater*. Topics this year included: *The Osbournes* from the then popular reality show, the characters from *Scooby Doo*, and Austin Powers complete with Mini-Me, Darth Vader, an Anna Nicole Smith lookalike, the Green Goblin from the *Spider-Man* movie and Gandalf. The show ended with the assembled cast dancing and singing to Neil Diamond's *Coming to America*. Rides and attractions open this year included: *The Amazing Adventures of Spider-Man, Doctor Doom's Fearfall, Incredible Hulk Coaster, Storm Force Accelatron, One Fish, Two Fish, Red Fish, Blue Fish, Caro-Seuss-el, The Flying Unicorn, Dueling Dragons, Poseidon's Fury, Jurassic Park River Adventure* and *Dudley Do-Right's Ripsaw Falls*.

> The original concept for the icon of this year would have been Sindy be a disfigured female version of the Phantom of the Opera. FUN EAR FACT!

Other notable events this year include the first time that *RIP tours* were offered. The park's advertisement offered, "The ultimate Halloween experience - a guided tour including priority entrance and preferred seating to Halloween Horror Nights houses, shows and select rides. VIP Tour - Non-private, 5-hour tour begins at 7pm - $120 per person or exclusive VIP Tour - Private, scheduled tours - $1,700 per group (15 people max)."

The event was also captured by the *Travel Channel*'s cameras in their film *The Art of the Scare* which had been filmed to showcase the level of work and detail that went into organizing the event every year. It also marked the first time an interactive website was built to help build the narrative of each island. The website, though primitive by modern standards, was the first time a website had been built showcasing the attractions that would be presented, along with the ability to download wallpapers and send e-cards. Previously the site would just be a holding page with the logo and contact details. The last notable event from this year was a far less haunting event. Presided over by the park 's icon the Caretaker, Regina Herron and Christopher Mygrant of Tampa got married at the theme park on October 13th. The marriage took place inside the soundstage where the icon's house had been built. The couple decided to get married at their favorite event as they had held their very first date at the event some years prior. Cast members and crew acted as witnesses, but they had other reasons to celebrate too...

The park's creative team along with the various other departments had all worked together to pull off the maximized event. Though the odds had been stacked against them and the objectives ambitious – they had succeeded. The event had returned attendance numbers that were back to where they had been. The Sentinel reported that, "On the Saturday night before Halloween, some employees said, attendance equaled the previous record of between 45,000 and 46,000." Most Saturdays at the event sold-out and reached capacity. This was music to the ears of the hard-working people of the park, and the park bosses, crew and the 600 scareactors employed that year could not be happier. The event that year would go down in Halloween Horror Nights history as one of the best.

Halloween Horror Nights 13

The Director will see you now

"You oughta be in pictures!"

An extreme year needed an extreme house; at least that was the plan for this year. Building on the successful move from the Studios to Islands of Adventure, the resort wanted to increase the scares and increase the suspense, as well as the tension and the spine-chilling creepiness of the whole event. This could be done by building another park-owned and created icon that could be tailored to embody all these attributes, and reflect them at the event. Various designs were undertaken before a combination of input from marketing and the park's art and design department created Paulo Ravinski, who would be known as the Director. Fitting nicely in with the resort's overriding movie theme, the Director would be an embodiment of the evils that would await unsuspecting guests within the event. Officially cranking the dial from downright scary to extreme, Universal knew they would be playing with fire and thus would court some controversy. The icon would be bounced off the idea of 'snuff-films', a relatively obscure film genre that had been going as long as cinema but had become more well-known due to the advent of the internet in recent times. These movies depict someone who is filmed actually dying. So the Director would be a movie director who needed victims for his latest snuff-films, where he would not just kill unsuspecting victims but also horribly torture them too. During this time a niche genre that was starting to break out to be mainstream (albeit for a short duration) was that of torture-horror. Later, movies called *Saw* and *Hostel* would go on to encompass this niche and have reasonable box-office success. Building on the emergence of this new genre, Universal was quick to add this into their character so as to keep the event as relevant as possible. Gone were the campy monsters of the past, as this event was squarely rebuilding its brand around the demographic it attracted, despite running the risk of making the event too extreme which could isolate their audience or upset the wider audience. It would be a gamble that would ultimately pay-off but there would be bumps along the road.

The backstory that was created by Universal was a twisted tale of evil: "Paulo Ravinski was born in Eastern Europe. Aspiring to be a filmmaker, he initially started out as a snuff film director, capturing actual human suffering, torture and death on his movie camera. His first project was a controversial feature known as *The Widow's Eye*. The film shocked so many of his country population that Ravinski was forced out, which is when he came to America. Law enforcement agencies and film critics call his work snuff cinema. The Director prefers his work to be referred to as 'art'."

Combining many connotations of popular horror with the new wave of horror movies that were hitting cinemas at the time, Universal had created an icon that could have the event built around them, much as they had with their past icon of Jack, but unlike how the event had been planned in the last two previous years where both respective icons had been scrapped at the last minute.

It was August 6th of that year when news broke in the local media that Universal were not just trying to make the event more extreme overall but that they wanted to make their first extreme house. The press reported that an 'inside source' had informed them that the house was being designed for construction, that you would have to be 18 years old to enter and would have to sign a full waiver before entering. The local paper went on to describe the house that was in full-planning, "No word on exactly what this horror-to-the-nth degree will entail or if, as some suggest, it will require an additional entry fee. One site said the stout of heart will wear a harness while the floor drops from beneath them - and that's before they spend some time in a casket." Rumors at the time said that the house would be built inside a soundstage, with controllable temperatures and management of footfall that could be better monitored, along with the space required for this rumored up-charge house. In fact, closely surveying the park maps of the time, it can be seen that one of the soundstages and the attached path are seen on the map but contain no number. It goes some way to show how close this house was to production and marketing before it was subsequently cancelled. The Jurassic Park area of the park managed to squeeze three houses within its boundaries, yet the use of the soundstages (which have always been popular haunt locations) would go underused; this adds to the theory. Despite the rumors then and now, the house would never come to fruition. It was also rumored at this time that Universal would be building a ghost ship house along with the extreme house; the former would be seen, though it is said that the extreme house was likely pulled due to concerns from higher management and the legal team. But this milestone in the history of the event goes to prove how serious the park was about organizing an event that was definitely aiming to increase the scares.

The house never truly got off the drawing board, however six horror filled scenes were planned. The house's entrance was that of a ruined church with a velvet curtain entrance obscuring the horrors that awaited. Once inside guests would see a number of church pews lined up while haunting pipe organ music filled the air. You would have entered eight at a time, before a large masked man would enter and affix blindfolds to each person. Once blindfolded you'd be pushed to sit in a pew per person and then separated from here on. You are individually selected and taken through another doorway by a scareactor who would be instructed to handle you in a rough manner. Scene One would see you thrown into an open coffin with the lid slammed shut. Here, you'd probably remove your blindfold and start kicking the door open, once the guest saw that the lid would not open, the sound of rats piling into the coffin's tight space would be played along with props prodding you to make it feel like they were crawling all over you. After a few minutes of this, the back of the coffin would open and drop backwards making you roll out onto a crash mat. Scene Two would see guests crawl through a chain lined tunnel where scareactors with torches could grab at you and propel you forwards. Scene Three would lead into a corridor of various doors. Here you would stay until the others in your group re-appear from their own coffin/tunnel ordeals. Once together lighting-effects would disorientate everyone before being chased out by a huge scareactor with a chainsaw. This scene was recycled from 2004's *Ghost Town*. Scene Four was particularly nightmarish where your team of eight would be taken from the corridor onto the usual school bus that has been appearing at Horror Nights for years. Once onsite burnt flesh zombies would terrorize you as the bus appears to be on fire on the outside. Initially the zombies would appear to be burnt out victims, then only come to live once everyone is on and seated. The effect of burning inside the bus would be created using a machine on the outside using real flames to simulate fire whilst dry-ice is pumped inside the bus to eventual zero visibility. Scene Five would see guests quickly escape the 'burning bus' and slide down into a cellar (the fire effect was later reused for 2010's *The Orfanage: Ashes to Ashes* house). The cellar is dark and damp, you're sprayed with water from a leaking pipe, blindfolded once again and sent into the final scene. Scene Six would see each of your group strapped into electric chairs. Each chair would periodically send a small shock to each guest, scareactors would shout fake screams too to heighten the effect for the guests strapped in. One person is a Universal plant and tries to simulate a true electrocution before the system fakes an overload and each member of the party is taken via wheelchairs to a recovery room with Horror Nights nurses (like the jello-shot girls). An interesting fact is that the 'safe-word' was "I'm a fluffy bunny" if any of the scenes were too much for you. As you can appreciate, claustrophobic persons, simulated fire and torture were all likely reasons why this impressive house never saw the light of day.

It was around this same time in early August that the park began advertising the forthcoming auditions for the event. Some 1,100 people were needed to fill the positions in the houses and scarezones, which would be a significant increase on the previous year's record of 900 scareactors. This was combined with early projections that the event would be attracting some 40,000 visitors on the busiest nights, with another 21 nights of fun to be had. These projections reinforced Universal's attempt to make the event more extreme and added to the need to hire more people than ever before. The move to the Islands park had also been a good move too, as industry experts had estimated that the park had received a 10% bump in attendance overall for the year, just by moving the event to the Islands park away from the Studios. So the decision to keep it at the same park from last year was made very early on.

The TV commercials began and the billboards were put up, and on their release Universal received a trickle of complaints. Many complained about the 'graphic' nature of the tortured victims in the 'snuff-film' advertisements that were seen and other complained about the general creepiness of the google-eyed monster from above the highway. Though surprisingly, the complaints were not as frequent as they had been in past years. Maybe Central Florida residents and visitors were getting used to the annual event? This year also marked the first use of media gifts – small, bespoke, handmade horror props sent to the select few in the media in the interest of providing further coverage of the event.
And boy did they start in style!
The first small number sent out to named people within the media were photographs of the recipient that had been altered by means of 'photo-shop', to appear to be in various levels of distress and torture. It was as though the Director had cast the recipient in one of his latest 'snuff-films'. "It's kind of disturbing to see yourself looking like that," said Bob Opsahl, anchor for *WFTV-Channel 9*. "I mean, I don't go see

movies like that."

Though most of the media took it well and saw the funny side of the gift, others were less happy. An anonymous anchor was reported as saying "With what is going on in the world today, and with the sickos Halloween Horror Nights attracts, this is all some borderline psychotic needs to think he has a message from heaven to knife one of us at a public appearance."

Channel 6, though, was quick to close-out these complaints, "I take security as seriously as the next guy," said Bob Frier of *WKMG-Channel 6*. "But you've got to be thinking way outside the box to think this thing is a safety risk. This was funny." Co-anchor at the time Jacqueline London followed Frier's sentiments by explaining that being a news anchor they would both see some pretty serious and horrific things on a regular basis, "but a promotion for Universal is hardly one of them," she said. London then quipped in reference to these comments that "they wouldn't want to pry my mouth open. They'd want it closed."

The commercials' frequency on TV were increased as the event drew closer. As more of the media than ever before were talking about the 'gifts' they had received, the *Travel Channel* played re-runs of their documentary filmed at the previous year's event, *The Art of the Scare*. This all led to pre-event tickets sales increasing significantly. In fact, by October 1st, just days before the event, advance ticket sales were running 8% ahead of advanced sales for 2002 from the same period. Universal knew that as long as the buzz maintained and the event was delivered to expectations (with the vastly increased number of scareactors), the gamble would pay off and the event would be a hit.

The house number would be increased to six and would begin with *Scream House Revisited*. It would reunite guests with the previous icon, the Caretaker, back in his dilapidated manor house built inside Soundstage 20. In fact, the house was left from the previous year and was redressed to look even more decrepit and evil. Roaming the house were partially embalmed creatures and scattered about were decaying corpses with tortured souls of the evil operations that the Caretaker had undertaken in the house. Along with the victims, the Caretaker roamed about in a menacing fashion lurking with mummified corpses and caskets galore. Though the layout of the house was similar, some alterations had occurred and the house generally was presented in a more terrifying manner. There was the addition of burnt-out rooms to indicate that a level of trauma had been suffered to the building that mirrored the horrors faced by the occupiers. It was also worthy of note that last year this house had been built for Cindy and not the Caretaker. It had only been repurposed at the last minute, so this year the house was a fully-fledged house of evil for the maniacal Caretaker, where more time had been taken to tell his twisted story.

The next house, and one that adjoined inside the same soundstage, was the *All Nite Die-In* and was this year's icon's house. Entering into a large, deserted drive-in movie theater that was showing various horror movies projected onto the big screen, guests would be taken on a twisted journey through some of the most horrific movies in history. Though many horror movie franchises were represented here albeit in an unofficial capacity, guests could recognize the horrors even if they weren't exactly authorized for use and were used based on the principle of 'fair-use.' Each room represented a scene from a famous horror movie with the Director inside lurking in each house to usher guests through the house.

The next house was *Funhouse of Fear in 3D* which would be this year's only 3D house but not the only comical house. Located in the Thunder Falls Terrace area the house was filled with clowns in every sense and in every room. Universal billed the house as "Nothing is what it seems in this mind-boggling maze of optical delusions and maniacal clowns that will have you running for the exit. Too bad there isn't one." Gory scenes were interspersed with disorientating illusions of scareactors jumping out on guests, and crazy mirrors used to show faux exits. And although the house was filled with clowns, Jack was completely absent from the proceedings.

Though the previous house was relatively small in comparison, the other two Jurassic Park houses were quite large and the first one was an extension of the scarezone in this area. *Jungle of Doom*, located in the Triceratops Discovery Trail area and in Camp Jurassic, the house would be filled with jungle people and zombies performing ritual killings and human sacrifices. All this, combined with cannibals eating human flesh to distractive attractive males and females wearing not much more than loincloths. The main difference in the house over the streets was the use of more blood and gore, with scares coming from the darkness within the area and the abundance of shrubs and plants that lined the area.

The final house in the Jurassic Park area would go on to become a Halloween Horror Nights staple, and would feature a house that would return time and time again. Such was the popularity of the house, where scares and stomach-turning sensory delights were provided in equal measures. *Psycho Scareapy* would be located in the Jurassic Park Discovery Center and take up most of the ground floor. This house was huge! Entering into the house from the rear of the building, guests would be taken into a ghoulish and nightmarish insane asylum of the murderous kind. Demented, ghoul-like inmates had overthrown the facility, killed all the guards, nearly killed all the doctors and were now running free in a world of unfettered craziness. Padded cells and electric pulse treatment chairs were scattered about in the various rooms, along with one very memorable scene in the bathroom where fake human excrement had been scribed over the walls with the park's art and design pumping in smells to match the visual delights. The aim to terrorize your person along with your sense of smell was hand-in-hand in this epic inaugural house.

The final house and the one that had been most talked about prior to the event was *Ship of Scream* located in the *Popeye and Bluto's Bilge-Rat Barges* queue housing. The house would follow HMS Friday, a ship that had been launched January 13th 1913 and had reappeared some 90 years later with no souls on board, merely adrift in the open seas. Ghostly crewmembers in full uniform and suitably attired passengers were hidden lurking in the misty shadows of the ship.

There were five scarezones this year. *Port of Entry* became *Port of Evil* and mixed gale force winds, bright lights and loud drumming music to push guests into the park. The *Opening Scaremony* was also back this year and featured in this location. The Director, complete with his minions, tortured various people with glass helmets filled with snakes, spiders and rats. This ended with a sound-off of fireworks before the event was officially open. *Marvel Super Hero Island* became *Toxic City*, and had hordes of mutated, melted-faced mutants running around in a foamy environment. The foam machines from the previous year had been redeployed to great effect. The original idea was to reimagine the scarezone that had been undertaken the year before, due to its popularity. However rumors at the time suggested that *Marvel* were less than impressed with what Universal had done to their characters, so stepped in to kindly request that the zone and house of 2002 were not repeated.

Hide and Shrieeek was located in the Toon Lagoon area of the park. Various sets had been built to line a path through the area that would act as places for scareactors to actively hide within but hide within plain sight. For example, black backdrops were used along with black clad actors so camouflaged scareactors could jump on unsuspecting guests. Though this was a technique that had been used before, it was the first time it was used to such success in the streets. The next scarezone was *Night Prey* and was located in the Jurassic Park area, as previously described. Podium dances and fired torches lit the path between scares from various locations, including from the hedges and shrubs where the raptors of the previous year had been based. The next scarezone was on the Lost Continent renamed *Immortal Island*. It would see an epic battle between fire versus ice, settled only by a ride of then *Dueling Dragons ride* to see who the winner would be. The Ice Queen who had been within the scarezones on the previous year in a smaller capacity was now back and located in this zone up against the Lord of Fire. Various battles would be held nightly and a range of minions on each side would pull guests into the action and ask for their cover. Complete with the battles of the area, guests were also greeted by the *Chainsaw Drill Team* who were dressed as orcs with very elaborate makeup and costuming. The fabled Rat Lady was also present, once again located within her glass coffin, out on the street rather than in houses as she had been in recent years. There was a final scarezone *Boo-ville* but this was merely a bit foggy and acted as a welcome reprieve for most guests.

The one common thread that all the scarezones had in common was the use of the number '13' throughout. Purposely deployed into every house and street, the number would be a reflection of the old superstition and would be used to great effect throughout. The other attribute that tied the streets together well was the use of music. 2003 marked the first time that the creators had used music from *Midnight Syndicate*, who are an American musical group that work mostly within the gothic genre of music. They started in 1997 and are based out of Chardon, Ohio. Music from their *Realm of Shadows* album was used to enhance the streets and provide a knitted-together experience that was unlike previous years. Universal would go on to use their music frequently in the years that followed.

The attractions that were open this year include: *The Amazing Adventures of Spider-Man, Doctor Doom's Fearfall, Incredible Hulk Coaster, Popeye and Bluto's Bilge-Rat Barges, Storm Force Accelatron, One Fish, Two Fish, Red Fish, Blue Fish, Caro-Seuss-el, The Flying Unicorn, Dueling Dragons, Poseidon's Fury* and *Dudley Do-Right's Ripsaw Falls*.

Expanding on the *Opening Scaremonies show* of the first night, a new show called *Infestation* would be located near the entrance to the Enchanted Oak Tavern. Universal advertised that, "Here's your chance to 'audition' for The Director's latest film, as you get to interact with a host of creepy, crawly, co-stars. You must be 18 or older." Members of the public would be doing basically *Fear Factor* tasks where glass helmets with spiders, snakes, scorpions etc. would be poured on the volunteers (real volunteers too!). The Director hosted the event and a wheel of misfortune where your fate would be to be randomly selected to have various creepy critters poured over you.

The other show this year was a marked return for the time-travelling due of Bill and Ted. This marked the occasion where J Michael Roddy had ceased writing the show and had now given the reins fully to Mike Aiello, who had co-written the script last year with Roddy. Mike said at the time, "This year was a challenge because we went about writing the script a little bit differently. It was a team effort by a group of people with lots of different ideas and viewpoints. Universal had a basic idea that they wanted a little more music in the show this year and we (myself and Kenny Babel) wrote first based on that. Gregg Birkhimer (this year's director) gave us many points and ideas for his vision of the show. It was a fun process and a great learning experience."

The show marked the first time the opening announcement of 'switch off your phones and do not record the show' was done in a tongue-in-cheek video manner to much guest praise. It also featured a return of satirical gags featuring the then Iraqi leader Saddam Hussein (who was actually played each night by Aiello) and various members of the Bush administration. The show also featured a return for Aaron Bailey playing the part of Bill, who had not played the character for a few years and it also marked the start of a new actor, Scott Stenzel who took up the part of Ted for the very first time. This time, being located at the *Toon Lagoon Amphitheater*, the show would feature: characters from *The Matrix*, *The Lord of the Rings*, Captain Jack Sparrow from *Pirates of the Caribbean: The Curse of the Black Pearl* which had been released a few months prior to the event, along with various stars from popular music. The show this year also coincided with Universal closing the *Wild West Stage Show* in the Studios Park to make way for the *Fear Factor show*, though this had no bearing on the event or the *Bill and Ted show* that year.

This year marked a few firsts. The first being that express passes were sold in strict quantities for the very first time. In fact, they had sold out on nearly all Friday and Saturday nights during the event, marking their return an absolute given for the event's managers. The other being that donors of actual blood (rather than the fake stuff at the event) were being offered discounted tickets to the event if they donated during the month of October at any of the Central Florida blood banks. At the time blood donation levels had reached their absolute lowest for many years and the local hospitals were demanding something to be done about the decrease. Incentivized donations with event tickets were just one of many drives that occurred at the same time that year.

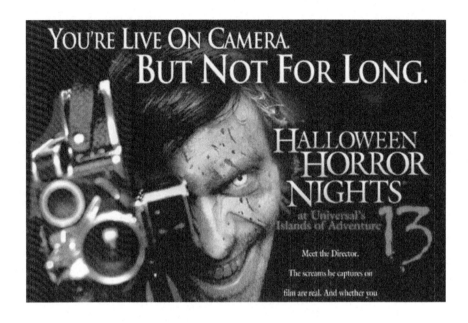

If you love The Director, hunt down the two episodes from the ScareZone podcast where author Christopher Ripley and Logan Sekulow interview the actor who played this character – he and his actual director (on another show) had some very funny stories to tell about this role, see www.scarezone.com

Halloween Horror Nights: 14th Annual

What's your breaking point?

Twice the fear!

In the formative years since the atrocities of 2001 the parks of Central Florida had struggled to attract tourists and push for growth. A real slowdown in the market was seen from 2002 and continued into 2004, though Universal had an ace up its sleeve and that ace was Halloween Horror Nights. Despite the bad headlines of visitor numbers being down and takings being slow, the event was growing and seemed to become bigger and better each year. In fact many analysts at the time directly attributed Universal's visitor number bump in 2003 to the Halloween Horror Nights event; this one event that had been held on various dates for one month could attract so many people that it could effectively push the overall yearly total of park guests up on the previous year – which was music to the resort bosses' ears. Building on results from the previous year and knowing that the event needed to grow with the visitor numbers it was enjoying, the park's management decided to put on the biggest event that they had in the event's history.

This year would feature: 7 houses, 1 show, the parade would be back, 4 heavily-themed scarezones with 12 rides/attractions open most nights. Not only was the level of entertainment increased but so was the geography, as for the first time in the event's history they decided to utilize both parks. A detailed plan was drawn up whereby the best locations for scarezones and houses could be presented but also to maximize footfall flow and the marketing that could be attributed to a two-park-one-ticket event. Pinch-points like the Jurassic Park area could be fenced off and expansive between-park areas (not open to guests) could be opened up to move guests between the parks. Logistically it would be a large undertaking but if Universal could pull this off at a time

163

when visitors were needed it could really benefit not only the event but the resort as a whole.

News of the plans came in July that year, when the local press ran articles of what was in store, "Aficionados of fright can experience twice the chills this fall when Universal Orlando expands its popular Halloween Horror Nights to include both of its theme parks. It's the first time in the event's 14-year history that it will take place in both Universal Studios and the newer Islands of Adventure." The article continued, "Universal said this year's Halloween Horror Nights will include seven new haunted mazes, bigger and more intense 'scare zones', a Halloween parade and a haunted cornfield that is currently being grown on one of the park's back lots." And it was the latter that Universal was aiming to intensify like never before. Once the plans early on in 2004 had been decided to undertake a dual park event, the organizers wanted to maximize the space on the 'backstage' areas to create large and detailed scarezones that they couldn't create in the usual guest areas. The usual scarezones were located in high-traffic areas that could not be closed off during the day to park guests, so all props and stages need to be relocated after the event finished each night; though some larger props that aren't too gruesome often remain if no parades are on that specific route. Knowing that areas could be managed better as they were backstage, the park's creatives were able to build scarezones that were as detailed as the houses in these select areas.

The largest scarezone built to date would be *Field of Screams* and would be over 2 acres in size. Located between the parks behind *The Cat in the Hat* attraction the scarezone would use real corn, that as mentioned earlier, was being specifically grown on the backlot. "Welcome to Hillside," the fallen-down, dilapidated sign read at the entrance to the scarezone. Rotting trees, bales of hay and straw-stuffed scarecrows lined the route. Lurking in the actual corn were scarecrow scareactors combined with chainsaw-toting farmers, that were selected for their ease of movement between the corn. Chants would ring out from the scareactors of,
"Stay off the path that is twisted and worn.
Where stalks all grow tattered and torn.
For all those who do, stay lost and forlorn.
Singing forever the Rhyme of the Corn."
The scarezone was so large and so detailed that people mistakenly believed that the whole installation had been a permanent attraction.

There was however one issue that the scarezones had to combat this year - and none more so than that of the cornfields of this scarezone - the hurricane season. Florida had received a battering that year from various seasonal weather events. Though not all reached the shores of Florida, the Atlantic area did produce: 15 tropical storms, 9 hurricanes and 6 major hurricanes over category 3. And by the time the event had started, the Central Florida area had received four hurricanes which had pummeled the parks and affected visitor numbers, especially those from the local area and neighboring states. Great effort was made to attract this important demographic as some 100,000 Florida residents registered with the Orlando/Orange County Convention & Visitors Bureau website were offered specially priced tickets in an attempt to get the locals back in the parks, after the storm issues of the time. And although the storms battered the cornfields in the first few weeks and a lot had been damaged during the summer, the scarezone was repaired before a welcome reprieve was seen when the storms eased off in mid-October. The idea of a maze had been the brainchild of Adrian LePeltier the Park's Show Director. He wanted to build an outdoor maze that was authentic and incredibly scary; he recalls, "I had the idea and I pitched it to Creative, they ran with it but I didn't realize they would take my idea literally and actually build a real bloody cornfield! I just assumed we'd buy in fake corn and dress it to look authentic. We laugh about it now but this was a real shock at the time."

The next big scarezone was *Fright Yard* and it was located again between the parks behind the *Poseidon's Fury* attraction. Universal described the house in this way: "An ominous industrial landscape of rusty trucks, stacked freight containers, and burning buses, *The Fright Yard* is infested with the worst society has to offer. You suddenly find yourself caught between "survivor clans" where The Demented lie in wait for The Twisted and both tribes are waiting for you. Armed with chainsaws and flame-throwers, they hide, lurk, and stalk guests in this heavy metal maze. Even with police choppers hovering above, this is a twisted and terrifying turf war that has no rules."

The area, though slightly smaller than the cornfields of the other dual park scarezone, was in fact much larger than most of the scarezones that had been seen up to this point; it was also extremely detailed. Large faux-buildings and fake train overpasses were erected and then partially burnt down, covered in graffiti or broken-down to show the chaos of a town where mob-rule was in existence. Burnt out cars, industrial waste and civic infrastructure items were left scattered and broken in the streets. Again, affording its unique location, the park's creatives could build sets and props that could be left in situ ready for detailing to be added. They also, for the very first time, decorated certain props within the scarezone with the usernames of the fan communities from the various fan websites for the event; a sort of nod to the fans for all they do in helping to publicize the event online (they also added the names in discreet locations within the website). Effectively these two scarezones were like additional houses, such was the level of detail and the ability to explore them that had been created by the Art and Design department.

Two other scarezones were seen this year, including a return of Midway of the Bizarre located this time in the Boneyard at the Studios park and Port of Entry located as the name suggests at the front of the Islands park. The former was very much like the scarezones that had been seen in the Amity area of the park at past events, though some new additions were seen. The latter zone was a mixture of lighting props and electrical devices that were removable and thus suffered no damage in the storms. Fake bolts of lightning were played out where scareactors would collectively run and hide; a tactic that seem 'all too close to home' considering the battering that the Central Florida residents had received at the time.

Seven houses had been constructed this year, with rumors of an eighth extreme house surfacing again, which as in previous years proved to be nonexistent. The seven houses however would prove to be very popular with a knitted-together theme of 'bad luck' and 'Friday 13th' attached to each house. Anticipation for the houses was built via the internet this year where the houses could be presented and unveiled like never before. Building on the feedback from the previous year, a website with full 'Flash' based animations was constructed to highlight the backstories of each house, to show the characters that might lurk within and the stories that had brought them together. Early on in the development of the event it was always key to the Park's creatives to create detailed and sometime elaborate back stories to enable guests to be taken into the worlds they were presenting. There was no better way of starting this journey than by releasing tidbits and clues via the site to build this anticipation. As the event unraveled to highlight the houses, so too did the media receive information for publication. Additionally, the billboards were put up, posters were released and for the first time elaborate house-specific queue videos were made, all designed to tell the relevant stories and move the narrative on. The latter in fact proved very popular, as the previous years' queue videos had been just collections of clips to prime guests before entering. This time, specially created videos were made teasing guests as to the impending doom that they were about to meet. And it was the first house that had the most detailed video which would quickly grow to be the most anticipated.

Castle Vampyre was built in Soundstage 23, which is a large stage for a large house. The house was so large that it actually had staircases and elevators installed. With such an asset built as this, the park's creative set about creating a *Blair Witch*-like documentary that could be screened in the queue to great effect. The video, which is about 8 minutes long, shows a frightened woman accessing the forgotten castle before ultimately facing her doom just as the camera's film would and by burning-up. Inside, the various rooms were decorated to represent every popular vampire from folklore and movie history (though not specifically tied to any franchise). The gothic castle façade would lead to rooms filled with caskets, to areas where humans were being surgically farmed for their blood, to a 'fang-tastic' disco rave with scantily clad vampires, to more well-known vampires such as the vicious *Nosferatu* vampire They then moved to the black and white gothic Dracula, to a leather clad 'Blade'-looking vampire squad to some just gruesome man-monster bats hanging from the ceiling. In total there were exactly 22 different types of vampire lurking within the house. The backstory was that every 13 years the various sections of vampire-dom meet to literally hangout at the castle, whilst guests are drafted in to explore the goings on. The tag line of the event had been 'What's your breaking point?', which Universal and its 22 selected types of vamps were eager to find out, in a house that pulled no punches.

The next house up was *Horror in Wax* which was located nearby in Soundstage 20. Universal billed the house as "The classic monsters themselves are all here... carved in wax, sculpted in resin and frozen in paraffin... perfectly preserved at the very moment tragedy struck. But this twisted enterprise was not abandoned - instead it became home to a deranged menagerie of the bizarre who lure guests inside for purposes that will become terrifyingly clear."

The website of the event also told the tale of Gunter Dietze who mysteriously died shortly after creating the wax museum that was to be explored at the event. The house contained various mutant wax-like creatures, with the classic Universal monsters in wax form and various past guests to the attraction who had been partly covered in wax suffering various burns and deformities.

Horror in Wax shared its soundstage with *Hellgate Prison*, another house which utilized the queue video technique to great effect. Universal described the house as, "Warden Robert L. Strickland's monument to himself where paying visitors suddenly find themselves lost and alone inside the penitentiary's cellblocks, corridors, and secret chambers... alone with a prison population of insane inmates, crazed convicts, and convicted criminals with nothing to lose before they walk the 'last mile' to sit on top of Old Smokey, the world's most excruciatingly painful electric chair." It was this chair which had been made into the centerpiece of the experience, where a prop chair, sparks, bangs of light and a fake electrical current would be violently injected into a faux scareactor to give the appearance of electrocution; the sight was horrific and proved that Universal was keen to keep pushing the boundaries further and further.

Hellgate Prison featured a storyline of a prison out of control. Prisoners ran amok and guards were left beaten and bruised throughout. The house included: a visitation room where prisoners behind glass threw phones at the glass and taunted guests with abuse, a demolished sick bay, a laundry room, a toilet scene (which was similar to the gross-out scene from *Shadybrook* in the previous year), and a boiler room with burned remnants of former guards and prisoners. The house concluded with guests entering into a multi-pathed labyrinth of chainmail fences where people often got lost and separated from their respective groups. Angry and aggressive inmates would shout abuse and throw items at the fences, combined with search lights and sirens which disorientated people. The house courted controversy due to its adult themes and use of simulated death, but it wasn't the only aspect which received criticism.

The event's mascot this year was a bald inmate of a mental health facility that had been put into a straitjacket due his possible murderous intentions or his lack of ability to handle the horrific aspects of the event that had been presented to him. Either way, the mascot which was featured in nearly all the marketing depicted a man suffering from mental health issues. This generated a fair amount of controversy at the time with people quick to point out Universal's insensitivity to the issue of mental health. Kate Hale was the president and CEO of the National Mental Health Associations of Florida at the time and she was quoted as saying, "Universal's public-relations department calls the promotion 'lighthearted' and says it never meant to offend anyone. But we are offended and angry." Towards the end of the event on October 30th a small silent protest was conducted outside of the studios park. The media made light of the issue and brushed it off saying that 'they should be protesting at the increased ticket prices' rather than the innocent use of this mascot. Regardless of the impact that the mascot had made on the event, the character would not return as mascot or event icon ever again.

The next house built at the event was *Ghost Town* and it was located within Soundstage 22. Universal described the house as "Strangled by gold fever, the violent town of Lightning Gulch disappeared in a fierce thunderstorm that swallowed up the settlement and all its ill-fated souls. Today there is no trace of the Gulch... except when vicious storms rage, once again revealing all of the buildings and the tortured ghosts that lurk in its streets, saloons, and alleyways. Still desperate to protect long lost treasure, these wretched spirits remain blinded by the lust for gold and enraged by greed."

A first for the event was that the house featured a western setting which the park creatives were eager to build. Universal on the West coast had a long tradition of making western movies, so much so that sets built for the classic westerns of the past are still sitting on their backlot to this day. A miniature town of worn-out timber clad buildings was assembled with gun-toting zombie-like cowboys with mummified call girls spread throughout the rooms and scenes.

2004 did not have an icon per say, however, original plans that were changed for budgetary reasons would have seen a 'headless horseman' type character riding through the streets at night striking at guests. He would have been dressed in all black and named 'The Master'

FUN FEAR FACT!

Located in the former *Hercules* attraction building, Universal built *Horror Nights Nightmares*. This was a series of rooms created to showcase the popular recent past icons that the event had created. Jack, the Caretaker, the Director and Eddie were all presented within the house. Jack had his infamous photo booth located within the house, likewise the Director had a newly re-imagined morgue to experiment with, and Eddie finally had the lion's share of the latter part of the house. Here he could chase guests in a mini-mockup of the *Run* house corridors that had been built for him (but not used by him) in 2001.

The next house offered this year was *Deadtropolis* and it was located in the *Earthquake* queue building. The house was Universal's first full zombie house which unofficially tied into the events of the Universal remake movie *Dawn of the Dead* which had been released in March of that year. Scenes from the movie were actually played in the queue to ramp up the anticipation for the horrors contained within. Entering via a quarantine, guests were bombarded by zombies at all different levels of zombification, much like in the popular movie. Soon guests would be exploring streets lined with crashed vehicles, to domestic settings like houses and garages with hiding and distracting zombies (like the vomiting one in the house). Moving on, guests enter onto the openness of the streets where dead homeless people minus their brains lay in the streets. Soon guests enter into China Town before an escape alley leads the guests out of the house. TVs and monitors line the house warning guests not to get infected and that just one bite or scrape could infect you instantly. Then in one fine, cheeky scare the event's creatives installed a dripping water pipe above that would drip water onto each guest's head. A final scareactor would announce to guests that they had survived the house but were now unfortunately infected!

The final house offered this year was *Disorientorium* and built within the underused Carnage Warehouse. The light-hearted house this year which featured a series of scary yet comical scenes was a welcome reprieve compared to the horrors of the other houses. The house's story was that it was supposedly a side-show carnival-like fun house that had been built by an outside company. The first scene was a return of the spinning tunnel filled with stars and moons which led into an area where camouflaged scareactors in black and green costumes were lurking. This would be followed on by a house of mirrors where the popular *Treaks and Foons* characters from the past year had returned to jump out on guests. The house would end with a return to the tunnel effect where guests would have to crouch down to exit whilst scareactors would reach out from all sides of the walls and ceiling.

The parade was back this year. It had also been completely overhauled to contain new floats. The floats along with the houses had been designed this year using state-of-the-art computer aided design programs (CAD) which allowed the event's creative teams to build the houses on the computers and then simulate walkthroughs. So proud were they of the addition and its ability to aid in the business of designing the best scares, Universal released a video to the internet this year detailing how it aided in house and parade design. The parade had a castle and ship float designed that were extremely detailed, like never before, which some had hypothesized was due to the use of CAD. Bill and Ted were also back this year, with popular themes and characters including: the Olsen twins, the Austin Powers characters, Michael Jackson (lampooning his issues of the day) and Paris Hilton. There was also a showing of *The Rocky Horror Picture Show* (the movie) which was projected continuously onto screens on one of the streets of the New York area, which marked the first time the popular movie had been seen at the event.

Though occurring this year but not about this year, the event became award-winning for the very first time. The local press ran articles of the event's success, "Remember those creepy television advertisements for Universal Orlando's Halloween Horror Nights, the ones that featured Caretaker, the skeletal mortician, inspecting an assortment of scalpels and other painful-looking instruments? The chilling ad campaign has received an Effie Award from the New York American Marketing

Association." The Association named the park's brave step in moving the event from one park to another and in attracting guests when other parks nationally had struggled since 9/11. The association also noted the resort's fortunes in increasing attendance, which had risen a huge 64% in 2002.

"The Crowds are back" read the headlines in the local press. Overall attendance figures for the year showed that the Central Florida area attracted an additional 8% more visitors than it had in the previous year. The newly constructed *The Mummy ride* which had replaced *Kongrontation* that year and the highly successful Halloween Horror Nights event had been directly attributed to the overall increase in attendance. Todd Pack in the local Sentinel wrote, "Revenge of the Mummy and an expanded Halloween Horror Nights helped lift its attendance 14 percent to 6.7 million." The gamble for Universal to spread the event over the two parks and increase the scares had paid off. At a time when most parks and resorts around the country were only seeing small and modest increases in their attendance, Universal was significantly beating the local figure. Universal's addition of a new ride linked to a highly successful multi-million dollar franchise and the expansion of the popular event were directly attributed to this third and fourth quarter success. Noticing that anticipation could be built with a detailed story, which could be presented and teased to the audience through marketing (though specifically through the website), Universal decided that next time they would push the narrative even further and take the event where it had never been before.

Halloween Horror Nights: Tales of Terror

No one will live happily ever after...

The mission statement for Halloween Horror Nights 2005 was to present an event where guests were taken on a journey into a new world where every show, zone and house would be linked and knitted together like never before. However, this endeavor would not be plain sailing and would ultimately be presented differently from how it was planned originally.

The dual-park situation was extremely popular and helped to ease crowds from the Islands park, that in places did bottle-neck and cause operational issues with public footfall flow. So the idea to retain the dual-park use was kept, as at least areas of the backlot not open to guests could be opened up and the massive soundstages could be used. Initially two icons were planned, one that would represent each park. 'Fate' would represent the studios where games of chance would be installed and a variety of different paths would be offered. The character would be a blind woman who would be clutching cards and dice to emphasize the point. The other icon would represent the Islands park and be called 'Darkness'. A turn-left only sign would be deployed and guests would follow a darkened path where a more straightforward story-like experience would be offered. Unfortunately, due to a variety of reasons, the concept was dropped early on.

The next concept, which ultimately was accepted and used at the event would tell a tale of Terra Cruentas. Terra Cruentas would be a land ruled by the Terra Queen, who was planned to be the event's icon. In this newly-created world, human blood, bones and flesh would be the world's only source creation, so a never-ending cycle of sacrifice would have to be played out around the park, but particularly at the Port of

Entry. A show named *The Terra Throne* at the entrance to the Islands park contained within a scarezone called *Terra Guard Run* would collect and gather members from each house and zone to partake in the sacrificing show. Blood from the victims would be taken for distribution in the Gorewood Forest area of the park (around Jurassic Park) where it would be given to the ground in the aim of producing iron. Likewise, the bones would be buried for this purpose too and the flesh would be collected to feed the demons and minions of the land. The iron that was created would be collected nightly to add to the Terra Throne, an evolving throne where the Terra Queen would sit to rule her empire and for more victims to be held and sacrificed, thus creating a cycle that would be undertaken to maintain the strange world.

The above tale was presented to the bosses of the resort and accepted for use. Unfortunately, a little later on when full development was underway some of the same executives who had green-lit the overall theme left the organization. New executives came in and knowing that the event was now responsible for year-on-year attendance growth, they wanted to ensure the overall theme was sufficient for the expectations they had. The new executives decided to leave the planning that had been undertaken as it was but requested that a new park icon was selected. Fearing that the Terra Queen was perhaps a little too sexy (and not creepy enough) or not sufficient to build an event around for the purposes of marketing, a new icon would be selected. So as to not ruin the carefully planned story that had been developed, the Terra Queen would remain as the event's mascot but a new icon would be developed. Various ideas were considered before the event's creatives decided on creating a character named the Storyteller. The new icon that the marketing would center on would be an evil old lady, almost witch like, who could be presented as the narrator of this whole world's story. As the story takes place within different dimensions and different times, having a character like that would generally add to the knitted-together thematic that the park wanted to go for this year. As well as appearing in all the marketing for the event, she would also appear in one of the houses and at the Port of Entry and not anywhere else. The website was built around her and her stories, and it teased the audience of the site every week with the frequent small updates that started in the summer and gradually unraveled all the stories before the event commenced in October.

It was then in August of that year that the New York Times and Orlando Sentinel ran mutual articles about the up-coming event and the need to fulfil the 1,000 vacancies that were required for the event. The largest story ever told by the event required the largest influx of cast and crew which had ever been seen up until this point. *The Sentinel* reported, "Think you have what it takes to be a professional in the scare business? Then Universal Orlando might be looking for you. Every Tuesday through Sept. 13, the theme park is holding casting calls for 1,000 performers to frighten visitors during Halloween Horror Nights 15."

The articles in both papers stated that the park was looking to recruit stilt-walkers, celebrity impersonators, scareactors and street performers for the month-long event. Anticipation really grew at this time, knowing that the event was once again making national headlines for the right reasons.

The opening night began and the *opening scaremonies* began where the Terra Queen and her minions were presented to the audience. Additional pyro-effects and fireworks were used to celebrate the fact that the event had started. The show would remain nightly and alter slightly, with the main purpose of the show to tie the aspects of the event together and to show a 'live' human sacrifice on stage. The final show of the event would see the humans replaced by the Terra Queen herself, where she would be sacrificed. The sinister monks would proclaim, as part of the legend of the Queen, that she would return in 15 years' time to present her world again (so can we expect to see her in 2020?). As well as setting up the narrative for the event, the show would tease and highlight to guests the horrors that awaited.

The first house that most guests this year attended was *Demon Cantina* and was located in the Carnage Warehouse behind Marvel Superhero Island. The house would be one of the most popular for this year. Loosely inspired by the legendary 1996 movie *From Dusk till Dawn*, the house would be the guests' own adventure into the cantina of this world, where instead of vampires, demons of all kinds would come to feast and drink within the bar setting. They feasted on the flesh provided by the Queen and drank the blood of foolish mortals who had stumbled into their realm. The website billed the house as, "Mankind tempts fate if anyone is foolish enough to step inside the Demon Cantina, flagrant trespass on the turf of the ferocious Bone Choppers of Ironbone Gorge. Celebrating their own last Season of the Queen, the meanest of the Queen's Black Guard enlist chainsaw-wielding maniacs to provide entertainment and seductive creatures to supply amusement... and all take one last taste of sweet warm Bloodberry wine."

The faux-wine in fact would actually go on to be sold at the event in specialty glasses, available at various re-themed outlets for the event. It was something that Universal had never done before but would visit again once more when Hogsmead would open where they would sell the ever popular 'Butterbeer'. Was this an early inspiration for the popular drink? The theme was diesel-punk and it featured various victims in various states of distress, where demons aplenty would appear to make even the sternest of guests jump-out-of-their-skin. The house ended with the puking drunk fake scareactor placed outside the house. The same prop had been seen in past houses.

The next house on the journey would take guests in to a forestry setting (Gorewood Forest) on Jurassic Park island where *The Skool* would be presented. The house would be a boarding school for the new demons, monsters and mutants that were being bred and trained to take over the processes at the other houses at the event. Smaller actors were used, all with masks on as the Halloween was not just celebrated on the one night but the whole of October at this ghoul school. No teachers were seen in the house, as guests followed a path around all the various classrooms and dormitories. The house would again like the opening show of the event, be a teaser for the monsters that were about to be presented in the other houses.

The next house in this area would also prove to be extremely popular and would ensure the creatures contained within would be back at the event time after time. The house located in the expansive Jurassic Park Discovery Center was *Body Collectors* and the house was huge. Set in a Victorian-like industrial environment, the house would serve as a warehouse for processing the victims of the opening show. Various rooms would be presented showing the victims being dismembered and their organs, flesh, bones and other items being harvested for movement to the areas of the park where they were required. Filling the house were these silent, white-faced, smartly dressed creatures that had fixed grins on them as they worked on their victims. The creatures were called the Collectors and they were directly inspired characters that appeared in the then very popular TV series *Buffy the Vampire Slayer*. They appeared in only one episode entitled *Hush* where the voiceless monsters were called the Gentlemen. They had been deployed within the episode to cut out the tongues and murder anyone that spoke to them, so the episode became very popular for the quirky use of no talking throughout the episode. One fan-favorite house had the Collectors ripping a backbone from a victim tied to a table to great theatrical effect. The popularity of the house and the regular 3 hours plus that the queue maintained on most nights ensured that the characters of the house would be surely back for future events.

Both scarezones on the island of Gorewood Forest would be supported by *Cemetery Mines* scarezone that would see a collection of mutants scaring guests as they chased them from hiding in the entrances to the many mines that were scattered about.

The next house on the journey would be *Terror Mines* and for an event first, it would be placed inside the *Poseidon's Fury* attraction. Walking the same path as the attraction, guests would be taken into a mine setting where mutants called gnome-rats would be lurking around every corner. The house also had a novel use of lighting. The park's creatives had explored the idea of giving guests the flashlights to use in the houses, but fearing they may unwittingly be used as weapons (by accident) by guests, or being stolen outright, the idea was never implemented. Instead the idea of giving every 12th guest a helmet with flashlight attached would be brought into play within the house and little other lighting would be used. The helmets could also be counted out as they were handed to guests to prevent theft. The effect worked well for guests who had the helmet or who were with the guest with the helmet, though less well if you were that 11th person since a helmet had been given out. The helmets would then be controlled by sensors that would automatically switch them off at certain points or back on to heighten the scares. The extremely dark house took guests around the various areas of the mine where the effects of the house had been altered to accommodate the mine theme. This also concluded at the water vortex tunnel where light and water were used in equal measure to disorientate guests. Outside, *The Fire Pits* scarezone saw the entrance to the ride and surrounding areas transformed into a medieval village complete with peasants, knights and, somehow, the *Chainsaw Drill Team*.

The next house would be *Cold Blind Terror* and it would be located inside Soundstage 20. The house would feature a polar landscape that was extremely cold (the air-conditioning had been ramped up) and the lighting of the house was controlled, which created a deeply cold and dark house. Universal billed the house as, "Bone-chilling cold and blind terror numb the senses as one cannot see, one cannot hear... and one cannot escape. In and out of total darkness, mankind find themselves shivering from both fear and the icy cold blackness. Strange sounds split the darkness, but one cannot be sure the source... one cannot be sure what lurks behind... one cannot be sure of what lies ahead. One cannot be sure if they'll ever see light again." Many complained that the house was less themed than the others but instead of a gory back story it was the use of the cold air and lack of light presented in a confined space that was central to scaring the guests.

Around the corner from the above house was *Blood Ruins* in Soundstage 22. Universal billed the house as, "Still ruled by defrocked monks, the ruin at the old Blood Abbey serves as prison, hospital and asylum to a population of fresh mankind "donors". In centuries before its walls began to crumble, the Blood Abbey was the place where terrible tools of torture were invented. Now these instruments have found new use as Ore Mongers fanning the flames of Dragon Forge demand a never-ending supply of blood for the tempering of the Blade." The house was originally planned to be located in the *Dueling Dragons* attraction's queue building. Pre-Harry Potter expansion, the queue building was a gothic setting that had been highly themed to build expectation for the ride ahead; a medieval dungeon-like setting located within the bowels of a castle deep in the forest would hold guests before they chose sides and rode the dragon. This was all changed and re-themed to *Harry Potter* in 2010, however back in 2005 the area would have served as a perfect location for a house (much like the *Poseidon's Fury* attraction building). However, when the executives changed, so did the use of the building. Park bosses were not happy that one of the most popular rides of the park would be offline for the duration of the event when empty soundstages were sitting there waiting to be used. And although it cost more to move the house to the soundstage (originally much of the original queue setting would have been untouched), the house had to be hastily redesigned from the ground-up. Creatives countered this issue of sets that weren't as detailed as originally planned by ramping up the level of makeup on the scareactors within. As the story unfolded it told a tragic tale of a rampant bubonic plague that was spreading amongst the villagers and monks alike. Makeup artists from the park attached fake buboes and ulcers to the characters and created deformed mutant-like appendages to increase the gore factor of the house.

The house 'Blood Ruins' was originally proposed for building inside the Dueling Dragons coaster queue line. Fearing operational issues to the ride, the house was moved to a soundstage instead. FUN FEAR FACT!

The final house presented was *Where Evil Hides* located in Soundstage 18. This house would act as the newly appointed icon's house with the character of the Storyteller appearing at certain times throughout. Universal billed the house as, "Beyond Maldaken Pass lie the very places in mankind's worst nightmares where night terrors are real. The places where the monsters live, the skeletons are stored and the bodies are hidden. The places in the imagination where terror plays hide-and-seek with the unfortunate dreamer. Once inside, one faces all of those dark hallways, passages and doors that open to exactly what one had hoped they did not."

The house told the tale of a psycho-killer on the loose within the setting of a suburban house. A white faced, boiler suit-wearing killer would be seen jumping out at guests throughout (from cupboards, under beds, through windows etc.) and the Storyteller would pop up at times to move the narrative along.

The attractions that were open this year included: *The Amazing Adventures of Spider-Man, Dr. Doom's Fearfall, Storm Force Accelatron, Incredible Hulk Coaster, The Cat In The Hat, One Fish, Two Fish, Red Fish, Blue Fish, Caro-Seuss-el, Dudley Do-Rights Ripsaw Falls, Jurassic Park River Adventure, The Flying Unicorn* and *Dueling Dragons*. The following attractions operated on peak nights (mostly Fridays and Saturdays): *Twister...Ride it Out, Revenge of the Mummy, Jimmy Neutron's Nicktoon Blast* and *Shrek 4-D*. Bill and Ted were back this year and the show featured characters from *Family Guy, Star Wars* and the new Tim Burton movie *Charlie and the Chocolate Factory* which had been released in July of that year. There was also a very memorable moment from the show where Ronald McDonald and the (Burger) King have a fight scene.

This year was also memorable for the staff of the event as it received no higher praise than winning the inaugural best Halloween event for 2005 from Amusement Today's Golden Ticket Awards. *Amusement Today* had been running the celebrated awards since 1998 but it was only this year that they added the category of Halloween. The judges of the event were extremely impressed with the level of detail within the houses and streets and how the whole event was tied together under one narrative. The event's run was to end on a high for whole team after securing this award. It would, however, be tarnished with sadness at it would also mark the final year that Adrian LePeltier, the Park's Show Director, would work on Halloween Horror Nights at Universal. An emotional farewell was given to Adrian as the props and sets were packed away after another highly successful year.

A new era was coming...

A final area of note occurring during 2005 was the possible acquirement of rights to certain characters that would eventually make a big impact on the event. A small article in the *Sentinel* ran on July 25th with the headline, "Big-screen horror characters come to life; Orlando firm teams up with New Line Cinema to create film-based haunted houses." The article told the story of how *New Line Cinema* was starting to look for licensing partners to utilize their recently-obtained 'fearsome threesome' of Freddy Krueger, Jason Voorhees and Leatherface along with their respective franchises of *A Nightmare on Elm Street, Friday the 13th* and *The Texas Chainsaw Massacre*.

Many discussions were held on a plethora of ideas, from video games to clothing, though *New Line Cinema* was very keen to bring the icons to a theme park or haunt attraction. Later on in November the company showcased a number of prototypes at the annual conference of the International Association of Amusement Parks and Attractions in Atlanta, where real costumes and latex masks had been made using profiles of Robert Englund's actual face. And although nothing was to be seen of the characters in 2006, it wasn't until 2007 that the characters would finally be released on the world...

(Author's note: but please don't skip the next chapter though!)

Halloween Horror Nights: Sweet 16

"Horror comes home!"

Halloween Horror Nights 16 was planned as the event's first ever retrospective event. All the best and brightest from the previous 16 years would be showcased in all seven houses, three (well, four) shows and four scarezones. Official news of the park's intentions came in July of that year when the media was drip-fed tidbits of information and a hint that the event would be a celebration of the overall event's brand. Slightly before that in June of that year Universal altered the archives and placeholder website in favor of a new teaser site which would build anticipation amongst the viewers over the coming months by releasing small background stories, faux press clippings and the like. Tickets for the event officially went on sale on July 14th for $59.95 plus tax; hoping that select days may sell-out again it would be a direct aim to get the tickets out there very early once more (in fact it was exactly 11 days earlier than when they had launched the tickets in the previous year).

Along with the various pieces of information released over the summer, it was also officially announced that the event would return to where it began, dubbing the new event as "horror comes home!" It was also around September 1st that the resort began to start advertising for new recruits to join the army of scareactors needed for the event. Like previously at the Islands park where numbers had increased to a new record of 1,000 members of the cast, it was decided to maintain that number to ramp up the scares for this anniversary style event. Needing people to do the scares in lieu of just relying on props or technology to do the scares (something that Universal's competitors at various locations around the country had done) was something that Universal wanted to highlight. "The scares truly come from the performers," TJ Mannarino of the resort's Art and Design department said. "They can be relentless, or they can be subtle, and you can't get that from technology."

Along with the 1,000 performers, the park would utilize hundreds of backstage crew and artisans along with 60 people to staff the makeup and prosthetics department for the month-long event. Their driving focus was to bring back the event's icons from the past events, bringing them together to celebrate all that truly scared the most and provided the most chills. "The icons will dominate the entire event from haunted houses to shows," said Mannarino. "It's their world."

The icons assembled!

An elaborate stage was constructed outside Mel's Diner at the top of the Hollywood section of the park. The stage would provide the opening show of the night called *The Arrival* and it would play on and off all evening with the aim that everyone who was in the park would catch a glimpse of it at some point. The show featured the horned beast himself, 'Darkness' from the movie *Legend* and although not an icon of the event, he had previously featured heavily in the event's parades. As master of ceremony he would bring forth and summon the icons to take center stage, introducing each one. His minions, made up of vampires, weird monks and mutants selected from various scarezones would be on hand to assist. Darkness, raising from the ground to the center of the stage, would first bring forth the Storyteller who would quickly introduce herself and her house before pulling out the tongue of a victim tied to a chair. Each icon would follow a similar route of introduction before torturing an actor with an elaborate staged magic trick; they would get more gruesome as they went on. Next would be the Director who would promptly electrocute a lady in a bathtub, followed by the Caretaker who would rip the prop organs from a man's chest, a man lying conveniently in a coffin at high level. The final and most elaborate gruesome act was Jack the Clown placing a man in a giant blender before then switching it on, to very bloody and splattering consequences. Once the introductions had been made, a series of fireworks were let-off and the event was officially open.

"Pain is temporary, but film is forever". This was the creepy catchphrase that ran out of the first house on our journey. That house was *All Nite Die-In: Take 2*, located on Sound Stage 23, a sequel house to the Director's popular house of 2003. Incredibly similar in style but with different movies, the Director would take guests on a journey through a drive-in movie theater to visit some of the scariest scenes from motion picture history. One of the first scenes took guests right into the living room and kitchen from the opening scene of the *Scream* movie with popcorn on the stove ready to explode, with an actress who was extremely similar to Drew Barrymore followed by the relentless 'Ghostface killer' who popped up with knife in various locations within the sympathetic recreation of the set. Other rooms within the house included scenes recreated from *Hellraiser*, *The Ring* and *Silence of the Lambs*, with the final room being an ensemble of various killers from the previous scenes and other movies to chase the guests out into the street.

Dungeon Of Terror: Retold would be the next house and just like in the years past, the original *Fright Nights* house would be located once more in the *Jaws* queue building. The house was billed as, "In its day, it would lure tourists by the thousands. Now, it is only visited by the occasional lost traveler. Enter the *Dungeon of Terror*, where mysterious whispers call you deeper into hell. A place where the Teller of Stories demands the undivided attention of her 'guests'. Once you make the mistake of entering the Dungeon, you'll wish you had not because no one can leave until Her story has been told."

Introducing the house in her typical rocking chair manner, the Storyteller would collect tickets before sending guests onto a murderous tale of a roadside attraction gone wrong. A souvenir stand, followed by various exhibits and then motel-like rooms saw a gang of mutant inbred weirdos (complete with pig masks), torture and kill various passing travelers, all headed by a buxom lady in a flannel skirt complete with chainsaw. And although the house was pretty unlike the original house of the same name, it fitted its location perfectly and provided some really good scares.

People Under The Stairs: Under Construction would see a return for the event's 2nd originally-built house from the 1991 movie of the same name and it would be located in a wholly new location for the event. Located in Sprung Tent 1 or its official name of 'World Expo Warehouse 1' would see the event construct two sprung tents just for the purposes of Halloween Horror Nights. Utilizing what remained of the original sets plus creating more sets to fill the tented environment, the house would see guests come face-to-face with the freaks of the original movie. Utilizing the same gimmick of the previous year, where every 12th guest would be provided with a helmet with flash light, the house would try to pull off the same technique but with marginal success. Unlike *Poseidon's Fury* building where the light could be strictly controlled, the sprung tent would be too illuminated for the effect to work properly throughout, with some guests reportedly leaving the helmets behind half way around the house. One memorable scene from the house, and one that received much praise was a scene where guests were shot with a shotgun that had been filled with water. They also added in some special effects, smoke and sound-effects to give the impression that they had actually been shot, just like in the movie.

Neighboring next to the above house in Sprung Tent 2 would be *Psycho Path: The Return Of Norman Bates*, which was incidentally the third house ever created for the event back at the start. The original house and motel had long since been demolished to make way for expansions to the Kids' Zone area of the park, and although nothing remained from storage from these large sets, Universal's craftspeople set about recreating an impressive façade that was wholly reminiscent of the original motel set. The house was billed as "There is a vacancy once again at the legendary Bates Motel. Unlocking the door reveals a portal into the darkest depths of insanity. Your eyes prove to be useless as your mind takes over and leads you through the macabre nightmares of a pathological killer. A killer named Norman Bates."

The house used elements from the previous houses that had been utilized from the *Psycho* franchise, whereby guests would enter into the motel, see the office and cabin room 1 before descending into the mad world of Norman's mind. Rooms filled with mirror knives and huge eyeballs floating from the ceiling portrayed guests' descent into the mind of Norman Bates. This amalgamation of both respective Norman Bates' houses made for good scares throughout, building up to the final room with disorientating projections, music, soundbites with rows and rows of showers lining the walls filled with knife-wielding mothers!

Although the above façade was impressive, nothing could beat the façade and setting of the next house. *Psychoscareapy: Maximum Madness* was an amazing house that would be Jack's own house this year. The set was so impressive that many fans of the event petitioned Universal to leave it in situ as a year-around attraction. Although this didn't happen, no one could deny that it was one of the most impressive sets ever built for the event. Located in huge Soundstage 22 the house was billed as "Shady Brook Hospital has been plagued with rioting inmates off and on for years. These small incidents of chaos have always been resolved quickly and contained with minimal casualty. However, Shady Brook's newest resident is about to change all that. If you think you know insane you don't know Jack. Step inside an asylum where the sideshow is death and the "big top" has padded walls."

Setting the house back in Jack's time before he was murdered around the early twentieth century, the designers at Universal studied hospital architectural styles from this time to build an Art Deco-looking façade whose design would be seen throughout every room of the house. Rows of padded cells and inmates running amok would lead guests to Jack, complete with straight jacket and lurking in his own cell. The inmates would slowly transform into disciples of Jack's with similar makeup styles and speech, before guests would be inevitably guided to the infamous toilet scene once again.

The next house would see a return of the icon that was never really an icon, that of Eddie. *Run: Hostile Territory* would be located in the Earthquake queue building. It would see our titular host chasing guests, chainsaw in tow, around tight chainmail corridors within a warehouse-style torture facility. Reminiscent of the recent spate of horror-torture movies that had been released recently such as *Hostel*, the house would actively portray scenes of deviant acts with the aim of distracting guests before Eddie popped up to chase them into the next room. A booming soundtrack of drum 'n' bass music, combined with an orchestra accompaniment and manic laughter, was pumped into the house. This, along with no air-conditioning, created a house that was hot, humid and loud but was filled with chainsaw-chasing maniacs.

The final house would see a welcome return of the Caretaker back in his experimental mortuary in *Scream House: Resurrection* located in Soundstage 23. The house was billed as "Through blood, bone and ash, evil has risen again. Abandoned for years, this gothic mortuary contains the eternally tormented souls of the Caretaker's victims. Aided by a cultish group of Followers, the Caretaker assures that you will enter on your own two feet, but leave sealed in a casket."

The story of the house combined the themes of loss and bereavement that played on the main character of the house. Guests were informed that the reason behind his killer ambitions was his search for a means to bring back to life his departed daughter Cindy. For the first time, Universal acknowledged the existence of Cindy and rewrote her backstory to fit in with the character of the Caretaker. No longer portrayed as a crazed torturing killer, the Caretaker was seen as a father struggling to cope with the loss of a loved one. He was still terrifying, though! A cemetery was presented near the end of the house, complete with this amazing lightning effect that made guests and scareactors alike jump! Both he and Cindy were seen throughout the house, which was very much like (but not the same as) the mortuary presented in previous years.

The 'Ghoul School' that was created earlier on by the Art and Design Department was later revised by Laura Wallace to ensure 'golden rules' of scareactor etiquette were always observed by the perfumers. This included how actors interacted with the public, how they took breaks and did cast changes

FUN EAR FACT!

There were four scarezones this year.

The first was *Blood Masquerade* which was located in Shrek Alley. The main premise of the scarezone was that the vampires from Castle Vampyre were assembling for a masquerade party and to "renew their vows to a darker power". The zone was nowhere near as brilliant as the previous house and nor was the makeup as intense but it did fill the wide alley well and present some good scares.

Next up in the New York area was *Deadtropolis: Zombie Siege*. The house was billed as, "A greenish fog crawls in pockets along the streets. Hunched forms cut through the haze slowly. These silhouettes appear human, however the moans and cries they sound chill you to the bone. This is the new reality. A new dynamic has evolved for the phrase "us" and "them": Us being the living and them being zombies. View the haunting sites of a new metropolis populated by the undead. A Deadtropolis."

This scarezone was intense! Firstly, Universal decided to increase the total number of scareactors within this zone. They packed it with broken vehicles, disorientating smog and sirens with a very loud soundtrack. But also of note was the makeup; the cast had been made up exceptionally well. The disorientating effects combined with the sheer ratio of zombies per guest was amazing; it was a very well done scarezone. And if the zombies weren't enough there was another huge beast waiting for you at the back of the scarezone...

Harvest Of The Souls was located in Central Park and was a repeat of the scarezone that was a sequel scarezone (like the *Vampyre* scarezone) from the previous year's *Field of Screams*. The sets were not as detailed as had been the previous year (where acres of corn had been especially grown) but this was offset by increased scareactor numbers in this tight, winding path. Demented corn-kids and scarecrows lined the paths with pumpkins and dead trees placed strategically.

Horror Comes Home was the final scarezone on our list and was located on Hollywood Boulevard. The park map declared, "Take a macabre walk down memory lane with the haunted sights and sounds of previous Halloween Horror Nights. Keep your camera handy as some of the most infamous characters prowl the streets, looking for prey." Banners lined the street here, depicting every year of the event. Selected scareactors from the past 16 years had been chosen to line the streets and provide the scares. All the major characters were there, with the exception of the Cryptkeeper.

The dynamic time travelling dudes were back again in *Bill & Ted's Excellent Halloween Adventure*, this time taking place for the first time in the newly-refurbished *Fear Factor Stage*. Popular references this year included: the highly popular (at the time) TV series of *24*, *Deal or No Deal*, *The Da Vinci Code*, *Mission Impossible* and a remarkable lookalike of David Hasselhoff.

Rising from the ground at the back of the New York scarezone like a mechanical phoenix from the ashes was the myth and monster himself, the 30 ton *Robosaurus*, who had return for this year after a 12-year absence. Although the show and location were also exactly the same as in years past, it did for the first time tie into the scarezone's narrative.

The story presented in the show, was that to stop the zombie uprising the plucky robot with marines backup team had been sent into the area to wipe away all the living dead. So as well as the chaos of the usual show whereby several cars are crushed and the like, it also went onto breath fire and move around clearing the gathered zombies. It was actually the best performance of the robot at the event and was incredibly popular most nights. Show director J Michael Roddy said at the time, "Robosaurus was a big hit in the early '90s, in the infancy of our event, I think people love Robosaurus because it's something real. It's not a trick. It's a 40-foot-tall, mechanical dinosaur that eats cars. There's no trickery. No illusion. When we were looking at the things that we could bring back, Robosaurus was at the top of our list."

Another show that was presented this year (though not officially as it was going through some tests at the time) was the newly installed Universal 360 globes that had been placed as various locations around the lagoon. The nightly show was started this year as an aim to keep guests in the park until closing to see the special show. These giant orbs that were used at various times during the event showing clips of the event's icons and various clips from recent horror movies. The orbs, standing 30ft tall by 36ft wide, would present a whole 360° viewing screen that could be seen from many of the locations around the lagoon. Combined with lasers, pyro-effects and fireworks, the film introduced by the Director (of course!) was a fascinating use of this technology.

Though *RIP tours* of the park, where guests are guided in both exclusive and non-exclusive groups around all the shows and attractions each night had been introduced in the previous year, this year Universal introduced for the first time the fan favorite tour of *Unmasking the Horror Tour*. Originally costing just $35 and limited to 15 guests, the tour would see two to three of Universal's great tour guides taking guests for a 'lights-on' tour of three selected houses (usually two from the soundstages and one from the backlot or 'hacklot' as it was known this year). The two-hour tour, held not during the events nights but during the day, would lead guests around the three houses where guests would be told all the back stories and shown all the details that can easily be missed in between all the carnage and scares. Often members of the resort's Art and Design department would be on hand to answer a few select questions, and guests would very often see workmen fixing-up the houses from the previous night's damage. The tours were so popular that they were promptly brought back for the following year.

Also premiering this year was a new pass for passholders to the park. The Premier Pass was rolled out for the mega fans of Universal. There were special extras to the pass, including all the benefits of the other annual passes along with two-park freedom, select valet and no additional charge, and free entry into this year's Halloween Horror Nights on all of the non-peak nights. Although the pass was not as popular as management had hoped for, it did increase the park's attendance for non-peak nights.

The ever popular 'Shark in the Dark' aka the Jaws ride (but at night) was always a popular ride for HHN. In the years that Jack the Clown featured as the icon, an actor dressed as Jack would be deployed to the boat house (about half way into the ride) and would give additional scares to the paying crowds as they passed through. This however came to a surprise halt when the actor playing Jack fell into the water with the giant prop sharks. Slipping on some splashed water, the actor fell into the water and the ride had to be emergency stopped to prevent the actor from getting seriously injured. James-Michael Roddy recalls "once that happened, Jack was never placed in that ride again, the actor was very lucky to survive becoming face-to-face with Jaws!"

FUN FEAR FACT

No makeup or masks allowed!

Halloween Horror Nights: Carnival of Carnage

Choose Thy Fear!

The year 2007 was for many a year of change, for not only the Horror Nights event but also for the resort. Two iconic rides (*Earthquake* and *Back to the Future*) would both close within 14 months of each other to make way for new attractions. Both the addition of brand new lands for Harry Potter's universe and Springfield USA (from *The Simpsons*) would be announced this year, along with executive changes and other organizational changes. Most of these revisions and reinvestments were due to the fall in attendance that had been seen overall for the year 2006 for both parks. This, however, did not reflect on Halloween Horror Nights, which actually increased their attendance and managed to again create a bump in attendance for the fourth quarter of 2006. The local *Sentinel* reported at the time, "Last year, the company reported a record gate of nearly 500,000 visitors for those Halloween Horror Nights, accounting for almost one of every 12 visitors to Universal Studios". Universal Orlando President Bill Davis also said at the time, "We're very pleased with our fourth-quarter results and will do everything we can to maintain momentum, we're seeing increases in attendance from Florida, our overall U.S. market, South America and the Caribbean. And, like the rest of our industry, we're hard at work creating aggressive marketing programs we expect to help us in the UK." And everything he could do, he did, as the resort announced that the event would again be bigger and better than it had ever been before.

New Line Cinema, founded in 1967 by Robert Shaye, is an independent film studio owned by *Warner Bros* which had started out distributing art-house and educational films to colleges and schools across the country. It later went on to undertake less distribution and

191

therefore concentrate on more of its own productions. The studio focused on lesser-known talent and allowing them to experiment and flourish, to mixed success. This business plan remained much the same through the 1970s and 80s where one movie even went on to receive a coveted Academy Award. It wasn't until 1976 that the company began making full-length major motion pictures. Their first was a movie called *Stunts*. The action thriller did mildly well and allowed the company to invest in three further motion pictures all based around the horror and sci-fi genres, which all underperformed to company expectations. It wasn't until 1984's release of *A Nightmare on Elm Street* and its subsequent sequels that had achieved so much success at the box-office, conferring the title to their Studio of *The House that Freddy Built*. This continued into the 1980s when the third film in the Freddy franchise managed to make back nearly 10 times the budget for the studio. It was also around the late 1980s, hot on the success of this movie in 1987, that by 1988 the company had acquired the right to use the characters from the *Texas Chainsaw Massacre* films. Leatherface was later joined by Jason and co when the company acquired the rights to the popular *Friday 13th* franchise in about 1989. The company went on to continue the same lucrative mix of reasonable budget sizes to these cult franchises, releasing them to good box-office returns for many years.

Long before *New Line* had acquired the rights to use Jason, they had tried to get a 'Freddy vs. Jason' movie off the ground. Many fans, particularly those who regularly attended the various horror and fantasy related conventions wrote to the respective owners of the icons to register their approval for such a move. In fact, due to various owners of Jason and varying degrees of success for subsequent sequels, it would take 15 years of 'development hell' before the project could be realized; *New Line* buying the Jason franchise was the true catalyst to the whole project. During these 15 years it would see $6 million spent on eighteen unused scripts and over a dozen writers all working on it. But the toils of the past productions were not in vain as the movie was finally finished in 2003 when the movie went on to make $114 million at the box-office. Also during this time the Texas franchise was fully rebooted by *New Line* in 2006 also going on to make solid box-office returns. The three characters were exceedingly 'hot' during this period and had made a real comeback from their earlier successes of the 1980s to draw in popular audiences around the world by 2007. And as mentioned in 2005's chapter of this book, *New Line*, a progressive forwarding-thinking company was also looking to expand the popular characters' appeal to not just movies but to other mediums. At the time, licensing agreements for toys, comics and video games were all considered and some were put into production. It wasn't until 2006 that the company officially licensed the use of the icons to Universal Studios for use in Halloween Horror Nights.

The official announcement came on June 27th, 2007 that the three icons of horror would be officially joining the event on both coasts, with the event taking place in Orlando in the Studios and not at Islands of Adventure. It would be the first time the cinema had officially granted the rights to use the characters in a theme park (though many had tried to bring them to events and park before). "We're obviously extremely excited about it. It's going to be a great addition to what is already a great event, we're thrilled!" Jim Timon, Universal's senior vice president of entertainment had said at the time. Universal promised that they were extremely excited about taking the three characters and exploring where the park's creative minds could take them. It was also around this time and just before, that the website for the event was updated to show a random field in the middle of nowhere where a coming carnival was about to take place...

Slowly over the coming weeks various vehicles and trucks assembled on the field with some becoming 'clickable', but only once visitors to the site could work out various puzzles and games to unlock secrets about the upcoming event. It was around this time that various fan websites started to notice increased numbers in memberships to their forums, especially *hhnvault.com* (which is no longer running). Plucky fans trying to decipher the clues and find solutions to the puzzles would discuss solutions and what the possible items on the site would mean. This ramped up the anticipation from the online communities which, combined with the increase of social media interactions at the time (Facebook had reported a 178.38% increase in signups during this period from the year previous!), all led to further conversations and marketing for the event as the online community for the event started to explode in popularity.

Eventually, via the website and various press releases, the event's official icon was revealed to be the ever-popular Jack the Clown (though unofficially various stores had put out marketing posters before the 'big reveal' date). The story behind the event was fully unraveled and was to be *The Carnival of Carnage*. The story went that the cold October winds were bringing a dark and sinister carnival to town. Jack, now your ringmaster, has taken hold of the event as he brings together the most diabolical combination of sinister sideshows, a midway of carnage and the most maniacal movie madmen ever. These were Freddy Krueger, Jason Voorhees and Leatherface, three of the most modern and current horror icons that the silver screen had at the time. It was announced that the freakish foursome would be unveiled at a special 'opening scaremonies' show before their official deployment to their own individual houses at the event. They would not however feature on the streets, together (other than in this opening night show) or in any of the other shows. However, they did feature together in all the marketing, particularly in a number of popular commercials that showed a man entering the carnival and getting literally accosted by the foursome along with a short sequence showing 'gory-getaway' guests getting attacked at the onsite hotels.

The house count would also be increased this year to eight and instead of having a number of carefully allotted scarezones, this year would feature the park being plunged completely into fear by being one giant scarezone (though technically four to five set scarezones were seen, with roaming characters). The move to increase the street scares and increase the house numbers was a direct result of crowding within the park and the excessively long queues for the houses that would be expected. Timon went on say, "We're making a good step forward with the lines and the waits. We have added a haunted house, so we have one more haunted house experience to help absorb some capacity. We're also opening up the show stadiums, which will help absorb thousands of people an hour in show capacity."

Despite there being a house called 'Freddy Vs Jason' in 2015's event, the original idea was to have this idea on the streets. The idea was that an epic scarezone would be built within Shrek Alley featuring a number of performers dressed as Freddy and Jason doing battle. Battles would be on stages, podium and even in the air. The narrative of the zone would see the two do battle over and over again all night with finally an appearance of Leatherface towards of the end of the night to finalize who was the victor. The winner? Leatherface of course. Unfortunately, *New Line Cinema* did not sign off on the idea and the scarezone was never built.

FUN EAR FACT

Along with the scares came five shows. The first was the *Opening Scaremonies* which only ran on the first night of the event. The show featured a carnival announcer who warmed the audience up by listing the various scareactors who would be present this show before introducing our new Ringmaster Jack. Ever the showman, the character jumped on the stage, complete with ringmaster jacket and cane to announce "I'm back", much to the gathered crowd's cheers and clapping. A disheveled looking woman was then pulled on stage, named "Jill" (which is ironic as originally Jack's girlfriend would be called Jill but she was dropped at the development stage of this event). Complete with her torn jacket and hastily applied clown makeup, Jill remained frozen on stage in fright as Jack introduced the three icons that everyone had gathered to see. Jill, who had now turned assistant under Jack's instructions, turned a number of giant playing card posters to reveal the pictures of the three icons. Once fully revealed, Jack announced "welcome to the carnival of carnage", the crowd cheered and a number of fireworks were let off. Then suddenly the lights were killed, and a spot light focused on the shivering Jill, with a buzz of chain sounds coming from offstage. Then Leatherface himself burst through his poster and onto the stage to face Jill. Taking a large swipe at her, she ducked and the monster disappeared into the darkness. Still trembling, she ran stage left towards the Jason poster, from which, with a burst of energy, the 6ft 8-tall Jason came bursting through the poster to the sound of Jill screaming. Swinging his large knife at her, she falls back to the center of stage away from both posters before the chilling Freddy rhyme is played out. Looking on in terror, she is quickly grabbed from behind from Freddy and taken off-stage. The lights go up, the crowd cheers as Jack re-appears to announce that the carnival is now open. Though only appearing on opening night, the show was massively popular and remained online for years after the event for all to see.

The first house inside the event was *Dead Silence – The Curse of Mary Shaw* which was located in Soundstage 22 and the house would replicate the movie in exacting detail. The Universal picture was released in March of 2007 and for many was a commercial flop due to limited success. Released domestically but not in many foreign markets, in fact it didn't even get made into a DVD in the UK until 2010 when reasonable Blu-ray sales in the US prompted the change of heart. The film for many was seen as poorly-conceived so nobody expected it to become a haunted house attraction. Created by the same people that brought us the *SAW* franchise, the movie tells the story of a man named Jaime who after receiving a weird package with a doll named Billy inside, witnesses his wife's murder. He believes this crime happens because of Mary Shaw. Destined to find out the truth, Jamie goes to the town of Raven's Fair where the ventriloquist Mary Shaw used to perform and is buried. Shaw had been buried years prior due to cutting the tongue out of a boy who booed her on stage. The psychological chiller starred Ryan Kwanten as Jamie, Amber Valletta as Ella and Donnie Wahlberg as the Detective Jim Lipton. And although the movie was considered a flop by many, the movie would actually be a perfect example from which a truly brilliant haunted house could be devised.

The house began where the main character travels to the town of Raven's Fair at the very cemetery where Shaw was buried. Standing by the gravestone was Walberg's character, complete with trench coat and flashlight, informing guests to not go any further, to turn back now. Eventually guests made their way through into the mortuary and then into the basement scene from the movie before eventually following the path through to the theater where it all started. A neat cat-walk trick was played on guests whereby the illusion of being much higher and then suddenly falling was played on guests. Soon guests were in rooms filled with dolls, some with moving eyes (there was also a cameo of the puppet from the *SAW* franchise (Billy) located here. En route, various Mary Shaws would pop up in bursts of lightning, and as guests passed paintings and photos of people they turned to the guests, looking like tortured souls. The end of the house featured one final scare of a clown puppet suspended at high level that would swoop at guests. It was a clown that people inadvertently thought was Jack, but it wasn't. The house was so detailed that many guests who had gotten hold of a DVD of the movie (or who had seen it at the cinema) remarked how well the house did at recreating all the main scenes from the movie. DVD sales did increase for the movie after its release. Guessing how many could be directly attributed to this event is uncertain but I would estimate quite a few, as I for one would never have seen it without it being featured at the event!

Next on the tour of the park was *Psychoscareapy: Home For The Holidays* located on Soundstage 23. The popular *Psychoscareaphy* crew would be back in an entirely new house that would be themed around a possible breakout of inmates who terrorized a small mid-western town during the Christmas festivities. There was some confusion about the name of the house as some outlets and merchandise carried the former name for the house: *Silent Night Psychotic Nights*. The name had been changed at the request of Universal's legal department so as to not possibly impact on third party movie franchises of a similar name from the 1970s (*Silent Night, Bloody Night* etc.). The house would be exceedingly bright and represent various buildings within the small town with inmates providing various levels of comedy and scares in equal measures, as the house would also be one of two comedy houses for the year. Along the snowy journey through the house, guests would see people of the town stuffed into turkeys, people wrapped into Christmas trees with lights tied around them to other townsfolk having cookies cutters pressed into their flesh. These scenes combined with the scents that were pumped in again, including fern tree scent and cookies to 'burnt human flesh' smell from some unfortunate person stuffed inside the oven. This was all finished off by one inmate complete with Santa outfit and chainsaw, like some demented and evil mall Santa, who chased guests into the streets beyond.

The neighboring house (sharing the same Soundstage) would be that of the first of our icons and would feature Freddy in *A Nightmare on Elm Street: Dreamwalkers*. Like all the other houses, the house would feature a specially developed narrative but would also add scenes from the movies to act like a mixture of recreation and sequel to the popular franchise. From the website and queue videos, guests would piece together that they were about to become guinea pigs for a new experimental drug that had been developed to aid in providing a good night's sleep. The drug would be applied to guests walking through a tunnel lined with black vinyl via misting vents that would spray a fog within the tunnel (really just dry-ice!). Once applied, sleep would be induced by a chanting woman announcer, telling people to "sleep, sleep, sleep..." As the fog would lift guests would find themselves inside the soundstage facing the infamous house on Elm Street, lovingly recreated to exacting details. "You'll definitely feel like you're at 1428 Elm Street," said J Michael Roddy, manager of show development, of the Freddy house. "Universal presents Freddy's surreal dream world, including a sleep clinic, a steamy boiler room, a gallery of his creative kills, and a hallway where you can't tell what's Freddy and what's merely one of his many, many reflections."

Once inside the house within a house, guests would pass the stairs into the first room. It would be the stairs where the first scare would come, as guests 'conga-line' into the house awaiting the first room. A quiet boo-door would open under the stairs with a Freddy popping up behind selected guests to whisper quietly in their ears: "Freddy's gonna get ya!" he'd say, before quickly disappearing quietly back to the stairs. Once inside the first room, a recreation of the Johnny Depp dream sequence (site note: Depp's first ever movie role), guests would be entering the room on its side where a recreation of the tortured Depp is lying on the side. As guests look on in horror, a boo-door would open up (now to your left) with a loud bang. A snarling Freddy, complete with pronged gloves, scratched through to welcome guests before loudly disappearing into the loft-hatch once more. Confused as to where to go next, guests would eventually see the bed on its side, and like in the infamous scene, guests would have to pull their way through the bed sheets to enter into the next scene. Not knowing exactly where the next step would be was a continuing attribute of this house, where it was presented more like an actual maze than a house.

Once through the bed, guests would see other guests suspended on tables being doped with the drug from before, having nightmares, twisting and turning in their sleep all having the same nightmare as you the dreamwalkers. Soon after, guests would be within the boiler room scenes of the house that would feature various paths, including a mirrored section. Originally, some of the walls were to be electrified in this area to give guests a mild shock for touching the wrong walls. This was however pulled before opening by the safety inspectors, fearing possible complaints. Likewise, another addition was pulled at the last minute, featuring Jason in the boiler scene before being suspended behind bars (like *Freddy vs Jason*, but Freddy winning). Although the prison cell remained, it stayed empty with guests wondering what should have been in there. It was later revealed by the event's creatives that New Line had stipulated that the icons remain separate in all the houses. Regardless of this feature, the house would prove very popular and would consistently have one of the longest queues for the event.

Next up was *Vampyr: Blood Bath* located in the Nazarman's area. Nazarman's had originally been the first place on the property repurposed just for Halloween Horror Nights. However this venue would have a different future after this year, marking this house the last to ever be held here. Soon after the event, the areas used for the house were cleared and created into storage space. Dividing into two, the Nazarman's back area would, by early 2008, become a *Starbucks* and *Ben & Jerry's* stores. Unfortunately, the final house would not be the greatest of send-offs as the house, in many fans' eyes, failed to live up to the house tradition it had drawn from. Taking the idea from the original (gangs of different vampires meeting up to feast) and now moving the setting to a New York nightclub in the present day, guests would be taken into the nightclub. There, unsuspecting dancers would be spirited away by flying vampires for their blood to be drained. The house was notable for presenting a number of 'sexy-vampires' of both genders on podiums dancing with little on that mixed into the horror of vampires feasting on humans and animals in the processing area. Unfortunately, the house did utilize outdoor portions of the Nazarman's area that with sunlight or rain became a dearth of scares. One neat attribute that many fans witnessed in this house was the use of scareactors pretending to be members of the public, who would either react more to the scares around them or would become victims inside the house. It wasn't unique to this house, and was also witnessed at the *Texas Chainsaw* house, the *Friday 13th* house and throughout the scarezones. It is unknown whether Universal ever continued this method of ramping up the scares.

The next house would be *The Texas Chainsaw Massacre: Flesh Wounds* located inside the *Earthquake* queue building. This building would have a name change after the event, to fall in line with the attraction altering to become *Disaster*. There had been some very minor controversy over the name of the house as various fans had thought it was called Fresh wounds, instead of Flesh wounds. It is likely that as *Psychoscarephy's* name had changed it could be that this house had a slight name change at the last minute (for reasons unknown).

The house was themed to the remake of the original movie which had been out in cinemas in the previous year, though much of the house was similar to that of the original movies. Starting at the family manor (complete with sliding door), guests would enter into the strange, depraved world of the Hoyt family. Passing through the basement of the house complete with a dining table seating all assembled family members, guests would soon pass the school bus. This contained the shouty Sheriff Hoyt from the remake, and you'd then be chased for your life through runs of bedsheets tied to washing lines as Leatherface himself chased guests through the area and onto the street. It was exactly like being in the movie of 2006.

The next house would also transfer guests right into a movie, with guests entering into scenes from *Friday 13th Part 2* in *Friday The 13th: Camp Blood* located in the *Jaws* queue. Scoring highly with fans and public alike, the house would be perfectly-suited to the timber framed fishing huts of Amity, making this house very authentic to its original source material. Jason was everywhere in this house, with only the largest of scareactors being deployed, with their towering presences intimating guests further than just the makeup. Windows in the house (yes windows!) were made to allow views of the Jaws Lake which acted as the infamous lake from the movie, with various Jason's popping up to scare guests. Decapitated camp councilors would be mixed with councilors thrown in body bags and tied from the ceilings. There were two very detailed show-scenes: one where a victim was decapitated 'live' as guests passed by, to another where the shrine to Jason's dearly departed mother had been recreated. The house ended with huge splatterings of blood where guests were sprayed with water to simulate the effect.

'Jack's Funhouse in Clown-O-Vision' would be next in one of the sprung tents and would be the final comedic house of the event. Using the popular 3D technology that had been used to great effect in the past, the house mixed scares and comedy in equal measures. Universal billed the house as "This Jack'd up funhouse plunges you laughing and screaming into an oversaturated world of color that leaps at you with more crazed clowns than you can shake a kid at. Before its over-you will know Jack!" Playing on all the five senses, the house mixed visual gags with smells and dynamic colorations to present a fun house gone wrong.

The final house would be *The Thing: Assimilation* located next door in the other sprung tent building. The house would be a direct sequel to the popular 1980s movie and directly tie into the 25th anniversary of the original release. The original Universal picture from 1982 had actually been a revamp of the book and 1950s movie of a similar movie, which took the main premise but transferred the action to the North Pole. Kurt Russell, who would be recreated in the Orlando house, starred in the original as the main hero and one of the sole survivors of the events in that movie. All the mutating creatures and special effects in the movie had been created by Rob Bottin and Stan Winston. Using these as a template, the Universal creatives set about creating monsters that would be in keeping with the creatures of the original but in a modern setting. The detailed makeup and animatronic characters would be throughout the house and if Universal had slipped in the design, it could be argued that they spent more time on creating the monsters than actually worrying about the scares in the house Whatever your opinion, the house would go down as one of the most unique in recent years.

Other than the *Opening Scareamonies*, the other shows that year would feature *Bill And Ted's Excellent Halloween Adventure* back in their new *Fear Factor Stage* home. Along with the time-travelling duo there would also be a *Freak Show* at the *Animal Actors' Stage* that Universal billed as, "This year, Brian Brushwood will appear with his world-renowned magic show. Stuffed full of the most intense, riveting, and disturbing feats you've ever seen performed live." A show featuring Jack and introducing his girlfriend, Chance, was held outside Mel's on a large temporary stage that featured various park 'guests' (6 in total) succumbing to various means of torture and magic tricks. This was all completed by the first appearance of the *Rocky Horror Picture Show: A Tribute* located on the *Beetlejuice Stage* (which was very befitting as the stage required very little re-dressing). The show would go on to return in selected years thereafter.

The scarezones were not officially separated, as select scareactors were allowed to roam between zones. The roaming scareactors included weird biker clowns on motorbikes with carnival horse heads attached, the *Chainsaw Drill Team* and various clowns in bumper cars. The fixed scarezones were located in five areas, they were: *Killer Carnies* located in New York with circus acts performing, *Motormaniacs* located on Hollywood Boulevard and *Plaza Of The Stars*, *Treaks & Foons* were back and located within Shrek Alley, *Troupe Macabre* located within the main path of Central Park (this featured turn-of-the-century French circus performers in black and white garb, chasing guests up and down Central Park), followed lastly by a large Ferris wheel erected by the lake outside the *Men in Black ride* (the wheel had appeared on the website and it could not be ridden). The various tours would again be offered this year, with the behind-the-scenes tour again taking place during the day where guests could explore the soundstage houses and the *Vampyre house*.

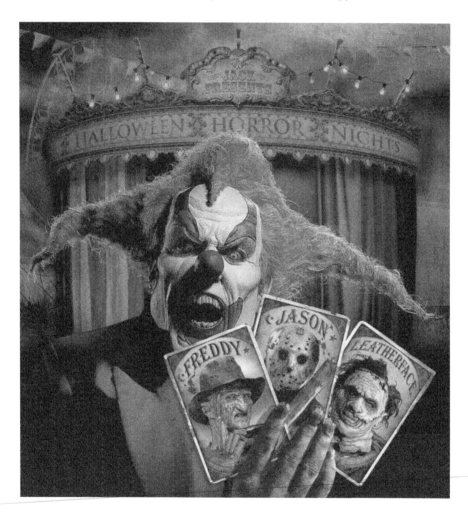

A truly great year for the event!

The Lost Icon

In the Summer of 2007 for the 2008 event Mike Aiello wrote a concept for a new icon. That icon was 'Nathaniel Crowe' with the premise of connecting 2007's *Carnival of Carnage* to a proposed 2008 event. The concept would be to link a number of previous icons to the specific site where the Carnival had been sited for this year. It would also feature the townsfolk who had barricaded in the caretaker of the town's funeral home (as in the Caretaker) and then burnt it down, for acts of heinous cruelty to the local community. The land would be nothing more than a windswept desolate place where Crow would attempt to grow and sell the pumpkins, though these would quickly rot when picked. Crowe eventually meets Jack who explains the land is cursed and nothing will ever prosper here. He subsequently pays Crowe to put his carnival on his land for the 2007 event. Eventually, Crowe is seduced by the horrors of the carnival; the sights, the sounds and the smells invigorate his soul and repurpose his existence. One by one many of the patrons visiting the carnival start to disappear but Crow does not, instead he witnesses more acts of horror and madness. He even asked Jack why he does not die while others do. Jack responded "you'll see."

Eventually, the Carnival leaves and an isolated Crowe is left to tend to his dry and barren landscape. Over time he becomes filled with hate and in a chance meeting with a former poster advertising the former carnival he begins to bleed from sheer anger with his blood spelling out a mysterious rhyme onto the now bare poster:

"Forgotten are the ways of old,
traditions blood black and cold.
Up through dirt roots grow and burst,
evils' return, you'll see what came first.
When ravens and crows made the night black,
Pumpkins were carved to keep the evil back.

When the howl of the wind sent shivers down spines,
Graves of our dead covered in vines.
When black cats crossed paths and wolves howl,
True witches did more than laugh and scowl.
Your time has come Nathaniel Crow,
outside the box you'll think, you'll grow.
Terrors traditions in ways you will demand,
Halloween's true self is at hand."

The blood quickly returned to Crowe's body as he imagined the possibilities of the rhyme he had seen before him. As the chant continued in his mind the original icons showed up and then he awoke, realizing it had fallen asleep in a field of pumpkins. Crow got up and soon realized that the pumpkins had all been carved into weird freakish faces with candles inside. Above the now lit pumpkins were dead trees that were filled with perched crows with glowing red eyes staring at him. As he tried to stand a number of cursed roots tied around him and pulled him back down to the ground; he was the land's prisoner. The moon rose above the clouds and the formerly perched crows all flew down to him and attacked the helpless man. Digging and clawing they tore out his eyes and his flesh. As the crows removed his flesh they replaced it with rotting pumpkin pieces. The roots that had secured him to the ground were now wrapping around his legs and arms to hold in the cursed pumpkin pieces. The roots dragged his jaw off and a selection of crows placed a lit candle within his mouth cavity. Eventually the crows were finished and flew back to their trees. The whole origin story would have played out in a long version on the official HHN website and in an abridged version for the televised commercials.

The proposed icon would have been the humanized embodiment of Halloween. All the most iconic fables and tales from the past millennia would now be wrapped within his dark soul hidden inside this grotesque body. The icon's purpose would be to present Halloween from centuries back and bring it up to date to shock and terrify all. His working title was that of 'The Crowe'. The reasons behind the fact that the proposed icon was never used have never been known. It may have been the name or it might simply have been the fact the *Bloody Mary* icon sat better with management. Whatever the decision, the central premise of presenting a year where all the houses and scarezones tied together in some way was still used. Likewise, using the website to tell an engaging origin story was used in both 2008 for *Bloody Mary* and then in 2009 for the *Usher*.

An artist's sketch of Nathaniel Crowe

Halloween Horror Nights: Reflections of Fear

I Dare You to Say it One More Time...

Halloween Horror Nights 2008 would again be a bumper year for the event, and much like last year this year would go down as being one of the absolute fan favorites. Much of the reason behind this informal accolade is due in part to the incredibly detailed backstory that was created for the event, which was probably the most detailed of all backstories ever given. In addition, there was a high level of fan and public interactivity that was created especially for attendees of the event, something that had not occurred on this scale before. And although this year would be a solid favorite, it would not be a smooth ride, with many challenges presenting themselves along the way in order for Universal to hold the world's largest Halloween event.

As we know, in the recent years at the resort, Halloween Horror Nights had been wildly popular, so popular in fact that it had helped tremendously to hike up the overall visitor numbers in the final quarter of each respective year. Building on this solid foundation and continuing with further investments in the parks and better, more targeted marketing, Universal Resort posted some of its then best financial results. In February of that year the resort posted a $92 million profit for the preceding year, which had doubled from the previous year. This included an overall visitor figure that was up 3% from the previous year. This sort of increase had not been seen since 2004, and a lot of which was directly attributed to the success of the event in the final quarter of 2007. Building on this legacy, the park's creatives decided to set about creating another immersive world that would start long before the event, via the website.

Another in house-designed icon would lead this year's event, a decision that was taken early on. The story would focus on the mysterious Dr. Mary Agana and her transformation into the urban legend of Bloody Mary. There wasn't any official backstory for the urban legend, rather, a series of comparative tales had been told and written about for many years. Some included the Tudor Queen Mary I and others were about a tortured soul from Normandy. Whatever the tale you had heard, most people had at least heard of her. Universal decided to ignore the tales of the past and create their own unique tale of how the character was created. "We take that which everybody knows and we build the whole part that everyone doesn't know," said Jim Timon, Universal Orlando's senior vice president for entertainment. "And then turn it around a bit: What happens when you get pulled into the mirror?"

Once pulled through the broken mirror, of course, guests would expect to be taken into a world filled with urban legends, fantasy, fairy tales and myths.

The backstory for the icon would be one of the most detailed ever created by the event's creatives. "We wanted a unique tonality to her. What does the inside of a mirror sound like?" said J Michael Roddy, Universal manager of show development. "It's a combination of underwater sounds, some echo chambers, and we hired three very talented actresses to combine three different elements of her voice so that there's a similarity to it, but also something supernatural about it." Mary would not just use sound to ramp-up the creepiness, she would be the first truly sensual icon that can get under your skin and affect all your senses. Roddy continued, "You can't connect with her because she doesn't have eyes. That is the connection people look for immediately," he said. "So now forcing people to look up at something and it's looking back at us and there's no way to relate to it. I think that's really effective."

Along with her creepy sound, glassy stare and extreme anarchic power there would be something truly disturbing about her, that would affect and attract people like no icon had before. Jim Timon continued, "It's a trace memory. It's reminding you of something you'd rather not remember," he said. "I'm thinking that's where we're getting them is on a sub-psychological level!"

She was officially introduced as Dr. Mary Agana on the event's website on July 1st, 2008. Viewers of the site would enter into her office and read her journal. The setting was 1958 at the time, but the overall story would take guests through time and eventually through dimension. The office was very tidy and had a desk abutted to a large wall-mounted mirror. Items would eventually appear and become clickable, revealing nuggets of information about the new icon; eventually a journal appeared which informed us who she was and that she was a psychiatrist. On a day-by-day basis to tie into events that were presented as happening in real time (events of July 18th 1958 were released on July 18th 2008 for example) and with each journal entry about her patients or experiments, it became clear she was slipping slowly into some kind of insanity herself, the possible catalyst being a rejection letter from the National Association of Mental Health (NAMH).

Slowly as the weeks went on and the updates came, it appeared that Agana was not just trying to cure her patients' fears or anxieties, she was trying to see where they manifested from, a process that would often require her to torture her patients to better treat them, or so her deluded mind thought. This level of immersive therapy continued until one patient was killed during the process. The very next entry in her journal was then filled with her excitement for what she had done, rather than her remorse; this was paired with the office becoming increasingly disorderly. As the next case arrived her style of writing changed, with far more doodles and pictures being drawn in her journal. Several patients were then killed before she started to question her own sanity. Finally, she began treating one of the doctors who rejected her, whom she later killed, and then a local detective named Boris Shuster. During the buildup to the event, Shuster would actually have a real window re-dressed as his office, which looked exactly how it had been on the website. A testament to the popularity of this character (who we as fans never actually saw!), the window is still there to this day and can be found in the New York section of the studios park.

Her last journal entry on August 27th showed a dilapidated office and broken mirror where she had become Bloody Mary. Later a paranormal investigation society created by *Shuster* (called the *Legendary Truth*), investigated the office in 2008 on the anniversary of the events revealing definitively that she was the inspiration for the urban legend we all know. It was later revealed that Agana herself was brutally murdered, supposedly by Shuster on discovery of the shocking acts she had committed, though during the event it was revealed she had been murdered by another man, an ex-convict who was either an assistant or a patient of hers.

The story was powerful, it was detailed and it became a must-watch for many fans of the event. The story was so strong that literally ever day fans of the event found themselves rushing back from work/school to refresh the site to see if there had been any updates; the suspense was as effective as a Hitchcock movie. Bit by bit the story revealed itself, until the full reveal of all information (when Agana became Bloody Mary) around early September actually crashed the event's website, such were the high numbers of fans, locals and tourists trying to access the site at the same time to see what the conclusion to this summer long epic was. It was a truly great time to be a Halloween Horror Nights fan.

However, whilst the story played out on the website, things behind the scenes and in the fan community were not as smooth-running. The first issue of the event came in August of that year when the plans were leaked. Though not displayed publicly, and only spoken about in specific circles, the house names were also leaked at the same time. One fan realized that Universal, unlike Disney, must seek permission for any building permits from the City Orlando. He knew that as long as you can travel to the City and complete the associated forms, any member of the public could at that time access the drawings that had been submitted. This led to five of the eight houses having their actual titles discovered, with three left for speculation. This process would later lead to a petition from Universal to the City to change the process to prevent these leaks. This was emphasized when Universal began the permit process for the new Harry Potter land that was going to be built at Islands of Adventure. To prevent leaks of this super-secret addition to the resort, the City agreed to not disclose the drawings for the purposes of themed entertainment as that disclosure may be used against the resort's intentions. This minor law change that came into effect was dubbed *The Potter Law* by the fan communities.

Not only had the drawings and house names leaked, but so did the title of the event, when Universal inadvertently included the name of the event on the event's website before the big reveal. Then the official commercial was leaked, though not in its entirety. The company that had been contracted in to make the commercial had placed a number of screen captures from the commercial and the making-of on their website. And lastly, some of the billboards were erected early by accident. The largest number of billboards were placed around the state that year (over 80 in number), and the huge boards contained the logo of the event with a glassy eyed Bloody Mary starring down at the passing traffic. Though little was made of this minor mistake, the billboards would go on to draw criticism from the local communities of Central Florida for their 'graphic' appearance. One local mother said at the time, "Each year, I grow more frustrated and disappointed by the choices Universal makes in advertising this event, which glamorizes violence and human cruelty. This year, I find the billboards truly unacceptable to our community." Though as you will have realized from this book, the billboards seem to draw complaints every year.

Building on this expanded and immersive event theme, it would be 23 nights in duration, featuring: 8 brand new houses, and a larger-sized and higher quantity of scarezones with fewer shows. There was also the hiring of the largest number of scareactors ever, with records detailing that the record of 1,000 in the past had been exceeded this year. The first show would not be an *Opening Scaremonies* this year but rather a media preview show that happened before the event in September located at the *Horror Makeup Stage*. A *Legendary Truth* operative introduced the show that included a terrifying sequence where Bloody Mary burst bloody and torn through a mirror live on stage, much to the gathered crowd's surprise and delight. The show would later be posted online for everyone to enjoy in lieu of any formal *Opening Scaremonies*.

The first house of the event would be *Body Collectors: Collections of the Past* and was located within Soundstage 20. The theme was that some of the most awful crimes of our history were not in fact created by the persons the history books define but rather by the demented Body Collectors. The Victorian theme was heavily influenced by Jack the Ripper and Sweeney Todd. Heavily detailed London Victorian streets were met with coaches, London fog and East-end prostitutes.

"Hello guvnor, how's about a good time?" one would say near the entrance. Walking down the first alley, guests would be confronted by one of the grinning collectors floating in mid-air, before a similar knife-swinging collector would come at guests from the side. Streets had their original street names from the infamous case (such as Mitre Square), along with the scents and smells of Victorian England. One façade even had "Aiello & Roddy" barbershop written above, as a sort of Easter egg to fans (both men are well-known creatives for the event). Eventually, guests would be led into the demon barber's shop before witnessing a man having his leg chopped off with spraying blood effect (just water) before entering an area that looked like a factory. One other memorable scene included a scantily clad prostitute on the street corner waving and chatting to guests before a collector jumped out from the shadows behind her, then grabbed her, pulling her backwards before slicing her throat there and then. The gore and the effects were staggering in this house and were worth many repeat visits in order to see how they actually created those effects with such brilliance.

Next door would be *Creatures!* in Soundstage 22.
Universal billed the house as, "Creatures straight from the cover of Atomi Comics' *Strange Tales* burst forth to rampage and massacre the backwoods locals. Join Johnny, Cleet, Jim Deedle and the rest of the gang at the Butchered Buck as they fight off this terrifying invasion of

creatures from who knows where."

This house told the story of a sleepy backwater which was being attacked by an alien that had landed in the area. Various Southern locals doing battle with giant prop aliens were seen, including recycled pieces of The Thing house that were taken from the previous year.

Over in the Sprung Tents, the first house was a very experimental means of presenting a house, called *Dead Exposure*. The story was that of a plucky photographer who, through the use of photography, captures the moments his town becomes overrun with flesh-eating zombies. The special effect, which had not been used before or since, included a completely dark house that was only illuminated via a number of camera flashes. Entering via a photograph, guests would see the use of blacklight strobes timed to camera click in every room that created the flashes of light. This was paired with illuminous paint on costumes and sets that created the sensation of capturing the moment with very timed and rehearsed zombie scareactors. The tie in to the narrative was that the main protagonist was one of Agana's patients whom she wrote about in her journal.

The original idea for the icon this year would have been 'The Evil Queen', the concept would have heavily geared the event towards mocking their mousy neighbor. There was even discussions of a house called 'Unmagic Kingdoms' where various familiar attractions had gone awry.

FUN EAR FACT

Next to this house in the other Sprung building, *The Hallow* delighted crowds. A combination of different phobias and legends were presented here. Universal billed the house as, "Where do the traditions we observe each Halloween come from? It is said that every Halloween within the blackest parts of the forest, Samhain, The Lord of the Underworld, lives again and the souls of the damned beckon you. For if you journey deep enough, you will see that Samhain's traditions are trapped within The Hallow."

An impressive forest environment was created for the house, complete with a large façade, and inside witches, ghouls, skeletons and demons acted out demonic practices that terrified audiences.

Next up would be the sole movie-based house this year. *Doomsday* was held within the newly-created *Disaster!* queue building which had opened with the newly-refurbished ride in January of that year. The queue building had not changed much, with only a few alterations to maximize use of the space for the event. There were easily moveable props for the ride, that could be wheeled out to make way for Halloween Horror Nights. The movie of the same name had been released in May of that year to mixed success. Capitalizing on the same thought process of last year with *Dead Silence* (a movie that didn't perform well at the box-office but would create a good haunted house attraction that may well increase DVD sales) the park's creatives went about creating an exact detailed environment that was reminiscent of the movie. The story was that of a post-apocalyptic Scotland, where they have bred a virus that ravages the population, leaving those left behind after the plague to survive by any means necessary. Punks and chainsaw guys filled this house to mixed responses.

Interstellar Terror would be presented in Soundstage 20 this year. The story was that of a scientific community based on board the first space ship to leave our solar system. Reappearing sometime later orbiting our moon, the guests of the event were sent in to investigate the strange reappearance of the ship and what might lurk inside waiting for us. Despite several houses being presented over the years at the event that feature aliens or spaceships, this was the first house that took guests into space. Slowly the story is revealed that after leaving the solar system, the crew discovers a mysterious relic that makes them all go insane and become murderous. The house used the space setting to great effect, creating houses that contained low-gravity and airlocks showing crew members being pulled out into space.

The next house would be the icon's house located within the *Jaws* queue building and was called *Reflections of Fear*. The house was an exact replica of the website and used details from it to create the sensation that guests had now entered the world of Bloody Mary. The only downside of this house was that if you hadn't been on the website, little in the house may have made sense to you, though most people had. Mirror effects were used throughout the house to create not only the story but also the scares. Guests were transported through time to various versions of the office as seen in the journal, as she treats and then tortures her unsuspecting patients. A neat cameo in the house was her desk where a bottle of 'Sleepwell', the drug from the previous year's Freddy house had been placed by the park's creatives for sharped eyed fans of the event.

The final house (and one of the most popular from that year) was being held in a new building. It was used for the third sequel in this house's franchise, that of *Scary Tales: Once Upon a Nightmare*, located in the Parade Warehouse (B-79). The building, located right at the back of the staff only areas of the studio, was built to house parade floats when not in use. The floats had been wrapped in cellophane and moved to a new location for the duration of the event. The house was required, as the Nazarman's area was now out of use (as mentioned in the previous chapter). The house had a huge façade that took guests on a twisted journey featuring strange versions of Cinderella, Alice in Wonderland and The Wizard of Oz.

The seven scarezones this year would be many and plentiful with an exceptionally high level of detailing. The first would be *American Gothic* located on Production Central. It was billed as, "Some legends allow a simple man or woman to remain immortal. Some deeds, so dark, take a simple person and transform them into lore. America's past has been filled with these dark deeds, sorted characters and unbelievable acts of horror. Reflect upon your own mortality as you venture through history with the infamous Lizzie Borden as your guide."
It would be a reimagining of a scarezone that had featured before in the early days of the event.

Tying into the nearby *Scary Tales* house, *Asylum in Wonderland* would delight guests in the Hollywood Boulevard area of the park. The zone featured highly-decorated and designed characters that had been lifted from the original text but with a contemporary spin. Borrowing the same theme was *Fractured Tales* located nearby in Kidzone, with fairy tale recreations around every corner from some of your best loved children's tales that had been twisted to horrific proportions. "The stories that we created are familiar, so you play that same kind of game where people kind of know a little bit about what they think it is," says T.J. Mannarino, director of art and design for entertainment at Universal. "But then when they come and see it, it's a whole different slant to it."

The Path of the Wicked was located on Plaza of the Stars near the entrance to the park and toyed with the simple idea of 'What if the Wicked Witch had actually won?' The Land of Oz had been presented like never before with flying monkey men, tortured characters and witches everywhere, with guests singing out "Toto, I've a feeling we're not in Kansas anymore!" After the carnage of this area, guests would often find themselves in *Streets of Blood: Body Collectors* in the New York Streets area. Tying into the house that year, that also featured the grinning ghouls, guests would witness New York re-dressed to simulate the terrors of 1888 London when the "Ripper" struck (or was it the collectors?). This neat house and scarezone played on people fears for the 120th anniversary of the terrible real-life events of Victorian England.

The final scarezone would be *The Skoolhouse* located outside Mel's Drive-In, and would see the largest-ever set built for a scarezone. Universal billed the area as, "Mr. Renshaw's class has always been good. Mr. Renshaw's class has never broken the rules. Mr. Renshaw's class has always been perfect little angels. All of that changes when the kids from the Skoolhouse "cut" class. The children of the quaint town of Carey, Ohio are out to teach everyone that their version of Trick or Treat may be the difference between your life and death."

Along with the school house that had been built as a set within the zone, the area was complimented with a high number of scareactors all dressed as murderous school children dressed in Halloween costumes with distinctive masks. The characters interacted with guests all evening every night to create a truly great scarezone.

There would also be an unofficial eighth scarezone in the park this year that, although not on park maps, would return nearly every year since. Located in the main path outside the *Gardens of Allah* that run through Central Park, the event's creatives installed exactly 500 jack-o-lanterns throughout the trees that had been individually lit by LEDs. They were timed to flicker and dance to the music that was pumped into the area. At points in the specially chosen soundtrack, a 'wind' would blow through with them all flickering out.

Brian Brushwood was back again this year, again located at the *Animal Actors' Stage* to bring his unique show of magic and wonder. The 20-minute show would be altered slightly from the previous year and would contain more tricks that Brushwood would perform himself. The main five routines would be intercut with punk music numbers, where the popular cell phone trick from the previous year was carried out much to the guests' delight.

Along with Brushwood, the time-travelling duo Bill and Ted were back again with their ever-popular show. This year it featured many political gags, as the presidential election was in full swing. References to *Indiana Jones* were made as his new movie had just been released that summer, along with *The Dark Knight*, *Hellboy*, *Predator* and a lookalike of Miley Cyrus, this was all topped-off with a cast dance-off to the *Aerosmith vs Run DMC's Walk This Way*. The show was noteworthy this year due to the number of rewrites that occurred. From casting to the final night some 30 rewrites had occurred to ensure the content was fresh and as funny as possible. Rewriting the script over the event is nothing new for raucous pop-culture comedy, though this year the shear volume of revisions was an event first.

The final show that year had returned like Brushwood from the previous year, that of *The Rocky Horror Picture Show* tribute. The popular show featured such classics numbers as *Dammit Janet, Sweet Transvestite, Touch-a Touch-a Touch Me* and finished off by a rowdy and rambunctious rendition of everyone's favorite the *Time Warp*. Other attractions open this year include: *Men in Black: Alien Attack*, the newly opened *The Simpsons Ride, Revenge of the Mummy, Jaws* and *Disaster*! A Major Motion Picture Ride... Starring You!

The Museum That Never Was...

Fans of the event haven't just been calling for a year-round HHN house in recent times; they've actually been calling for one for years! The first time that Universal gave true credence to the concept of a year-round house was back in the late 1990s. The problem with considering such a project was the fact that the resort was going through a massive transformation, from singular theme park to resort destination and for want of a better reason, the idea fell off the table.

After Islands of Adventure opened in 1999 and the newly-created resort was in full swing, the idea to take Halloween Horror Nights into a different direction was finally agreed but it wouldn't be until 2000. Read more about that HERE. The event would be completely revised with the introduction of new characters, new worlds and with a better emphasis on the overall event narrative. The personification of this step change came in the form of Jack the Clown.

Jack would usher in a new era for the event, taking it in a fresh but distinctly familiar direction. It was now that the idea to create a new chapter for the event would also require some kind of physical keynote to what had been in the past. It was true that many of the older props and sets had been stored in one of Universal's massive off-site hangers, so they had plenty of physical heritage that they could call upon.

Not wanting to forget the event's rich history, the decision was taken to present a small museum that would tick all the boxes. This was combined with a desire from the Marketing Department to install an attraction that could act as a year-round commercial for the autumnal event (they needed to fill them newly built hotel rooms somehow!). Initially a year-round haunt was considered, but as the newly founded resort was trying to aim for a more family-orientated audience the thought of irate parents clogging Guest Services to complain about what little Jimmy saw was just a step too far.

The first idea that nearly came to fruition was *Dr. Oddfellow's Carnival Exhibition*. Dr. Oddfellow was Jack's former employer and ringmaster of the Carnival Of Thrills, and his backstory was eventually unveiled on the official HHN website. The idea had been drafted to coincide with the introduction of Jack and would show how a combination of events had come together to create the evil clown we all know and love. The Brown Derby, which had only been seasonally used up until this point, was the proposed location. Whether it was budgetary issues or timings we don't know, but for whatever reason the idea was shelved, though as their mousey neighbor would confirm, good ideas never quite die!

Skip forward a few years and the new chapter of HHN could not be more popular. It was at this point that the Art and Design Department decided that after each of the new icons had received each of their respective introductory years (Jack in 2000, Eddie Jack again in 2001, Caretaker in 2002, the Director in 2003 and the Storyteller in 2005), that a retrospective celebratory homecoming year would be undertaken in 2006. This would become *Sweet Sixteen*. The year would combine old favorite houses (including a rehash of the very original house from 1991 *The Dungeon of Terror*, though it was not anywhere like the original) with new houses all under the banner of it being the event's first anniversary year. This gave the designers the chance to relook at their 1999 plans and see whether a museum could be viable again...

The plan this time would be to convert the *Lucy: A Tribute* building into a year-round museum of the weird and wonderful from the past years of HHN, with construction commencing shortly after the event had wrapped. Plans and mockups were soon drafted and presented to management. The concept was simple: careful removal of the Lucy props and sets with a light, almost reversible layover of HHN props and sets from years gone by. The concept included an audio tour where interactive voices guiding guests around the exhibits would be offered, based on the era. This would conclude with a year-round chance to get your photo with whichever icon was on duty that day and a small gift shop selling HHN merchandise.

The Lucy Tribute, which was not an opening day attraction (though it did open just 2 years after the park opened), was seen as "tired" and in need of something more "relevant" to the park goers of the day. The proximity to the park gates made it an unhelpful location for park executives wishing to not terrify guests as they entered, however the size and layout would be perfect for the proposed museum.

A number of minor factors fell together to ensure the 2006 idea would not take off. As mentioned above, the park's executives were not comfortable with the location and proximity to the park gates; nobody wanted a family's first impression of the new family orientated resort to be that of a kid-murdering clown. The next factor was news from the west coast that the Lucy Tribute there was already scheduled for removal, and that the fan community of Lucille Ball spoke out strongly against this. Whether it was because of the same rumblings from the west coast or not, the Marketing Department were keen to remind everyone that the attraction, though modest in execution, did attract a number of diehard *Lucy* fans to the resort every year. They knew that the 'haunt-freaks' would come every year, come what may. The project was officially shelved, though one remnant of the proposed museum did survive and that was a waxwork of Jack, as seen below. Lucy would now be safe until 2015 when she was packed away to make way for *Hello Kitty* in 2016.

The following year the idea was redesigned (but to a much lesser degree) when the Brown Derby was converted into a small museum for guests taking the *Behind-the Screams tours*. The small space housed all the main costumes and props from the 2007 commercial, featuring Freddy, Jason and Leatherface. It also included the gypsy's tent and the waxwork as mentioned above. Below is a photo of the small tribute built inside this small closed merchandise location.

It was then decided around this time to start ramping us the collection of props and sets inside the lobby of Universal's *Horror Make-Up Show*. It is here where you will find the Jack waxwork. In 2015s event the decision to convert the now-redundant *Twister* merchandise store into a HHN-themed store for the event was wildly popular. It is said that the layout and theming of this former store are the closest representation of how the museum, if built, would have looked inside the Lucy building. The public have also been able to see many of the past props and sets in a number of exhibits, including small fan gatherings at the park during the event or at Orange County Regional History Center.

Whether Universal Orlando will ever get its museum or year-round haunt is uncertain. What with Hollywood having their year-round haunt for many years and soon to open *The Walking Dead* attraction, it is unclear whether this will make its way to Orlando. Whatever the outcome, as the event continues to grow and grow and Universal is buying up plenty of potential future building plots, so the chance to have such an attraction has never looked so promising…

Halloween Horror Nights: Ripped From The Silver Screen

"It's Showtime!"

This year's event theme would be a year unlike any previous year. The event would not just dedicate a house or two to a particular movie but the film-based Studios park would play host to an event that would see every house and scarezone based on either actual movies or inspired by different movies. It would an ambitious project but it was handled by one man synonymous to fans for his dedication and knowledge of movies. That lead creative was J Michael Roddy, and unbeknown to fans, this would be his last year of working on the event. The man who had started way back in 1991 as a Norman Bates scareactor, was now Show Director and creator of Jack the Clown. He would ensure the event would see him leave in style by putting on the largest event to date. "We're turning the front gate into the facade of the Universal Palace Theater. There will be a box office, there will be a movie screen showing trailers," said Roddy, then show director for Universal Orlando Entertainment. "And then once you walk in, all these environments, all these movies are ripped from the silver screen and come to life." Due to the size of the event and the level of complexity, planning for the event this year started earlier than it had ever done up to this point. Roddy said at the time, "We've been working on 2010[event] since July [2009], so it's starting to actually be more than a year-round process. There's not a time where we're not in some capacity working on Halloween Horror Nights."

The event began its mammoth marketing for the event in April of that year with the highly-detailed website that slowly unraveled until June, when more and more information for the event had been issued via the website. The website over many months told eight different tales, all of which alluded to clues about the houses and scarezones that would feature that year. The clues didn't stop there either. As previously, fans had gotten hold of the blueprints for the various permits issued by the

City of Orlando right before the 'Potter Law' came into force. Universal's Art and Design team, knowing of the leak from the previous year, had already issued the paperwork to the City referring to each house in code names rather than their actual names (as had been the practice before). Getting hold of these names and clues from the website brought fans into an absolute frenzy trying to decipher them and work out which horrors were coming for us.

The event opened on September 25th with queues clogging up the I4 with eager guests excited about entering the park. The first house up was *Silver Screams*. This would be the icon's house this year which was located at the back of the park in the Parade Building. Once inside, guests would enter via the front of the *Universal Palace Theater*, which had morphed into a dilapidated state. Greeting guests at the front, complete with flash light was the Usher. He would stare at guests in the line and whisper, "tickets please". Once inside, the house would have a corridor then room, corridor then room setup, then repeat. The corridor would not only act as the respite between the horror, but it would include posters showing which film you were about to enter, this way it ramped up the anticipation, as prior to the event no guests knew which movies would be presented.

The first movie, and quite aptly would be the first true Universal horror picture, *The Phantom of the Opera*. Guests would enter a stone built, vaulted ceiling basement where the illusive phantom is playing his impressive organ. As he plays the organ, various pipes and bursts of air can be seen while the gothic music is blazed out in full volume. As guests delight in seeing him play with such a passion, another phantom (without mask) appears at the end of the room to give the maximum scare. The next corridor leads to the set of *My Bloody Valentine 3D* which had been released that year in theaters. Entering into the famous hospital scene of the movie guests are first confronted with a blood-stained wall that reads, "Happy Valentine's Day". As guests ponder this message the gas mask-wearing pickaxe man would come running down the hall; he then pops up again until guests move on to the next scene. Whereas in 2007 the event took guests on a sequel of *The Thing* (1982) movie, this year we would not be back within the first movie with various creatures in varying states of mutation attacking, before heading to the next room where the *Evil Dead* franchise was represented. Guests here witness Ash doing battle with chainsaw against a large ghoul-like creature. In the next room, we witness the original death of our icon before moving to the next scene to see the popular *Shaun of the Dead* movie. Guests are now back inside The Winchester pub right at the climax of the movie when the zombie hoards are attacking the boarded-out windows. Both our hero Shaun and a zombified Ed are seen inside as various popular *Queen* hits are played on the jukebox. The final scene of the house is from the 2008 movie *The Strangers* before guests head out as the Usher provides one last final scare.

The next house on our tour would be highly anticipated. *Saw* was brought to the event inside the *Jaws* queue building, though this wasn't the first *Saw* attraction as there had been one open in the UK a few months before the event. Our event's *Saw* would lead guests on a tour of the greatest hits from the popular horror franchise. *Saw's* producer Oren Koules, who actually at the time lived in Tampa, said during the event, "Having people experience the Saw films live, not just on the screen, but to have people walk through it, taste it, touch it and feel it - is amazing for us." So impressed was he with Universal's dedication to detail, the producer was actually spotted with colleagues, attending on various nights. Roddy went on to say, "I think Saw is the most popular of our brands this year, I think it will be one of the major draws. It's prevalent, it's contemporary, people know what that is." He continued, "You're actually going to walk into Jigsaw's lair. As you walk in, it's an industrial building, almost nondescript. And as you enter, you're immediately in his workshop. You'll see all of the TVs and the cameras, and you'll come face-to-monitor with [puppet] Billy, who'll give you your task, which is to make it through this maze."

"For us, it's a big, big challenge that we replicate this 100 percent," said T.J. Mannarino, director of art and design for Universal Orlando. "Saw will have to match that intensity, that excitement." And meet the intensity it did!

The queue for the house would feature clips from past movies in the franchise and posters for the upcoming *Saw VI* that was released during the event. Guests would enter into a warehouse environment before being confronted by Billy the puppet who asks "Do you want to play a game?" before sneakily throwing a burst of air at people's ankles as they walked passed him. Various scenes from the movies were depicted throughout the house including the infamous head-bear-trap sequence, a man in barbed wire and even a medical scene with Jigsaw. The creators had actually used a high number of props from the original movies, with no less than Billy the puppet, which had been given to Universal from the last movie's production, along with Jigsaw actor Tobin Bell who had recorded new dialogue especially for the event. The house was finished by an effective scare where a circular row of Jigsaws complete with pig masks were all waiting for guests. Five of the six would be dummies and one human; but which one? They would rotate the dummies so that guests entering for repeat visits would not know which one of the six would be jumping out at them. They also deployed scareactors into the queue for this house, where they would queue and chat to people in character in the queue lines, but once inside would be grabbed and tortured by Jigsaw to increase the intensity of the house.

The next house and possibly one of the most immersive ever built was The Wolfman located inside Soundstage 22. The house had been built with cooperation of the Universal production staff who were working on the movie at the time of the house's design. The aim was for guests to experience the movie and then experience the house. However, due to production setbacks the movie's release date was delayed until after the event, with the new ethos being, 'enjoy the house and then enjoy the movie' (guests had to wait until January 2010 before they could see the movie). Regardless of this issue with timing, the house was exceedingly impressive. The first area guests encounter was a gypsy settlement with foreboding stories about 'the beast' before we are led into the forest. The forest was possibly one of the most detailed scenes ever created, with guests staring in wonder at the immersive level of detail the park's creatives had designed. Real trees, moss, grass, hills, fog, gravel, even a moon(!) etc. were combined with the sound of pounding feet as the mysterious beast was drawing closer and closer, before an inexplicable howl rang out within the area. Guests could be forgiven for thinking they had actually been transferred to the moors of England! "We were basically given access to all their designs, and this is a big-budget version. A lot of amazing production value has gone into it." Roddy said. "Although the house is built inside a soundstage, it has an outdoors feel with a gypsy camp, a forest and the sensation of being chased by a lycanthrope. This is the only place you're going to be able to see the Wolfman (at the time). It doesn't open until February, so that's pretty cool for us," Roddy said.

After exploring the moors, guests enter into the village, the mansion and the crypt from the movie before the beast actively targets us, the guests. Eventually we are led back into the woods (a different scene) with the Wolfman chasing us and jumping between hills and hedges as he chases us down. Finally, we reach a mound where the Wolfman jumps onto a large natural plinth howling at the moon above. Just as we stare in fright, having been caught, a hunter emerges from the side complete with blunderbuss and silver bullets to fire at the beast. This sends the scareactor flying back to the hill below (he must have been wearing a harness for such a stunt). Before guests make their final run for the exit, the Wolfman, now scared and battle damaged, attacked guests for one final scare. Despite the movie being released after the event, it did not dampen enthusiasm for the house, which in this author's opinion was one of the most immersive ever created.

The next house would be the event's comedic house and was presented in Sprung Tent 2 as *Chucky: Friends till the End*. The house was a funhouse created by Chucky with toys in various states of play combined to scare guests witless. Quirky sets of freakish teddy bears or scareactors whose costumes were hundreds of plush dolls knitted together ambled around. They would lure guests into a false sense of calm before a knife-wielding Chucky would pop up from a boo-door complete with large butcher's knife. This was the first official house to feature Chucky in the Orlando event, whereas he had been present in both shows and houses at the Hollywood event for some years.

Next-door in Sprung Tent 1 the park presented *The Spawning*, an original house created by the resort's creatives that had been sponsored by the media company *Fangoria*. The house had been based on the concept of mutant creatures living in the sewers below a town that were emerging to attack the water plant workers who maintained the tunnels. The mutants were named, 'sculders', and were presented as freakish, scaled monsters with huge claws. The name of the beasts, along with the setting, led many to believe that the house had been inspired by various episodes of *The X-Files* though no official tie-in was given.

The next house would be *Dracula: Legacy in Blood* and was located in Soundstage 23. The setting was Eastern Europe around the turn of the last century with a huge façade built within the stage of a mysterious castle perched on the side of a cliff, complete with speared heads and foggy atmosphere being pumped in. The house featured Dracula and his many, many brides through the claustrophobic stony areas of the castles, seemingly popping up at every turn. The house was epic due to the high number of brides in various states of vampirism from beauty to feral to beast-like, who were seen jumping out and feasting on poor unfortunate souls throughout. The house was so popular that it was awarded in-house as 'house of the year' for 2009.

Also sharing the above soundstage was *Frankenstein: Creation of the Damned*. Universal billed the house as, "It has been a fortnight since his creation caused the castle to be engulfed in flames. Doctor Frankenstein now continues his work to perfect the art of resurrection and regeneration surrounded by his creations. The Creature has also returned to make the Doctor pay for the pain and suffering he has had to endure. The Creature will destroy everything in his path to gain redemption, and you are now caught in the middle of the epic battle."
Completing the lineup for the big three from Universal's classic

horror monsters, the house would feature another huge castle façade where Dr. Frankenstein is seen experimenting on various body parts before guests are confronted by the legendary beast. Various laboratory and dungeon scenes were depicted in pure steam-punk fashion and featured the Doctor, the monster, Fritz, the bride and various other characters. The house was impressive for its use of electricity effects, pyro and smells. It left guests reeling from the sensory overload that had been thrown at them to make this house outstandingly popular.

The final house would be one of the two original concept houses for the event that were sponsored by *Fangoria,* that of *Leave it to Cleaver* located in the Disaster queue building. The house told the sad tale of Sam Meetz, a butcher who owns and operates Meetz Meats, in Carey, Ohio (who was actually played on the website and queue videos by park creative Mike Aiello). The house featured guests on a tour of the factory where various Meetz Meats mask-wearing employees were undertaking varying cannibalistic activities for processing flesh for human consumption. The house had been inspired by various B-Movies from the 1950s and 60s.

FUN FEAR FACT

A scarezone based on *Ash and the Evil Dead* franchise was proposed for this year. For various reasons this did not work out, however the idea never died (much like the characters of the movie!) and a house based from the remake of the same movie was seen at HHN 2013.

The scarezones this year included *Lights Camera Hacktion,* located on Hollywood Boulevard. The concept was that the *Chainsaw Drill Team* of the event is being included in a movie about a murderous chainsaw-wielding mad gang. The problem is: production has hired the original murderous chainsaw wielding gang from the event. After action was called, the team sets about setting about all of the production staff whom are in various degrees of injury while the gang chases production staff and guests alike throughout this zone. Next up was *Cirque Du Freak* located in Kidzone Plaza. Inspired by the Universal movie of the same name that was released during the event, the zone featured characters and sets from the movie that spread into Central Park and onto the edge of the new Simpsons area.

The scarezone *Horrorwood Die-In* located outside Mel's Drive-In was presented where a big screen had been erected with parked cars to simulate the appearance of a drive-in movie playing. The screen would play clips of Universal horrors movies from the past and present whilst characters from the movie world of horror would prowl the streets (mostly for photo-opportunities). The monsters included: Norman Bates, The Barlow vampire from the made-for-TV movie *Salem's Lot*, characters from *The Strangers*, *Saw*, *The Exorcist* all ushered (excuse the pun) by the main icon himself, the Usher.

Next up would be *Apocalypse: City of Cannibals* located in the New York area of the park. Here, various scenes of destruction were witnessed with hordes of cannibals running around creating mayhem. Nearby on the Plaza to the Star would be *Containment*, a small scarezone that featured a misty green fog with various scareactors in medical overalls in varying states of mutation; this abutted Shrek Alley by *War of the Living Dead*. This noisy scarezone featured WW2 zombie soldiers of different armies fighting a battle to the death (well they're already dead, no?). Gun battles and fog played host to this popular scarezone.

The above six scarezones were the official scarezones of the event but in the final week of the event the park's creatives decided to use the Sting Alley area of the backlot to showcase an additional scarezone which would act as the preview for the coming year. This additional scarezone was named *Shadows from the Past*, and featured nearly all the past event icons, including: the Caretaker, the Director, Eddie Schmidt, Jack the Clown, the Storyteller and the Usher, plus various other characters including Alice and the Terra Queen. The Frequent Fear Pass was also extended towards the end of the event to encompass additional nights for fans desperate to see this later addition to the event.

The original plan for the 'Dracula: Legacy in Blood' house was to see a final depiction of a fully winged Dracula at the end of the house. Due to budgets and space issues the character was never built.

FUN FEAR FACT

Two shows were offered this year. These were *The Rocky Horror Picture Show: A Tribute* which was presented in the same way as it had been in the previous years, along with another version of the popular *Bill and Ted show*. This year's show featured references to the new *Terminator* movie, *Avatar*, a lookalike for Britney Spears, all topped off with a medley of songs to commemorate the passing of pop's Michael Jackson which had occurred a few months prior to the event. Rides open for this year's event included: *Men in Black: Alien Attack*, *The Simpsons Ride*, *Revenge of the Mummy*, *JAWS*, *Disaster! A Major Motion Picture Ride... Starring You!* and *Hollywood Rip Ride Rockit*.

There was also the opportunity on selected nights to attend special signings with various celebrity guests. Steve and Tango from the popular *Ghost Hunters* TV show were on hand on various nights, including Tippi Hedren (from Hitchcock's *The Birds* and other movies) who had been happy to sign autographs and pose for photos and also, John C. Reilly who had been there promoting his movie *Cirque du Freak: The Vampire's Assistant* with other members of the cast onsite. Along with the unique popcorn prop that had been sent out as media gifts, there was a special rare prop given out to select guests this year. These were specially created beads for guests booking on the Gory Getaway packages this year; these black and red beads would feature medallions of the main house icons from the year and are now extremely collectable.

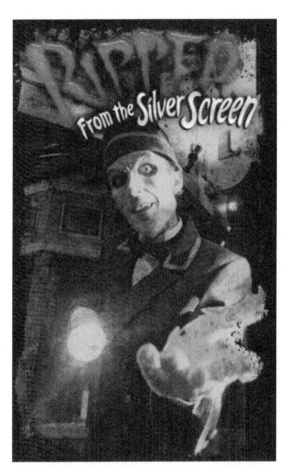

The Usher would also be a fan favorite at HHN25

Harry Potter and the Forbidden HHN Code Names

Why does Universal use code names for HHN, have you ever wondered? The truth is, up until 2008 they never used code names at all but the story behind how they were created them is a fascinating insight into how the event is created. So pull up a comfy chair and allow us once again to delve into the history of the world's greatest Halloween event...

Firstly, we need to separate Universal from Disney to show how these two theme park giants are setup in Florida. When dear old Uncle Walt decided to build what we know today as Walt Disney World in a quiet area of Florida he went to the State and got a whole bunch of unique abilities and permissions, that to this day have never been bettered by any other organization.

It was the creation of the Reedy Creek Improvement District that enabled Disney to effectively do what they wanted within their vast property without having to go through the same channels as other businesses. They could then wholly control within their boundaries the waterways, power, utilities, personnel, zoning, airspace etc. And in return Disney would drive employment opportunities for all and substantially increase tourism. And although that is a vast simplification of the process, it does allow Disney to build what they want, where they want, with some limitations but without the requirement to get the City of Orlando to sign-off on absolutely everything. Universal on the other hand, did not have this luxury.

So when Universal wants to build anything it has to go to the City and get full permission to do so, just like every other business in Florida. And it was 2008 where this became an issue. It had been known to the then small HHN fan community that the permits for these houses would be put onto the internet by the City, with the reference of houses being "temporary haunt themed buildings for the purposes of seasonal entertainment." It wouldn't name the houses but it would list any approvals and inspections occurring by the City (fire checks, disabled access etc); this was the limit of the information that was provided online.

However, it was soon found out by a number of fans that if you visited the City's offices in person as a regular citizen you could go and look at the physical plans being approved. I remember speaking to the City's officer in charge of the approval process back in 2006 and she would readily go through the plans providing every last details, which at the time would have been by about late spring.

The first issue of this process arose in August of 2008, when plans for the event were leaked all over the internet, including the house names, house locations, layouts and facade plans. This led to five of the eight houses having their actual titles known, with three open for speculation.

Universal were livid that the City would allow this situation to occur as the fan (who shall remain nameless) had taken photos of the blueprints using his mobile phone and had posted them on various online forums. Universal who unbeknownst to the world at the time had just signed a huge master licensing agreement with JK Rowling and *Warner Bros* (in a huge coup against Disney) back in May 2007 and were gearing up to agree themed lands and attractions with their new partners. Universal's level of annoyance at this issue would only intensify if they were to submit these plans to the City only for them to be leaked by the fan communities or agents of Disney (conspiracy theory? Nah, just kidding on that last one). How would this affect their new *Harry Potter* agreement and all future HHNs if everything they did would be leaked? Universal proposed a solution.

Universal petitioned the City to make a local change to the way in which themed entertainment building processes could be handled. In many ways Disney had it far easier as they not only had their own law making district but also at the time they only used their own properties. Universal had to get full approval for everything they did plus they used largely third party IPs – all of which put Universal in a precarious position. The City agreed to Universal petition (a petition that was supported by the other local non-Disney theme parks) and from then on, the City would never release drawings of proposed themed entertainment projects to the press or public without prior permission.

This swift step change from the City would be nicknamed by the HHN fan community as "Potter's Law".

And although it was too late for 2008's HHN, the law would come into effect for every Universal project including all the *Harry Potter* additions and every HHN since late 2008. So in the following year that it was decided that HHN houses would be given code names as Universal needed a formal process of referring to their properties with the City. They initially used a numbering system but this was complicated by the many third party vendors who confused drawings and issues. The City also did not like the numbering system, so it was agreed that codenames would be used for all within the production process and would simplify matters. The City could say the house named "Flashlight" had it's disabled access approved and everyone from the technician to the Universal CEO would know what "Flashlight" was and how the construction of that house was progressing.

"Flashlight" by the way, was the code name for the Usher's house of that year. The very first HHN code names were:

Soundstage 22 – Brute – Frankenstein: Creation of the Damned
Soundstage 23 – Agana – Dracula: Legacy in Blood
Soundstage 23 – Big Boy – The Wolfman
Sprung One – Geppetto – Chucky: Friends 'til the End
Sprung Two – Civic Duty – The Spawning
Parade Building – Flashlight – Silver Screams
Disaster Overflow Queue – Pleasant Vielle – Leave it to Cleaver
Jaws Queue – Hammer – SAW

You can see above how the Orlando code names are used as mental triggers and connect to their houses, making them essentially guessable for guests but not without some serious detective work (that's what us at HHNU are for!). So whereas Murdy from Hollywood's HHN will use code names can be weird and wonderful, the Orlando ones are far more technical and practical – which is why they are not as forthcoming with releasing their code names as what Hollywood are. Indeed, the only way we all learned of the code names for 2009's HHN were to speak to the City as that was the only information they could tell the public following Potter's law (not with Twitter as it is done now). So there you have it, the history of the Orlando code names and why they are used.

Halloween Horror Nights XX

Twenty Years of Fear

"A New Era of Darkness Begins!"

The event in 2010 would be the second-ever retrospective anniversary year, but unlike the 'Sweet Sixteen' event, this year would seamlessly mix everything that had been from the past with new horrors in an interesting way. "It's not just this big Carol Burnett special of Halloween... It's not a clip show," said Jim Timon, senior vice president of entertainment at Universal. "That would have been the easy thing to do - a let's-rest-on-our-laurels Halloween. There was no desire creatively to do that."

And although the park would present horrors from the past 20 years of back catalogue, the emphasis would be on setting the event up for future scares. "We want to make sure we touch on, in some sort of house form, some sort of street form, something that bases us in the 20 years of Horror Nights, but then that's it," said Mike Aiello, show director. "Everything else about the event, we want to make sure we are pushing this event forward, establishing a groundwork for the next 20 years." They also had to pull something out of the bag as the economy had been bumping along for a while and this impacted Universal at the time; no so much on ticket sales, as they were steady, but definitely on room sales. Around this time, hotel occupancy across Central Florida was down to 57.5%, which was a fall of 6.7% on the previous year. A real push was subsequently seen at Universal to sell hotel occupancy, by means of discounts and special promotions. This trickled on for most of 2010 as the economy started to grow and newer attractions came online such as *Hollywood Rip Ride Rockit* (2009), *The Simpsons' Ride* (2009) and *The Wizarding World of Harry Potter* (Hogsmeade) on June 18, 2010. These efforts lifted attendance through the spring and summer of 2010 but it would be Halloween Horror Night's job to continue this increase into the fall and through to the holiday celebrations.

Starting to plan the event for 2010 as far back as the summer of 2009, the park's creatives originally wanted to go with a Halloween tree theme where the roots of evil are never quite dead. In fact, the scarezone that was hastily brought in for the final weeks of the event in 2009 (*Shadows from the Past*) had a tree theme as its icon when it appeared on the official website at the time. There had also been the inaugural 'Entertainment Designer Forum' held in April of 2010, where various props and costumes from year's past were showcased, along with the event logo surrounded by tree branches. The initial idea was to bring Cindy back, the un-used icon from the past who had morphed over the years into the Caretaker's daughter. The concept would be her destroying the Halloween tree and what had been seen before, in favor of new horrors that she would unleash. It is not known why she was replaced with the new event icon of Fear, but it must have been late in the planning phase as a whole house had been developed for her inside the *Jaws* queue building which would remain for the event, whereas, the new icon did not have his own outright house.

It was around this time that the website started to update, bringing forth the now annual consumption of rumor and anticipation-making for the fandom of the event. *The Legendary Truth* website that had started in 2008 also became live again and worked hand-in-hand with the main website. Various charred photos and symbols were released, with the fan community spiraling into a frenzy trying to connect all the pieces together to work out who would be the icon and what houses etc. we were likely to see coming up. Soon the items assembled to create a lantern with branch-like pillars creating the roman numerals XX on the side. Soon after, the icon of Fear was unleashed and the icon left the first message on the website: "Nineteen years... Nineteen cycles... What has been decades for some has been Eons for me... On the Twentieth cycle... I shall be revealed!" It was soon presented on various media outlets, where it was claimed that Fear had possessed the staff of the resort's creative departments to bring about more terrifying scares than ever before. Soon the lantern became clickable on the website and the various past icons would be seen in the fire. "Fear is going to show himself this year," Aiello said at the time. "The one thing we've been growing and bringing to the guests every year is going to physically manifest itself this year and be that sort of puppet master or string puller. He's been the one entity that's been pushing this event year after year to create fear to feed him.."

Fear would be prominent within two scarezones that abutted each other: one on Hollywood Boulevard and the other at the top outside

Mel's Drive-In. The former was a collection of all things Halloween Horror Nights from the past 20 years, presented in the warehouse style from the commercial that also ran at the same time. A fake warehouse reflected the event's own actual warehouse that had housed the horrors of past events for over a decade now. The scarezone was named *Twenty Years of Fear* and directly tied into the Parade housing building's house of Horror Nights: *The Hallow'd Past* where guests were taken into a replica of this warehouse to face the creatures of the past brought back to life in a sort of 'greatest hits' for the event. The Mel's Drive-In scarezone was more of a meet-and-greet with the icons. All the past icons were present, excluding Bloody Mary (due to a copyright discussion that was occurring at the time), they all appeared with the mark of Fear (war paint or a scare etc.) across their persons to show their creation from Fear himself. "These icons were a piece to the puzzle that all had to exist physically in order to bring fear, to open that lantern and bring Fear into existence," Aiello said. Another interesting fact was that the Cryptkeeper from the early days of the event was seen not with his fellow icons in this scarezone but rather in the former scarezone sitting on a throne right at the start of the zone; in a way saying, here's the original icon at the start of the event and the scarezone.

The former icon of the event's house would be *The Orphanage: Ashes to Ashes* and was located in the *Jaws* queue building. The house was billed as, "Ashes to ashes, forever now dust. For years she has existed in the shadows, never getting her due. Misunderstood by all around her, she has had enough of her playthings at the Good Harvest Orphanage - now is the time for vengeance. This burned out shell contains the souls of the forgotten and the lost who all scream one name: Cindy." The *Jaws* building lent itself well to the development of this house, much like it had in 2007 for the *Friday 13th* house. The charred remains of the orphanage complete with burning embers, smoke effects and 'burnt flesh smell' was complemented by the first ever use of real fire inside a Halloween Horror Nights house. Towards the end of the house, located outside of a window aperture was a gas-powered fire effect behind a pyro-glass panel that gave the effect that the fire was still ravishing the building and now was the time for guests to exit. Complete with the burnt out environment of a building still on fire (yes Universal used actual wood they had burned themselves to create the effect), the occupiers of the orphanage jumped out at various points around the maze complete with Halloween masks and fire-damaged costumes.

Next up was *Legendary Truth: The Wyandot Estate* located within Soundstage 22. This huge house was constructed to resemble an actual house inside the enormous soundstage. The house directly tied into events taking place on the sister website to the main event website - that of *legendarytruth.com*. Here, online guests had again been appointed as field investigators for the event. Entering into the soundstage, guests would be amazed at the 1:1 size of this temporary haunt attraction, something that was enforced by the use of an actual parked vehicle outside the house where the LT investigators had setup their recording equipment. Guests walking passed the vehicle could study a number of monitors of 'rooms inside the house', where various haunting experiences were taking place. Though not actual CCTV footage, the vehicle acted a means of heightening the anticipation for a house that would go down in the event's history as one of the most chilling.

The house would be like a grown-up version of the haunted mansion, where ghosts would come at guests from all angles. It was also the first ever exclusive ghost-only-house that the event had created, something that seems unfathomable in the event's 20 year history but it's true. The backstory was that the house had been constructed in the 1920s by the then Wyandot family as a family home and guest house. The father of the family, Malcolm Wyandot, then became possessed at some point and by October 30th 1929 he had murdered his family and the 13 guests that were staying at the time. The house would then take guests on a journey showing the tortured souls that had returned. The house actually utilized more special effects than any house had ever used before, with ghosts using not just the campy pepper's ghost effect but also misdirection and lighting effects to open up areas that were presumed to be something. It was the later of these which produced a great scare where a ghost is seen charging at guests but would then 'jump' into the floor. Another scareactor timed and dressed like the former would then appear under the floor and would be dragged on a pulley system screaming under the guest's feet and disappear into the wall ahead. Lighting was used to show that guests would actually standing on clear glass, so when the light went off the appearance of floor boards would remain. This scare combined with a creepy bed scene with exact timings and a ghost chair to terrify and delight guests in equal measures. The house also had a cameo by the Storyteller; she like all the other past icons would make cameos in each respective house throughout the event.

Next was *Havoc: Dogs of War* and was located in the Sprung Tents. The house was billed as, "Ten years ago, the Shadowcreek Enterprise was tasked with developing an elite corps of soldiers. They succeeded. Through an inhalant that includes a compound of testosterone, adrenaline, and other anesthetics, Shadow Creek's latest run of volunteer test subjects are ready for inspection. The project name: HAVOC. The subjects are known simply as Dogs of War." This noisy house was completed with security/army officials trying to secure the deranged misfits that stalked this house. The sound of their firepower would ring in guests' ears as the jumpsuit clad mad-men and women would come at guests from all angles.

Hades: The Gates of Ruin was located within Soundstage 23 and was an impressive mix of horror and myth where the ancient Greek god of the underworld was present along with all his terrifying minions (no not them minions!). Guests were taken through an impressive cave façade (that resembled a demon-like face complete with nostrils and smoke effects) directly into the underworld of his controlling, where guests were confronted with impressive sets and equally impressive detailed scareactors. Notable scareactors as the Cyclopes, Medusa, a Minotaur and a Kraken were all seen. The Medusa was particularly notable for the extensive detailing to her costume complete with her unabashed insistence for staring down guests to give them the ultimate spooky experience. The house was also notable for being the first house to feature ancient Greek mythology as the sole theme of the house.

Also located inside the same soundstage was *PsychoScareapy: Echoes of Shadybrook*, another house from the popular event franchise. This time guests would be returning to a boarded-up Shadybrook some 15 years after the infamous asylum had closed its doors for the last time. Left behind in the padded cells is a collection of residents that time forgot, who were equally as menacing and maniacal as they had ever been. It happened to feature one of the most psychologically terrifying scares ever showcased at the event. This was 'the corridor of hands'. Half way into the house, a corridor of cell bars ran down both side of the walls, and hundreds of hands grasped the bars, with 90% being fake and that creepy 10% left to reach out and grab at guests (though no intentional touching was seen). The only problem was: which hands were fake and which were the real ones? It was noted at the time that this scare terrified people. Organizers had to hold the lines up, to allow enough people to have passed beforehand so particularly freaked-out guests could run ahead. The house also used the relative new function of 'red-buttoning' which had come into use several years previously, though the button in this house was very prominent. Once pushed, a boo-door would open to reveal Jack the Clown who had been an inmate of the original asylum.

Catacombs: Black Death Rising was another house located in one of the Sprung Tents. The house was billed as, "In 1534, an undisclosed outbreak plagued thousands of citizens in Paris and Marseilles. As a group of doctors quarantined the most infected against their will, the townspeople turned and sealed them to their doom. After almost 500 years, they remained without escape. Until now... they are rising, ready to take vengeance on any living being that dares to enter the Catacombs." The house started in a mausoleum with crypts containing rotting flesh and skeletal remains. The guests would then travel through a labyrinth of catacombs with doctors (complete with birdlike breathing appendages) who were attempting to work on the plagued victims. The final area of the house was a construction site of sorts within a museum, where various corpses had been unearthed and were now poised to attack.

The final house was *ZombieGeddon* and it was presented in the *Disaster* queue building. The house was billed as, "It's Zday +6 months. The US government has taken back the continental states while clearing the remaining Canadian infestations. They license and sanction private companies to capture 'un-live' subjects for target training. Dozens of independent training 'companies' appear, promising the best training that money can buy. Then there's ZAP...The Zombie Awareness Program."

The house would also act as the sole comedy house this year, a spot usually reserved for the *PsychoScareapy* houses, though this year, as noted previously, it was far more horrifying than usual. The house had zombies of all ages throughout and linked directly into the neighboring scarezone of *Zombie Gras* which had been located right outside the exit to the house. The idea had been that many of the zombies being tested by 'ZAP' inside the house had escaped and had decided to crash a *Mardi Gras* that was happening within the town of the same setting. Outside smashed-up carnival floats were seen with zombies now in full *Mardi Gras* costume whilst chewing on pieces of human flesh would jump out at guests both exiting the ride and guests walking through this pinch point to the rest of the studios. This was particularly heightened when the nearby *Bill and Ted show* would kick-out after each performance.

The all-original line-up of houses was complemented by an all-original line-of scarezones. The next scarezone was *The Coven* on Shrek Alley where witches both aesthetically pleasing and haggard were present to jump out at guests. This was flanked on the Plaza of the Stars with *Esqueleto Muerte* where technicolor skeletal scareactors were hired to jump onto guests from their black caskets; it was a particular scare-filled zone when the sun had set. The final scarezone would be located within Sting Alley, entitled *Saws N' Steam*. It would house the now steam-punked *Chainsaw Drill Team* within a wet misty environment that would petrify anyone who chanced their luck down the dark side street.

Returning shows this year included *Brian Brushwood: Menace and Malice* located this time on the *Beetlejuice stage*. The popular show returned for the last time and took up the stage that had usually housed *The Rocky Horror Picture Show*. The other show that returned this year was the popular *Bill and Ted Show* located again in their new home of the *Fear Factor Stage*. Notable topics for lampooning this year included: Tiger Woods, *The Jersey Shore*, Justin Bieber, the *Twilight* movies, the *Kick Ass* movie and the *Black Swan* movie (all of which had been released that year).

Rides that were open this year included: *Revenge of the Mummy, Men In Black: Alien Attack, Jaws: The Ride* and *The Simpsons Ride*. The *Hollywood Rip Ride Rockit* rollercoaster, the park's most recent ride addition had been due to be open for the event but had been closed since September 14th. The unique 17 stories-tall ride, complete with 90-degree lift hill, had opened to much fanfare in the August of that year but had been down periodically due to maintenance. "The overwhelming majority of guests who ride *Hollywood Rip Ride Rockit* rate their experience as 'excellent.' Our maintenance programs are intense and thorough, with guest safety always the most important priority," Universal Vice-President Tom Schroder said at the time. "We don't share specifics about this kind of work, but I can tell you it is something we don't rush. Each attraction is different and requires its own schedule," he added. "We will reopen Hollywood Rip Ride Rockit as soon as we can do so, but only after we are satisfied all our work is complete."

It was therefore decided that as the ride would be worked on during the event, and because queues would be directly below much of the ride's path, they would close the ride for the duration of the event. Eventually, the problems would be solved and the ride would re-open to day guests on October 27th, 2010. Despite the ride being down, Universal routinely surveyed guests on exiting the park on their overall experience of the event. It had early on pulled the highest guest satisfaction level ever, even without the new signature ride, so the decision was therefore taken to keep the ride closed throughout the nightly event but open for day guests from 27th.

The level of satisfaction was not the only performance indicator that was ranking high during the event; the level of hotel room sales had drastically improved, something that the Universal management were keen to secure for the final fourth quarter of 2010. New came during the event that room sales were up 12.3% from the previous year for the Central Florida area. "Things are hopping at Universal. And it translates into occupied hotel rooms," said Scott Smith, a lodging instructor in the University of Central Florida's Rosen College of Hospitality Management at the time. It was reported that a combination of the recent opening of the new *Harry Potter* attractions and Halloween Horror Nights had made the resort's hotel room occupancies increase more than the local average to a rumored 16.5%.

The positivity of the event was not just seen in the statistics and figures of the resort's accounts, but also the romantic-yet-horrific competition that was seen at the time. For the first time ever, Universal began marketing the chance to get hitched at the event. The event had held several weddings previously but this was the first time that Universal had marketed via their travel company the ability for couples to marry there. To mark the occasion, Universal was going to celebrate this gruesome additional by offering the first marriage for free via a bloodthirsty competition. A press release was issued that read,

"Couples can enter by e-mailing a Halloween-themed picture of themselves to hhnwed@universalorlando.com. Photos must be accompanied by a description (no more than 200 words) of why they want an HHN wedding. ... Among the grand-prize benefits are food and beverage (including wedding cake) for 20 people and access to a haunted house for the ceremony with 10 scare actors in attendance - including the famed chainsaw drill team."

The winners of the competition were a couple from Vermont; April Richardson, a graphic designer, and Adam Cochran, a pharmacist. The wedding was held on Friday October 15th inside Soundstage 22 at the *Wyandot House*. The couple, who had been engaged since May of that year won a prize worth more than $11,000, which also included park tickets, a hotel stay and other perks. The worthy winners who had been dating for six years were also lifelong fans of the event who would regular throw Halloween parties back in Vermont. The ceremony was attended by all the main icons and street scareactors. After the ceremony the couple boarded a hearse and were driven by the Caretaker himself to their reception, whilst flanked by the *Chainsaw Drill Team*. Driving through the park, much to the delight of guests, the couple were escorted to their reception which was located backstage in Soundstage 33 (which is used exclusively for special events). There, the couple was presented with a tiered and cobwebbed cake before enjoying the rest of sights and sounds of the popular event.

Another final first this year was the addition of a VIP Lounge for the fans of the event. For an additional upcharge of just $9.99, guests could enter inside Cafe La Bamba Cantina for not just a drinks bar but also a museum of props from the last 20 years that had been gathered from the actual Halloween Horror Nights warehouse. On selected nights various icons would come into the lounge from the neighboring scarezone for photo-opportunities, with Thursday nights reserved for exclusive lectures from the event's creatives. Popular topics were alternate icon discussions, alternate themes, further backstory of the developments of both Dr. Mary Agana and 'the Thing', along with houses and scarezones that never quite left the drawing board. Popular with fans of the event, the lounge was positively packed on these nights.

Halloween Horror Nights 21

Are you in?

As in the previous year where the event's icon became a personification of emotion, this year it would be another intangible aspect with Lady Luck herself being brought forth to terrify guests. She came about when the park's own fortunes were going great, where hotel occupancy was up, and so was attendance. You could say, though, that this wasn't luck, this was forward planning and heavy investment by the corporation. To continue this success, it was around early June that the website was updated and the public was informed of the event dates, prices, tickets etc. though no word yet on which houses and street scares would be enjoyed. June 28th came and the official event site updated to reveal the overall theme. Pictured throughout were two playing cards, an ace and a queen of spades which totaled 21, next to a severed and bloody hand.

June 19th came around with the first announcement of which house we would be experiencing. It was *The Thing*, based on the new movie that was going to be released during the event. The Universal picture was a prequel of the 1982 movie of the same name. The basic premise of the movie was that a team of American and Norwegian scientists discovers an extraterrestrial being buried deep in the ice of Antarctica. The movie would end with a direct setup for the 1982 movie by showing the escaped and affected dog running away into the night (soon to be discovered by the characters from the Kurt Russell movie). The star-studded premiere would actually be held on October 11th 2011 at Universal Studios in Hollywood during their Halloween Horror Nights event. The synchronicity of the premiere and house with the joint marketing had been deployed very successfully, despite the movie not performing to expectations at the box-office. This process had also been planned in 2009 for *The Wolfman*, but due to production issues the movie was released after the 2009 event instead of during. The message for cinemagoers was that once they had seen the movie, it was now time to experience the movie in real life, with houses developed at both coasts for the event.

Located in Soundstage 23, the house really did bring guests right into the heart of the action. Beginning their journey, guests would travel to the South Pole and find themselves in a snowy environment where they would approach the research station featured in the movie. With the soundstage's actual thermostat cranked down to the minimum level, guests explored the base from the movie, where various scenes had been recreated to show the scientists and inhabitants mutating into the alien creatures. This was later combined with the unaffected scientists doing battle with the aliens. One interesting scene had a human-alien mid-transformation doing battle with a scientist whilst they were suspended on a harness timed to move with the gunshot from the ground character. Then after this, guests would find themselves entering into the actual alien ship when the iconic flamethrower was used to dispatch the mutating alien.

Shortly after the announcement, the tickets went on sale via the event website. This was followed by a number of games becoming available throughout the month of August. Week by week, new and exciting games would be released that would ultimately reveal clues to the other possible houses that would be forthcoming. More games, along with leaderboards, became available on the 1st September along with the full reveal of all the planned event activities. There was also around this time the first ever fan 'tweet up', where fans of the event were asked via social media to attend a park get-together. Similar events, though, had occurred for the reveal of the Bloody Mary story in 2008. Anticipation was at its highest when the event officially opened on September 23rd that year. The tone for the event had been set when Jim Timon, Vice President of Entertainment announced, "None of our past is here. This is truly - by every aspect and by every design and by every costume, every house, every prosthetic, every scare zone, every piece of makeup -- absolutely new. Everything." And "new" everything would be; with no more Jack and co, guests would be brought into a new era where new franchises and themes could be explored.

During the build up to the event a fast-spreading rumor started that the old *Hard Rock Café* would be used to house one of the event's mazes.

The Café which had opened with the park back in 1990 was at the time the largest chain in the world. The café, which had been shaped into the size of a giant guitar, would subsequently close in 1998 when the new café built in the new City Walk took its place. 1999 saw the neck of the restaurant demolished (this acted as a walkway from the carpark where guests could formerly access the park via the restaurant). The building had been left for storage and occasional staff training, with the entrance to the building inside the Kidzone area of the park. It was around the summer of this year when fans of the event started reporting a great deal of activity inside the building, when various containers and furniture were cleared. Speculation soon ran rampant that the venue would be a perfect location for a house. Speculation was soon quashed when the event opened and no such house had been constructed inside the impressive venue. It was then around early October that Universal issued permits for an 'accelerated demolition' and by the middle part of the event the building had been fully demolished. It is unknown whether the rampant speculation at the time caused the building to be demolished, possibly fearing trespass in this vulnerable location or whether the building was just removed to make way for future expansions.

The next house in the lineup would be *Nightingales: Blood Prey* which shared the same soundstage with *The Thing*. Universal billed the house as, "Within every war, the Nightingales have appeared. Able to transform themselves to fit any setting, these savage banshees feed on the weak and the helpless. Patrolling WWI era trenches, you discover that you are more than just at war…you're being hunted." The house took guests right into another battle for survival, right into the trenches of the Western Front of World War One. Guests would explore the labyrinth of trenches where the nightingales (a freakish combination of Edwardian nurse meets a toothy, winged demon) are picking off their prey. This noisy house had these demon nurses from hell coming at guests from all angles, including again from above like the preceding house.

Nevermore: The Madness of Poe would be located inside Sprung Tent 2 and would take guests through the warped imagination of the writer Edgar Allen Poe. The house would begin with guests entering into the writer's own parlor before beginning the journey into his works, which were presented in chronological order. Pushing giant pages of his literary works aside, guests enter first into a diabolical scene from *The Tell Tale Heart* before quickly stepping into *The Raven* where the feathered ebony devils would attack from all angles. This even included an interesting special effect where a broken window would smash onto guests (though this was just sprayed water timed to go off with the sound effects and visuals). The house would end with various characters from all his books and poems seen in the house attacking en masse.

Next door in Sprung Tent 2 would be the event's 3D house, *The In-Between in 3D*, which would be the first 3D house since 2007. It happened to coincide nicely at about the height of the fad for 3D glasses at the cinema. Building on this tradition, Universal decided to use more distorting effects that would affect the wearer's perceptions of distance, substrate and depth perception rather than the use of fluorescent paints. Telling the story of two college students who get sucked into a wormhole, it took guests into an incredibly unworldly domain filled with demons and ghouls which utilized the distorting effects of the 3D glasses to great effect.

Winter's Night: The Haunting of Hawthorn Cemetery would be presented in Soundstage 22 this year. Again, another snowy and exceedingly cold environment had been created in the cavernous soundstages that took guests through a creepy graveyard at midnight. Event designers had taken great inspiration from London's creepy Highgate Cemetery, where overgrown grave stones and crypts were presented in this first-ever house to be solely based in a graveyard. A ghoulish caretaker of the grounds (not the Caretaker), a number of zombies, and ghosts torment guests throughout the house mixing psychological scares with jumping-out scares to great effect. The elaborately detailed house could be seen as one of the most detailed the event has ever been produced.

The last ever house to be presented in the place where it all started would actually be the first house that had ever started as a scarezone. That house was *Saws N' Steam: Into the Machine* presented in the *Jaws* queue building. "It's the very first time that we've decided to take a former scarezone and turn it into a haunted house," said show director Patrick Braillard at the time. "We've never done that before and in that way it becomes a new product."

This hot, wet, humid and steamy house would be perfectly suited to the nuances of the *Jaws* queue building. The house had been billed as, "Spinning blades and massive, crushing pistons await you around every corner as you are forced deeper into the bowels of a mechanical nightmare. Give yourself to The Machine." This steam-punked workhouse environment would utilize the steam (or dry-ice) very well in that it was used throughout to present some great scares that combined nicely with the gory splatterings of blood and guts in the various fake machines that had been set up. It was a great house that would ultimately send off the house that started it all in great fashion.

The next house would be *The Forsaken* and it would be presented in the Parade Building. The house told the story of the four ships that left for the Americas with Columbus, and as we know from history only three made the journey. The forth would be the main subject of the house and would show the crew of that ship die in a watery grave before rising from the depths to attack a Spanish fort. Passing through the ship, a church on the main land and then through the fort, guests would witness the zombie crew doing battle with the Spanish soldiers. The house would prove popular with guests for its imaginative use of narrative and scare but would ultimately prove difficult off-stage for the management. The special effects had been difficult to manage from the outset, which did not help matters when in the first week the set allegedly flooded from one of the effects. Custodians were deployed hourly to mop up water, clean down the backstage components and ensure the house was checked thoroughly to prevent it from occurring again. This was combined with the tremendous floods that were seen in the opening weeks where the bad weather was initially thought to be the cause of the water damage; though as in 2012 the area was known to management for the ceaseless flooding that has occurred in this area during the stormier months.

The final house would be *H.R. Bloodengutz Presents: Holidays of Horror* and would be the event's comedic house this year. Located in the *Disaster* queue building, the house would have a lengthy queue video that set guests up for the coming horrors. Introducing the titular main character of H.R. Bloodengutz, the house would represent successive scenes from various holidays dressed as scenes from his latest TV show. Similar to the cinema/drive-in movie houses of the past (corridor-scene-corridor-scene) the house mixed comedy with scares in equal measures.

There would be six scarezones this year. The six would be highly detailed and a real step change from previous years with more money spent on them to create new experiences that had never been seen before. The first would be *Nightmaze*, not only the first time an outdoors maze had been presented at the event but also the first time that park creatives had decided to move walls to constantly change the layout of the maze each night. This made for a different experience for regular event goers.

"When you enter it, you might see dividers and openings ... but once you get in it, those things are constantly moving it," said T.J. Mannarino, director of Entertainment Art & Design. "We're always going to force you to the place you don't want to go." This foggy and creative scarezone was presented in Production Central.

The next scarezone would build on the previous theme of showing guests something that they had never seen before by literally bringing the house down. *Acid Assault*, located in the New York area of the park, would use state-of-the-art projection equipment to show the buildings in the area crumbling to dust. Using similar technology to that use by Disney for their various projection shows, the effect would show the buildings being pelted with acid rain that would eventually lead the buildings to appear to collapse right in front of your eyes. The neat effect had never been used before but had been mixed so that it timed effectively with the scares of the area.

The next scarezone to offer something completely new would be located in the Hollywood area and be simply entitled *7*. The scarezone was again doing something completely fresh by altering to prescribed parameters throughout the night. Featuring various female scareactors that started each night off with impeccable attire dancing to popular music that would over the duration, morph into hideous, demonic sirens with rock music ramped up. The sirens would represent the seven deadly sins and would morph periodically throughout the night into their final ghoulish presences.

A smaller scarezone of *Canyon of Dark Souls* was presented at the front of the park that mixed stilt walkers with hooded monsters and static sets to great effect. *Grown Evil* was presented in the Central Park area of the park at the event, and would feature a number of animals that were morphing into humanoid monsters. The overgrown area was combined with various sets and props to afford scareactors the best chance of jumping out at guests. The final scarezone would be *Your Luck Has Run Out* and would feature the event's icon (as she had no house to call her own outright this year). Located on Sting Alley, the theme of change was heavily presented where the main icon would again morph inside the alley from fresh-faced Vegas Queen to hideous monster.

Only two shows would be presented this year, one old and one new. The old being the return of the popular Bill and Ted dudes to packed audiences. The highlights of the show this year included references to: *The Marvel Cinematic Universe*, *Scream 4* (which had been released earlier in the year), the latest *Mission Impossible* instalment and the newly revised *Planet of the Apes* franchise. There had been some controversy this year, not with the content of the show, but with the fact that select performances early on at the event had to be cancelled due to the flooding around the area. Sewers being overwhelmed with downpour from the late September storms caused a number of early shows to be cancelled.

248

The other show presented at the 2011 event was *Death Drums* a high octane musical performance and dance group which would delight guests in the area outside the then *Hercules* building. Presenting three different shows each night, the shows would combine drumming performances with glowing sticks to popular dance tracks while an assembled cast of performers danced right in front of the gathered guests.

Setting out to present a different event for a new era, Universal had been highly successful in their mission, which resulted in an experience quite unlike any that any guest had ever experienced before.

The Rat Lady on break…

Halloween Horror Nights 22

Once you're inside, there is no way out!

The build up to the 2012 event would actually begin in 2011, such was the level of popularity and love for the event by this time. The inaugural exhibition held at the Orange County Regional History Center was 'The Serious Art of Make-Believe'. The exhibition would run into December and would showcase all the artistry that had been created in the past 20 years of Universal Orlando's history. "There are some things in here that even the rabid fans have never seen. They never saw the light of day," said Andrew Sandall, assistant director of the history center. Everything from the Terra Queen's motorcycle to oil paintings of Jack the Clown, right down to concept art for attractions that had never been built were all showcased at the event. The event was topped-off by a final Q and A session on December 8th that featured many of the creative minds behind the exhibition. It was at this very session that Universal started to tease the 2012 Halloween Horror Nights event, when the previous event had only finished a fortnight ago. Promises of "huge announcements to come" and the development of "partnerships" with other media bodies were mooted at the event.

Such was the popularity of the history exhibition, that the resort along with its fellow competitors from the area decided to hold another forum on design at the very same venue in February of 2012. On February 24th representatives from Universal Orlando, Walt Disney World, Busch Gardens and *Nickelodeon* gathered for a special Q and A session to raise money for the American Cancer Society. The forum, now in its third year also held a special silent auction for various Universal Studios built props, including ones from the most recent Halloween Horror Nights. Much like the preceding design event, fans were teased on the scale of the upcoming Halloween event and that this year, like the last, the new era of entertainment would contain "new ways of doing things".

And new ways they were, when in July 15th an unexpected announcement occurred from a wildly different location that was broadcasted to the world's media (and not just via the event website like in previous years!). The announcement came from the world's largest fan and 'geekdom' event in San Diego that is *Comic Con*. "For the first time ever, we're tackling a video-game franchise and bringing it to life at Halloween Horror Nights," Jim Timon, senior vice president of entertainment at Universal Orlando said at the event. Universal had considered making a video game based house in the past but had never found the partner or space within the haunt calendar to build such a maze, so this would be their first foray into the very popular domain of gaming. Jointly announcing the event with John Murdy, creative director at Universal Hollywood, the house would be based on the very popular *Silent Hill* games. The house would be designed to tie into aspects of both the games; the 2006 movie of the same name and the upcoming Universal feature film of the time *Silent Hill: Revelation 3D*, which would be released on October 26 during the event. This would be a similar marketing technique that would link both coasts to new movies appearing in the cinema at the same time as the event; this cross-marketing would prove very fruitful for all partners. The house would be exceedingly close to the look of both the movies and video games, when guests entering into Soundstage 22 would first be confronted with a faceless nurse walking awkwardly in high heels before being shot at. Then sirens would sound and guests would be literally plunged into the underworld of *Silent Hill*, complete with all the characters and falling ash. A tall Pyramid Head character on stilts would terrify guests half way through, before they left the town with one final scare from one of the mutants.

Before the next house was officially announced (which would be very soon after), the fandom having been tipped-off from sources unknown managed to figure out that there was a strong likelihood of a Penn and Teller house at this year's event. The magic performing duo already had strong links to the event and had even designed their own house for the Hollywood event in year's past. Checking the schedule of their shows for the coming months, it appeared that a gap was seen in July and then a larger gap would be seen in the Fall. This seemed slightly irregular, seeing that the duo was based in Las Vegas performing their trademark show to packed-out audiences most nights on the Strip. Semi-confirmation was seen when in the diary gap, Penn and Teller teased followers of their Twitter account by showing pictures of them in Orlando. It wasn't until August 4th that the duo officially announced their involvement with the event. Stating that they had been officially invited to design their own house for the Florida event, Penn Jillette said at the time, "We blow up all of Las Vegas. It goes terribly, terribly wrong." The house would feature a post-apocalyptic world of Vegas but would be presented in the duo's unique and abstract sense of humor, acting as the event's comedy house for the year. "[They will aim]…to take all the lights and the sounds and all the clichés of Las Vegas and turn them upside down into a fun nightmare," Jillette said. The house wasn't just a house designed by the park with endorsement from the duo; this house would be fully designed in partnership with them. Jim Timon, senior vice president of entertainment had brokered the deal to ensure the pair could have complete creative control of the house. He said, "They're not just putting their name on a haunted house, they're actually designing it."

"It was heaven for me because I orchestrated that sort of stuff," Teller then said. "Working with the Universal's Halloween Horror Nights veterans has been a pure joy," he said. "These are people with a proficiency level in a very curious art form that is completely staggering to me."

The house would mix comedy with the current day clichés of the entertainment destination with horror, to create a very unique house. The house would be located inside Sprung Tent 2 and would be presented in 3D. The official name was *Penn and Teller: New(kd) Las Vegas 3-D.* The pinnacle of the house, though, and what made it exceedingly unique was that Penn and Teller would actually feature inside the house. On select nights the pair would appear in one of the scenes to not only terrify guests but to also shock them. Some guests were heard saying, "was that the real Penn and Teller!?" Yes, it was and Universal did not use stand-ins when the duo weren't performing, choosing to leave their section of the house empty so as not to confuse guests. Fans of the event had worked out that the house had been in development with Universal had used the duo's website to work out the timings. Again, approaching the website and seeing when they were performing in Vegas led fans to almost always accurately work out when the duo would be performing inside the house, which was something that Universal refused to publish (obviously fearing the house could get overwhelmed on selected nights). The house seamlessly mixed half-naked zombie show girls with a grossly large and bloated evil Elvis to gross scenes of puking inside the human buffet room. The house was a huge hit for the event.

Skipping back before this house's announcement was an altogether larger broadcast which would unknowingly at the time set up and define the event for the coming years. This was the announcement on July

19th that the popular *AMC* TV series of *The Walking Dead* would be coming to the event. Much like the previous *Silent Hill* announcement, the house would be a joint venture with the Hollywood park and would directly tie into the marketing for the third season of the popular show which would air during the event. This would mark another first, in that this was the first time that Universal on both parks had made houses from a TV show.

"For fans of the series, we're going to put you in the footsteps of the characters in the show," John Murdy, creative director at Universal Studios Hollywood, said at the time. "You're going to have to try and survive the zombie apocalypse."

The house would be set in the *Disaster* queue building and would be entitled, *The Walking Dead: Dead Inside*; making reference to the words scrawled on the infamous hospital doors from season one. The clue would also be in the name, as the house would take guests on the journey that the main character Rick Grimes suffered. They started from the hospital but then went into the many popular scenes from that opening season. After visiting the hospital, another popular show scene would be the shopping center where it seemed as if hundreds of 'walkers' were banging and scratching at the frosted-glassed doors trying to break into the area, to get the guests. The attention to detail and the fact that the house made guests feel like they were straight into the series proved very popular for the event on both coasts. This was an attribute that the event's creatives were keen to fulfil, so they worked closely with the actual designers from the series who were based in Georgia (as the show had been shot there), making the chance to work with the TV Producers of the show even more possible. "Having a chance to be involved in a live event is a completely new challenge for me," Greg Nicotero the co-executive producer said at the time. The level of detailing for the house wouldn't stop at the sets and props, and the level of goriness of the performers would be taken to the next level to match the aesthetics of the show. "It's the proximity of having people close to you that are kind of hideous and decomposing and gory. It's fun from the performer side of it, and it infects the guest in that kind of fun", said Nicotero.

Shortly after the above announcement around late July, the resort revealed that they were working with another icon from an altogether different media, that being the musical idol Alice Cooper. The house would be based off of a house from the previous year in the Hollywood event that would be entitled, *Alice Cooper: Welcome to My Nightmare*. The house that was built in Sprung Tent 1 would showcase various horror scenes that had been aided in design by Cooper himself and then feature an all-Cooper soundtrack throughout. Cooper, who was a huge fan of the event on both coasts, was excited to work again with Universal when he had been approached by Hollywood's creative director John Murdy. It was Murdy who had spotted Cooper enjoying the event with his family back in 2010 as ordinary park guests. Universal billed the house as,

"Journey into the legendary rocker Alice Cooper's twisted mind and witness the natural melding of horror and Cooper's four decades-long career. Here you will follow Steven, the iconic character from many of Cooper's works, as you come face-to-face with a myriad of tormentors who threaten an already-decaying sense of sanity." Entering via a huge façade of Cooper's face and through his mouth, guests were taken on a journey through Cooper's mind that mixed loud blasting rock 'n' roll from his various albums to timed scares (some of which were in the pitch black!).

It was also on this very day (the Cooper announcement) that Universal pulled the permit that had been on the *Hercules* building to have it replaced with another permit for demolition. Speculation then ran rampant over the possible demolition permit, though it was later revealed that the Soundstage would be torn-down during the event to make way for a new ride. That ride later turned out to be *Transformers*. This led to the eight houses that had been planned now reduced down to seven. Little is known about the house that was partially constructed inside the *Hercules* building, though one former Universal team member, who didn't want to be named told us:

"Construction on Transformers Orlando was said to have been planned to start after Halloween Horror Nights 2012 ended so A&D could use the space for a maze. Universal Orland corporate decided to expedite the construction timeline for the project and it displaced the maze being constructed in that location. A&D were removing props up until the final moment the building was cleared to be demolished (the night before it was torn down to be precise). The house was far along (the walls were up, some props were in place, and some of the puppets were present), but it was not in a finished state.

I've heard over the years that it was a house based on Mayan lore. It would have taken guests through a Mayan temple with creature puppets. One creature was described as a winged bat-like beast and the other as a large serpent. This concept has yet to be used at Halloween Horror Nights since the house was demolished in 2012. My speculation is that *Tomb of the Ancients* (2016 house) was inspired by this "lost haunted house" in terms of layout and structures, although the former was admittedly based on Egyptian lore whereas the latter was based on

Mayan mythology. The original location was labeled Soundstage 44. It was first used for "Murder, She Wrote Mystery Theater" from June of 1990 to 1996. "Hercules and Xena: Wizards of the Screen" opened in the venue a year later and closed in February of 2000. Soundstage 44 was used for storage, but for all intents and purposes remained unused until 2004 due to the rumored presence of asbestos in the structure. The Halloween Horror Nights 14 maze "Horror Nights Nightmares" was placed in the space.

Unfortunately, Hurricane Charley struck Florida and damaged Soundstage 44. The storm also damaged scarezone construction that year and made 2004 a difficult year for everyone involved in the process. The building remained vacant and damaged for a number of years. From what I understand, it was condemned due to the damage incurred by the storm and could not be used until improvements were made."

We do know that as the *Hercules* building had been cleared out and repaired at some cost, as the *Jaws* building which had normally been used as a haunt location had also been torn down to make way for the *Harry Potter* expansion. It was felt that the relatively new majority shareholders of the resort, Comcast had funding to fast-track *The Transformers* attraction using blueprints from the Hollywood and Singapore iterations of the ride, so that the attraction could be built in record time. This was seen as a movie to increase the attraction numbers of the park whilst the popular Jaws attraction was being moved to make way for future expansion.

This level of construction also impacted on the streets of the event where popular street locations from the past had to be opened up to cope with the level of footfall the popularity of the event was enjoying. It was then announced by the resort that plans had changed in August, and that the static scarezones of the past would be adapted to make way for the construction.

"Scarezones in the past have been defined places and spaces. Now we want to play with that a little bit," said Jim Timon, Universal's senior vice president for entertainment. "The characters and scare actors will ebb and flow and move and change, so you won't always see the same 'scareactors' in the same places as you may have seen them earlier in the night," Timon said.

Having to accommodate the relatively new *Superstar Parade* that had been showcased for day-guests, along with improving footfall, the static scarezones of the past could not be deployed. "There are some physical realities out there that we have to adjust and accommodate," Timon said. "It encouraged us to do stuff with the scare actors that we haven't done in our program before."

Though some physical sets were built for the scarezones, most were located in areas where the parade did not travel and where footfall couldn't bottleneck. The streets would be entitled, *The Legions of Horror* and would be the first time the whole park had roaming scarezones. It was the second time since 2007 that the event would allow all the streets to be one giant scarezone. The roaming hoards would include: The Iniquitous, The Vampires, The Beasts, The Warriors, The Prisoners, The Traditionals and The Walkers. The different factions would be based on the various online games that were popular on the event's official website.

The next house would be *Dead End* and it would be located in Soundstage 22. One of the two original concepts for this year, the house told the story of a haunted mansion overrun with ghosts that would terrify guests. Rumors quickly spread that the house would be one of the most psychologically scary houses ever created by the resort. "It's stuff that people have always fantasized of as 'classic haunted house.' For me, that is a combination not just of the scenery, it's a mixture of the sound design that we have in there and some of the wonderful special effects that we have that really puts this on edge," said TJ Mannarino at the time. "We do houses that are spectacle, we do houses that are comical, we do houses that follow a wonderful story," Mannarino said. "This one is truly scary."

The other house, located in the same soundstage, would be *Gothic*. This house would feature an elaborately-designed cathedral setting during restoration. Having never taken guests inside a cathedral, the journey would showcase to guests just how detailed the park's creatives could be by building a full cathedral set using the forced-perspective technique. Throughout the house, various gargoyles, a hunchback and statues would attack guests with everyone getting that feeling, 'is that statue a scareactor or an actual statue?', with us all finding out when it was too late! The brilliance of this house was later reflected when it won 'house of the year' by the in-house awards based on the feedback from guests.

The final house would be located in the Parade building and feature Universal's *House of Horrors'*, which some believe to be a late addition to the event due to the rapid decision to demolish the *Hercules* building. The building had at the time been housing the new Superstar Parade floats which had to be hastily removed then wrapped in protective film every evening in a nearby temporary housing for the event. The house was then allegedly constructed very late on inside the building using the footprint of the previous year's house, *The Forsaken*, but none of the same sets and props. Instead a black and white world of horror was presented where guests were taken into the classic world of the Universal horror movies. The problems didn't end there though. As in the previous years, the first two weeks of the event were beset by heavy rainfall that periodically flooded the area around the queue location, which had been moved to behind the building to cope with footfall for the other houses. A former Universal Team Member who didn't want to be named told us:

"Universal's House of Horrors was a concept A&D had been working on for a couple of years. It was inspired by *Dead Exposure*. In the past, Universal's A&D had explored different interpretations of the classic movie monsters at Horror Nights and 2009 was the last time they had been used. The concept was chosen because it was minimalistic in nature and could be constructed in the compressed timeline they faced. The entire maze was constructed in black and white as a tribute to the classic monsters. "Black" structures were accentuated with glow-in-the-dark paint as "white" for the black-and-white film stock effect they were aiming to accomplish. Guests walked through the opening of the maze which was an old film archive. The story was that guests were walking through during a thunderstorm and into the films themselves. "Lightning flashes" (accomplished with black lights) were used to "illuminate" the maze's scenes as well as the costumes. All of the monsters' costumes were black with glow-in-the-dark paint added for the finer details so guests could spot them when the black lights illuminated them.

Universal's *House of Horrors* was the last maze completed. Things were finished throughout the opening weekend. The night of rehearsals, A&D were still inside the maze finishing aspects of it. The maze had a reputation of being "thrown together," but it was as detailed as A&D could manage given the time constraints and minimalistic style.

I'd describe it as a gem caked in a layer of dirt that needed more polish. It was still quite good. The black light technique was effective and guest feedback was overall positive. It had a more mixed reaction amongst the dedicated fanbase because parts of it did feel "bare,' particularly the transitions.

There was more detail and ingenuity to it than the dedicated fanbase gave it credit for. *The Mummy* scene had a tunnel sequence (complete with a good distraction scare) that they've since reused in other mazes. Both of the *Frankenstein* scenes had details such as blacklight-painted stonework, chains hanging from the ceiling, and recreations of props from both of the original films. *The Creature* scene had skeletons in the "water" that surrounded guests to their right and left, seaweed with fog and lighting to look like water, and a boat mounted to the ceiling. Another cool scene was the finale. They hung individual film strips of each monster and crammed all six of them in the room, complete with music, sound clips from each film, and intermittent black lights flashing. At the time, it was a Horror Nights' first: six actors crammed in one space is a difficult thing. For instance, they couldn't just take any table and put it in the room as a prop. It had to match the source material, being painted black and gray, and then touched up with blacklight paint, then nailed down to the ground to ensure it couldn't be moved by guests."

Bill and Ted were again back this year and featured popular references to: *Mad Men*, *Magic Mike*, *Ted*, *The Dark Knight Rises* and *The Hobbit*, all topped off with various bouts of the craze that was sweeping the world of 'Gangnam Style' dancing. Completing this show was a new addition, unseen before, that of *20 Penny Circus: Fully Exposed* located at the *Beetlejuice stage*. The show mixed gross-out humor with magic tricks to delighted audiences nightly. Another highly-praised addition to this year was the *Hitchcock Lagoon show* that played nightly throughout the run. The show would start with the infamous and haunting main theme from his movie *Vertigo*. Interwoven would be clips from a variety of his most famous films before the infamous shower scene with the sharp and theatrical Bernard Herrmann score. This would be concluded with a fast-paced montage of clips with lengthy cross sections of clips from his movie *The Birds* with the main theme from *North by Northwest*. Fireworks and blazes of fire would signal the end of the show and the end of the night. It had truly been another great year to remember.

Halloween Horror Nights 23

What evil has taken root?

As in the previous year, the speculation began with the presentation of 'A Year in the Life: Backstage to Onstage at Universal Orlando Resort' which was held at the Orange County Regional History Center in February this year. The exhibition would showcase all the designs and stories from the past years at Universal Orlando, plus teasing for what would be about to unfold later in the year. TJ Mannarino said at the exhibition, "It's always fun to pull up the archives and start looking at stuff that really was the beginnings of some of the bigger projects. Some of these events have grown to massive size and they actually touch, in effect, the world. Halloween Horror Nights is now in four separate parks, from Singapore to Japan to Hollywood to here in Orlando."

As well as the gathered props, blueprints, set pieces and costumes that had been put on display, the exhibition featured a huge wall that showed the timeline for planning the events we all love. Halloween Horror Nights was now seen to be an 18-month affair, from initial concept through to the execution of every night. Apart from the various showcases at the event, it was highly rumored and teased that the *Legendary Truth* (the fan interactive collective experience) would be back and that this year would again feature a high number of outside-owned properties for the houses.

This was swiftly followed in March by the *Entertainment Designers' Forum* which was held at the same center, where discussions took place about how the houses are brought from concept to design. This was followed by Spooky Empire's *MAY-HEM/Halloween Extreme* convention on Memorial Day Weekend of May 23rd -25th in Orlando, where the Universal panel again hinted about the return of the *Legendary Truth* but also that this year would see a massive increase in merchandise. The increased merchandise would also be readily available on the website for those who could not attend the event.

Later on in the year to June, the building permits were issued to the City of Orlando, confirming that again we would all be enjoying 7 houses. This was rapidly realized when around the end of that month (June 26th) Universal announced the first house would be based on the modern cult classic movie *The Cabin in the Woods*. This was combined with the event's website updating to reveal the tree/root theme once again, with the tag line "What Evil Has Taken Root?" on the following day.

The house would be based on the movie that had been released in the previous year to much success. Officially labelled as a horror-comedy, a genre which had been weirdly absent for many years at the cinema, it mixed tongue-in-cheek post-modernistic humor with straight-out gore, culminating in possibly one of the bloodiest finales ever. The movie starts pretty traditionally by recounting the tale of some pretty clichéd high school students who eventually end up in a cabin in the woods. Little do they know that they are actually a part of a horrible experiment, which inevitably goes wrong and all hell breaks loose (literally). The movie had been produced by largely the same team that had brought us *Buffy the Vampire Slayer*, headed up as executive producer by Joss Whedon. The house would effectively stick to the original storyline and would take guests right through the many famous scenes of the movie, to make everyone feel like they were right there inside all the action. "We are building the cabin completely. You're going to walk through a forest to get there. You're going into the cabin. You're going to go into the cube cells. We're literally taking everything we can in the film and giving you a kind of best-of montage of the film with this kind of linking story," said Mike Aiello at the time.

This was achieved by extensive research by Universal whilst working with the original filmmakers, which led to the creation of extremely detailed sets that not only mirrored the movies but were filled with detail. The most notable scene from the movie which led to the most notable scene from the house would be the elevator scene. Guests would enter into a room filled with elevators, then just at the right moment the elevators would 'bing' indicating that the monsters had been selected, thereby every elevator would open to feature a whole array of monsters to terrify guests. There was even the popular merman that would spray blood (water) onto guests inside the control room. Drew Goddard the director of the movie said, "My wish for Cabin was always that it would live on outside the film, that people would take that ball and run with it, and I can't imagine a better fit for what we were trying to do with the movie than to make a maze out of it." The house had actually been one of the largest ever created, having been built inside the enormous Soundstage 21, which had never been used for the event before as this stage was usually occupied by production companies.

Fun fact: Both Jack the Clown and the Caretaker appeared as cameos in the elevator scene but only for the briefest of seconds.

The Evil Dead house would be announced next. The house would not be based on the original series of movies but rather on the recent remake which had been released earlier in 2013. As in previous years, the house would be across both American events at the same time with each coast undertaking their own creative touches to make two unique houses from the same property. John Murdy from Universal Hollywood said at the time, "If you're familiar with what we do with Halloween Horror Nights, we create living horror movies. So we want to make our guests feel like they got up from their movie seat, walked through the screen, and now they get to live through the world of *Evil Dead*. So we're bringing it to life with movie-quality sets, makeup, costumes and props. It'll be like living the experience for real."

Working closely with the original filmmakers, Universal was keen to build a house that not only featured all the classic components of the movie but also all the best scares that could be created in a way that wasn't predictable, so they would be presented totally fresh and incredibly scary. Fede Alvare who directed the 2013 movie said at the time, "It was mind-blowing. It was really like walking into the movie and having the chance to witness every crazy, gory moment of the movie firsthand, with people walking next to the characters. So it's amazing. It's so flattering and so great, and I think it's a great way to honor, not just the movie, but the Evil Dead franchise in general."

The event would also tie straight into the release of the Blu-ray for *The Evil Dead* movie, with copies of it available for sale at the event. Inside the house, all the classic elements of the movie were there, including the initial book reading, to exploring the basement, the tongue splitting scene, right down to the iconic approach to the cabin through the forest. The house was very popular and there were always long queues on every night of the event.

It was around late July that the announcement came that *The Walking Dead* would again be returning to the event. Building on the success and level of immersion of the previous year, Universal was to bring the horror TV series back to the park and showcase season 3 in the house and seasons 1 and 2 in the streets, where every scarezone would be dedicated to the popular show. The New York area of the park would show the fall of Atlanta from season one. This would be followed by the woodlands in the Central Park area. A Survivor's Camp was setup in the Kidzone area, which had been recreated exactly like the scene in the series. Mel's Drive-In area would feature the Farm, with detailed sets and props built with a mini-show that would be unlike anything seen at the event before, where a live disemboweling by various 'Walkers' would take place. This would be attached to Hollywood Boulevard where the Clear would be presented. This would be the first time in the event's history that the entire park would have a scarezone based on one single property. And if planned in advance, guests could walk all the scarezones in their order from the two seasons (as though they had been thrown into the actual show!) before enjoying the delights of season three inside the house. It was a hugely ambitious plan which was executed brilliantly at the Orlando event. Across the country in Hollywood they, too, had a house based on season three, that differed from the Orlando one by adding in a few additional scenes.

Proving their abilities at the last event, the producers of the show allowed the event's creatives to flourish for the planning of the house. "We didn't have any specific characters last year, but this year we're able to use Milton and Merle and Penny," Mike Aiello said at the time. This included recreating the house of Penny from the show, a house that has never been seen on screen but working with the producers the event could provide their version of what it could look like. Working with the Georgia-based producers of *AMC* enabled the event's Art and Design department to build a partnership that would not just last this event but would continue to the next year as well.

The house for the event was presented in the Parade building with the event's creatives again working closely with the original producers of the show. John Murdy said at the time, "it's fabulous to work with partners who are equally passionate and also get what we do." Walking the course back in the Spring of that year, the park's creatives and designers from the TV show especially chose the parade building to house the large maze. Mike Aiello said, "We knew we wanted to do the chain-link maze that has the tower as its focus point, that could not have been done anywhere but in a soundstage or B79 [parade float building]." Construction of the tower along with the prison scenes took all year, with the parade floats again relegated to another building. The house was topped-off with the inclusion of the twisted Governor who was seen throughout, taunting 'walkers' and guests alike. A neat addition to the house was a scareactor costumed as a 'walker' who had been chained up to the left, combined with a chainmail pen to the right, just outside the entrance. Scareactors working in tandem would work to make guests jump out of their skin as the lines snaked up and down around this area. It provided some entertainment watching unsuspecting guests, as there was no queue video.

Around August of this year all the other houses were announced via the event's official website and via their new Twitter account that had gone live at the end of July. Possibly the most anticipated and best house to ever be constructed at the event (this writer's opinion!) was the Universal picture *An American Werewolf in London*. The one house that Universal had been designing and planning without success for over six years, would now finally be brought to the event. Based on the original British-American movie from 1981, the house would take guests right back to that era for a journey through the moors of Yorkshire before heading down to London. The rumor was that the house had to be postponed from the year previous due to the construction of the new *Transformers* ride. The house would, for the first time, replace scareactors with huge puppets that would be controlled by a number of scareactors to great effect. Working in partnership with legendary movie director John Landis, the Orlando staff would work tirelessly to recreate the look and feel of the original movie. "It's something we've always wanted to do, and we've finally figured out a way that we'll be able to," said creative director Michael Aiello at the time. "The only way this could have happened as authentically as we've been able to do it was with John's involvement with us." Landis helped in all areas of the house's development, providing original source material and props that Universal could work from to create the scares. Weeks and months of planning were put into the exacting look of each werewolf where, like in the movie, full sized 8ft tall puppets were built. "They are using the exact same - now sort of dated but effective - technology that we used," Landis said. The creative makeup genius that is Rick Baker had originally made the puppets for the movie back in 1980. He spent just as much time back then building the animals and then working them on set as Universal was doing in 2013; Baker's tireless efforts to create the fiendish lycans actually awarded him his first Academy Award for makeup for that actual movie. "The attraction is really homage to Rick's work," Landis said.

But it wasn't just the werewolves that would be created to the exact specifications of 1981; the sound too would be directly recreated from the movie. "We had to go back to the original elements of the soundtrack and break down the tracks," Landis then said. "They used the sound effects from the film and the music from the film... They create a whole new ambience - but it's a new mix for this specific environment." Mike Aiello confirmed the dedication that was seen in creating the sound of the house by confirming the iconic howl of the werewolves had to be recreated to exacting parameters. "Capturing the sound of the wolf was incredibly important," he said. "We didn't want to try to replicate or re-create those sounds if we knew we could have access to them." The only way the house differed from the movie was that an active decision was made to tone the humor of the movie down inside the house and ramp up the scares instead. Starting off on the moors then travelling to the Slaughter Lamb pub, guests were then taken to London to see all the iconic scenes of the movie, including an indoor recreation of Piccadilly Circus and the London Tube. This culminated in one of the most elaborate scenes ever constructed where a scareactor costumed as the lead character from the movie (David) actually slowly transforms before your very eyes into a werewolf. Landis said at the time, "What I've come away with is I'm very impressed with how ambitious Mike is - they're building these very elaborate sets, fully realized reproductions of the Slaughtered Lamb, a bit of the tube station, Piccadilly Circus, the hospital. It's really an attempt to 'recreate in the flesh,' so to speak, an experience for the guests."

The house took the longest to build that year and was one of the last to be finished before the event. Built inside and occupying the whole of Soundstage 22 the house would combine intimate scenes such as the hotel with larger scenes like Piccadilly Circus where London cabs, double decker buses and even a police box (Tardis maybe?) would be recreated around the carnage of a werewolf loose in London. An impressive team of 60 scareactors would be deployed to work the house including an equal number of operations staff to keep the house alive and moving. It was possibly one of the most ambitious projects that had ever been created at the event. Landis was extremely positive and impressed with Universal's dedication to not only create the house but to painstakingly recreate all the scares from the movie. He said, "First of all, it's a theatrical event, an all-immersive theatrical event. It's very different from a film. What I hadn't considered before sitting down with the team was they have these practical realities of getting a certain number of people through, and just the logistics of the whole thing is complicated." Proud of the team he said finally, "These guys really are passionate about this stuff, there's a level of enthusiasm that's just infectious and wonderful. They love it, they really do!" The final touch of the house preparation and for one that Landis was present for, was the final attachment of the long running 'Easter egg' of every Landis movie, that of *See You Next Wednesday*. This time it would be manifested as a movie poster for eagle-eyed fans upon entering the Soho cinema scene of the house.

Next door to this house was another installment in the park's wishes to bring video games to the event. This was *Resident Evil: Escape From Raccoon City* which was located inside Soundstage 21. The house was billed as, "Raccoon City is overrun with Umbrella Corporation's most terrifying experiments, and the only option is complete destruction. You'll need to duck and dodge Lickers, Hunters, and Nemesis himself if you want any chance of escaping *Capcom*'s video game terrors before missiles send everything back to hell."

The event decided to not make the house from the recent franchise of movies that had been released, but to rather stick lovingly to the original *Resident Evil 2 and 3* video games. This even included a special scene towards the end of the house that included a 'paused screen', as the house was one giant video game that guests were experiencing, with the player of the game pausing it to go use the bathroom etc. This was a nifty idea but not popular with fans, who found the scene interesting but not scary. Working closely with the video game's creators *Capcom*, the house followed the story from the early noughties, and presented sets and costumes that looked very authentic to the original game.

The next house, located over in the Sprung Tents would be *Urban Legends: La Llorona,* a house that had been at the Hollywood event in the previous year. A house that was so popular it would go on to reach 'house of the year' status on the West coast. The house followed the tragic Mexican myth of Llorona or 'The Weeping Woman' which detailed the story of a mother killing her children before being damned to walk the earth for eternity. The house had borrowed half the sets from the Hollywood version of the house, before creating an entirely new path for the remainder. This noticeable difference saw guests enter into a small Mexican village, followed by chapel and crypt to then descend into the watery made world of the urban legend. The house was chilling and intense that mixed a variety of scares to create a truly terrifying experience.

Next to this house was *After Life Death's Vengeance* in Sprung Tent 2. The house used the 3D technology again to great effect. Universal billed the house as, "Serial killer Bobby "The Blade" is about to meet Ole' Sparky. 2000 volts are going to send him to a horrific realm of pain. His victims have waited an eternity for vengeance. They're bound to turn Bobby's afterlife into an unimaginable, infernal torment." Like the previous house, this one would be one of three that were entirely new concepts for the event and not linked directly to any other movie, TV or video game property. This would be the first house to use the 3D technology without using comedy; in fact, this year did not have a comical house at all. The house starts where we witness the execution of a serial killer, using a prop from a past year that had been entirely redressed to great effect. Soon guests descended via the turning vortex (used every year) into the afterlife, which allowed the 3D technology to confuse and disorientate guests throughout.

The final house of the event this year was a sequel to the popular *Havoc* house franchise that had been built up over the years. *Havoc: Derailed* would be presented in the *Disaster* queue building where actual train carriages had been set up to give the appearance of the misfit maniacs on the loose following the derailment of the train they were riding in. The house design was especially created to allow the event's creatives to experiment on a number of scares that they had been planning for a while. "Although the train cars are not moving, the house features a before-and-after motif. The crash point is accompanied by blinding light and very loud sound effects [to create the illusion of a train crashing]" Mike Aiello said at the time. "The back half was an easier build than the front half for us because building confined train cars is something we've never done before." This experimentation included the use of 'air-bladders' that were installed in the final scene to create a sense of chaos that would be used to push guests towards the exit while scareactors were attacking from all directions. "We're either (a) going to be really good at it or (b) we're going to learn from it," he said. "We do stuff like that every single year because it's the only way this event moves forward with the type of effects we do." It was truly inspiring to see the event still experimenting with ideas and concepts, which for an event that is over 20 years old is something very special indeed.

The two shows this year would see a return of two of the most popular. Bill and Ted were back with their usual comedy-music fest with references to: *The Big Bang Theory*, *Les Miserables*, Disney's construction of Avatarland, *The Man of Steel* and various lookalikes of Miley Cyrus, Justin Bieber, Anne Hathaway and Kim Kardashian featured in the final dance-off. The other show presented was a return of the popular *The Rocky Horror Picture Show - A Tribute* located again at the *Beetlejuice stage*.

Halloween Horror Nights 24

You've been warned!

It was late March of 2014 when we first received the news via the official event's website that there would be 8 houses, 2 shows and many street experiences. Dates for the event followed soon after. It wasn't until June 10th that we got our first indication of a house. The news websites and papers ran headlines such as "Walking Dead will overrun Universal for Halloween nights", and although it was an impressive feat to see the popular TV show back for a third year, some fans were less than impressed, though these seemed to be in the minority as most fans could recount the excessively detailed and memorable scares from the past two years (live disemboweling for example!).

The new house would feature all the key scenes and plot twists from the fourth season of the popular show. The news promised that the house would feature more scareactors and more elaborate scares than ever before. Guests would enter into the prison, walk through the cell block and then into an impressive scene with a crashed helicopter. In order to encompass the huge number of increased scareactors and massive set pieces, the house would be based inside Soundstage 25, which had never been used for the event before. The 11,000 square feet stage is one of two specially adapted stages that are just for the use of television production (due to the addition of additional rigs and a high-level gallery control room). Mike Aiello, director of entertainment for the event, said at the time, "We're bursting at the seams, as far as Soundstage 25 is concerned, by how much we're cramming into that space to ensure we're hitting all the necessary beats that are within season 4. Building the house inside this huge stage would effectively enable the house to be twice the size of any other. This fact was heavily marketed along with the tie-in that the event would begin around the same time as the show's fifth season.

The house started more or less in the queue where an impressive façade (probably the largest ever) had been created, complete with fencing and barbed wire. Guests queued along the façade until they entered. Once inside the house it did not feel claustrophobic, as the event's creatives had filled the giant scarezone with a labyrinth of rooms and set pieces. The number of scareactors deployed was very noticeable, there were 'walkers' coming at you from all angles, be they real actors or props. Moving on from the grocery store, guests would find themselves at the Country club and then finally at the walls of Terminus. Two very interesting scares were the use of lighting to make some prop 'walkers' appear to be running down a hall, when in fact they were stationary; the other being the forest scene where there must have been over 20 scareactors dressed as 'walkers' and a similar number of prop walkers disguised with the light effects. It was a hugely impressive house that probably made all the naysayers' jaws hit the floor, such was the detail and expansive size of the house.

It was then announced around July 16th that the next house to be revealed for the event would be *From Dusk Till Dawn* and would be located in Soundstage 22. The house would be based on the recent TV show and not on the movie of the same name. The original first season of the show ran on the *El Rey Network* in 2013, which had been produced by Robert Rodriguez who had originally directed the 1996 movie. Rodriguez and his team would work with Universal on both coasts to bring the house to both stateside events. "We will feature the over-the-top gore that the show does so well and our guests will come face-to-face with Robert's unique and wickedly cool take on the vampire mythos that is completely authentic to the show," said Aiello at the time. The house would be designed to reflect scenes from the first season but to also prepare guests for the second season that would debut during the event.

Entering in via the infamous Twister bar façade, guests would witness various half-naked vampire sirens that would titillate and terrify in equal portions. The house was the master this year of the distraction scare, where pole dancing vampires or vampires feasting on a dead patron would distract the eye just as another more hideous version would jump out from the side.

A few days later and the *SyFy* show of *Face Off* was announced with *Face Off: In The Flesh* to be debuted at the event in the streets. Laura Tyler, a Universal Orlando makeup artist, who had won the fifth series of the popular show would be on hand to oversee the scarezone and bring her award-winning scares to the streets of Hollywood Boulevard. "Our goal is to bring to life the macabre artistry displayed in the characters seen week after week," said Aiello at the time. Over the seven seasons of the show, ten iconic looks had been especially selected and then recreated for the scarezone. Each of the ten selected were then presented with their own set pieces from which they could scare and provide great photo opportunities.

This announcement was followed a few days later at the end of July by the announcement that *The Purge* was coming to the event. The popular film franchise would feature on the streets in the New York area as *Anarchy*. The two Universal pictures, which had been released on small budgets in 2013 and 2014 respectively, featured a dystopian world where the new government allows one night a year where there are no laws or police/ambulances etc. available. The wildly successful movies would be both used to simulate short show sequences on the streets to make it appear that the Purge was happening on the streets for real. This process would then mix characters from the movies with non-costumed scareactors (who appeared as guests), running and chasing them through the streets causing chaos and confusion in equal measures.

It was then on August 4th that *AVP: Alien vs. Predator* would be featuring at the event in Soundstage 24. Taking what Universal had learnt the year before by seamlessly mixing puppetry with real effects enabled them to create the alien species to great effect. Marking the double celebration of the 10th anniversary of the first *Aliens vs. Predator* movie and the 35th anniversary of the original *Alien* film, Universal wanted to present the characters in their true and terrifying presences in a way that would delight guests by showcasing their awesome wizardry.
"We're employing our full arsenal of tricks and techniques in translating the AVP: Alien vs. Predator brand into an authentic and horrific maze experience. Our guests are going to be thrown head first into this epic battle where only the strong will survive. This is truly going to be an out-of-this-world maze experience that the fans have been waiting for," said Aiello at the time.

In what was probably the best house for this year, the house told the story of base LV-426 that had been set up by the marines on a far and distant planet, only to be gate-crashed by a massive swarm of aliens and various predators hot on the prowl. All of the aliens featured were puppets, designed for the scare much like the American Werewolf puppets had been, the year before. These were met with huge predators over 6ft doing battle with various marines. The agreement with *Fox* for the use of characters enabled the creatives of the event to not tie the house to one specific time or place from any of the franchises, but would rather present various iconic scenes from the different movies.

Impressive scenes such as the chest-bursting predator on a sick bay bed to the marine being pulled down through the floor by a huge alien would all culminate with guests having to bend down or crawl out via a service tunnel with aliens attacking from above and both sides. It was truly an epic house that will go down in the event's history as one of the best.

Dracula Untold: Reign of Blood was next to be announced in early August. The house based of the recent movie of the same name would also be located in Soundstage 24. The movie, which wasn't released until October 10th would act as an 'immersive preview' that would take guests into the heart of the movie by exploring key scenes from a destroyed village and a network of caves before ending at the famous vampire's own castle. The house would also be shared with Hollywood where much of the same technique would be used, with the house choosing to focus on the horrors of Dracula, and the movie exploring his origins. John Murdy, creative director of the Hollywood event, said at the time, "But there is much more to the tale than just a dark figure lurking in the shadows, drinking blood. While *Dracula Untold* will reveal the origin story of the man who became Dracula, our 'Halloween Horror Nights' maze will invite guests to experience the atrocities Dracula imposed on his victims in the most frightening and immersive way possible." Like never before would Universal be giving guests the chance to preview a movie in this way before heading to the cinemas, a process which will likely evolve over time and become more important to the event.

The final IP house to be released for this year (announced on August 28th) would be based on one of the largest movie horror franchises of all time. *Halloween* would be presented for the first time at the Orlando event in Sprung Tent 2. "Guests will come face to face with Michael Myers as we re-create the kills committed the night he came home," said Aiello at the time. The house had been presented at the Hollywood event before mixing various scenes from various movies, whereas on the east coast the house was designed to encapsulate the horrors from the first movie. "It's our holy grail of horror films. It started the slasher genre and did it so well. It has all the right pieces essential to make a great horror maze: great character, inventive kills, really great story and iconic music," said Aiello. Rigidly sticking to the 1978 movie, the house would put every guest back into the scares from the iconic movie. Entering via the house façade of the movie, the façade would feature an impressive projection of the masked murderer to the front that appeared to show him smashing through the boarding to stare down at guests. Initially guests would see young Myers as he starts off his murderous career before witnessing all the key murder scenes from the movie through the rest of the house.

This release was followed by the final release of late August when Universal announced the final three houses to feature which would all be newly created original content for the event. These would be *Giggles & Gore Inc.* located in the *Disaster* queue building. The gory house would feature a factory of evil clowns with murderous intentions. Then the next house would be *Dollhouse of the Damned* located in the Sprung Tents. The house would feature an impressive façade of a giant doll's house, with dry ice and hysterical shrieks coming from within. Inside, a maniacal mix of mad people with grafted doll faces would terrorize guests throughout. The final house would be *Roanoke: Cannibal Colony* and would be located in the Parade building. It told the story of a recently relocated bunch of sixteenth century murderous cannibals as they adjust to their new surroundings whilst looking for food. Three houses were not easy concepts to bring to life when you have to start from scratch with an original idea, tell a story and make it come to life. "That's probably the hardest step in this process, and it's also the first one so that we can really make sure that, we're delivering on the expectation of what people know from Halloween Horror Nights but also surprise them with some things," said Aiello at the time.

Two further scarezones were presented this year, including *MASKerade; Unstitched* at the Plaza of the Stars area. The scarezone featured scareactors in impressive ball gowns dancing into the night as the skin on their faces is falling off. An impressive use of makeup was used to create the concept of wax and stitches being used whilst others were rounding up victims to have their skin removed. The final scarezone would be *Bayou of Blood* and would be located in the Central Park area. The zone would feature voodoo worshippers in a blood-filled frenzy attacking others to be provided as sacrifices for their rituals.

Two popular shows returned this year, those being *Bill and Ted* and *The Rocky Horror Picture Show Tribute*. The former featuring references to: the *Teenage Mutant Ninja Turtles'* movie from that year and the *Guardian of the Galaxy movie*, with an overall theme inspired from the movie *Neighbors* from that year.

Halloween Horror Nights 25

"25 Years of Fear"

HHN24 was not even over before a glimpse of what was coming for HHN25 was teased to Universal's social media followers on Halloween night. This was another first for HHN - they started teasing the coming year before the current event had finished (it had two nights left to run). The video showed a recap of the video from HHN24, followed by announcement of the dates for 2015 along with a final shadowy figure lurking in the background... an altogether familiar shadow at that! Fans were quick to notice that indeed, Jack was back.

It wouldn't be until around late May before Universal formally announced the crown prince of HHN would be returning to once again run amok; fans could not be happier.

Mike Aiello said at the time, "Among all the characters that have headlined Halloween Horror Nights over the last 25 years, Jack represents the event in the purest way possible - he is the embodiment of all the tricks and the treat." Aiello also announced that the event would run for a record 30 nights and would employ double the number of scareactors than in the previous year. Universal were ramming home the message that the 25th Anniversary would be the biggest and wildest HHN celebration ever.

On the same day as Aiello's announcement, the park also released the official dates and time along with a revised website showcasing the fact that we could all expect a record 9 houses (!), 5 scarezones and 2 shows. Many had questioned why Universal had released the house number so early. It was likely that a leaked document into the fan community some months earlier may have been to blame. The leaked list was eventually proven to be correct, albeit with the exception of one house that just happened to be changed at the last minute.

May gave way to June and another huge announcement followed:

Freddy Krueger and Jason Voorhees would be coming to HHN25. The duo would be making their return to East coast, following their last successful stint at the event for 2007's *Carnival of Carnage*. Aiello again took to the airways to explain the duo's return, "Guests walking through the house will first see Camp Crystal Lake. The first portion of the maze features 'all Jason' and his various kills. Fans of the brand will recognize many of the scare scenes from the movie franchise. The second portion focuses on Freddy as guests are transported to Elm Street through the dream realm. The maze ends with guests caught in the middle of a Freddy-and-Jason fight, complete with machetes and Freddy's knife glove flying, as the two battle it out to a gruesome, bloody end. The maze's end should appease both fandoms. Each set will alternate between Freddy emerging victorious and Jason pulling out the final win."

Just like the movie, the house would end in an epic battle of evil vs evil. The film would leave it somewhat ambivalent as to the winner of the battle; however Universal would rotate the winner to ensure a fair balance between the two. It was said that every 45 minutes there would be a cast change and each cast would have 'their winner', in order to keep things fair (just in case you were keeping score!). Two stuntmen were employed to film a number of the battle sequences, sequences that were filmed on site in the same soundstage and then projected using HD projectors onto the walls of the house. They added the odd real physical effect plus an epic soundtrack to ensure that the guests felt that they really were surrounded by these two doing battle.

Universal had promised double the number of scareactors, and they weren't messing around, with various Jason(s) popping out at unsuspecting guests right from the entrance. It is interesting to note that all the actors that played Jason were specifically selected for their body size, along with being all being between 6ft 3 to 6ft 8 in height. Elaborate sets, along with detailed environments, and an experimental underwater scene were all added. These were complemented with full-sized mannequins of some of the most famous kills from their respective movie franchises.

July rolled around and another house was announced to high praise; *Insidious* would be coming. The house didn't make headlines, but fans could not be happier; many speculated how such a house could be achieved and what it might contain. The speculation reached fever pitch during the early months.

It was located in Sprung Tent 2, and Universal released the following description: "Enter The Further and travel through all three parts of the Insidious saga. Denizens of the afterlife try to find their way back into the world using the living to guide them. The house isn't haunted--we are."

Many were a little disappointed at the news the house would be situated in the Sprungs. The Sprung tents by this time in the event's history were seen as perhaps the poor relative to the superior soundstages; however, Universal had further tricks up their sleeve to really enhance the Sprungs. With another event first (see a theme here?), Universal would provide the Sprungs with two new experimental devices that the other houses did not share. The first would be to finally correct the ills of the previous years with the Sprungs, and to finally blackout the light. Many had complained over the years that the Sprungs simply weren't worth entering until darkness had fallen; this was especially noted as in past years they had often opened first to guests in the penned areas. Universal set about correcting this fault by installing a number of blackout sheets, first to the ceilings and then to every wall. Finally, the park creatives could work in spaces where light was no longer a problem and the idea of closeness and intimacy could be really exploited for the better gain. The second aspect of the house that was an event first, was the installation of a post-house scare. The Sprungs could exploit their setting of being out back to good use with the additional space they had, which was unlike the Soundstages which often had very little room to operate (though they also did have some post-house scares too). The post-house scare would see guests leaving via the exit and walking along a rather straight platform to regain the path back to the park. Unsuspecting guests would then chatter about the delights of the house they had just experienced without knowing that those stacked crates along the path hid the Lipstick-Demon, who would infrequently pop-out at guests and give them all once last fright; top work Universal!

Shortly after the *Insidious* statement, there was an announcement that for the fourth time, *The Walking Dead* would again be returning to the event. This was met with a collective sigh from the fan community, who craved something new. However, everyone was reminded that the show was wildly popular with the general public and after all, we were getting a record nine houses this year! It was also announced that the house would be based on the then current fifth season, which was mirrored in Hollywood's event too. The house also featured many event firsts and proved to be a great house that was unfortunately not without its faults. The designers started by making the house the tallest house they'd ever produced. Many houses start off with huge lush facades that gradually become confined and narrow in their presentation along tight corridors, but not with this house. Every show scene would maximize as much head room as possible to give guests the feeling that they were fully enclosed in every scene. Nowhere better was this device used than in the supermarket floor cave-in scene. The notorious scene in the series saw our heroes fall through a rotten supermarket fall into a basement filled with water and flesh-eating zombies. It would be here that guests would do battle with another (!) event first, the installation of scareactors in water. Guests would see 'walkers' lunge at them from specially-created water pools that would splash and distract the flow of guests to provide better scares. What 99% of people walking through this scene missed, was that an actual lifeguard was sitting above the entrance watching the actors as they performed. This was the first time in the event's history that such a role had ever been required. The park's creatives had always ensured that each time the *Walking Dead* could come back, but on the basis that the house would outdo the previous year's incarnation. If 2014 would see the largest ever HHN house, then 2015 would be the tallest and the wettest. A promise that was performed perfectly well.

The next house to be announced with more gusto than some of the other houses was *The Purge*. "Just like in the film, guests will find themselves within arm's reach of the most sadistic collection of killers imaginable. Their only want and need is to express their right to purge and purge they will." said Aiello. Universal billed the house as "This year's Purge is more brutal than ever. From the moment you step inside the house, dozens of vicious vigilantes will descend upon you as they exercise their right to purge."

The house would spark much debate within the fan community as rumors swirled that the house had been added in at the last minute. The rumors continued when the event started, as the setting within the house appeared to be all too familiar to a fellow horror franchise. The rumors were compounded further with the leakage of the official HHN trailer showing Ghostface from the *Scream* franchise ready to slay unsuspecting victims. The true answer to what happened will surely never be fully known. Safe to say, the house looked as though it may have been built for the *Scream* franchise, and that for whatever reason, the decision had been made to adapt the house into *The Purge*, a Universal property. A former Universal Team Member who didn't want to be named told us:

"Word "officially" came down that things would not pan out for the *Scream* maze two weeks before rehearsals were scheduled for the performers. It was admittedly an issue that the company was aware of prior to this, but the hope was that things would work out.

The performers are able to see their role name and location based on an internal scheduling software. This changed and the word spread amongst the scareactors that something was awry. *Scream* is owned by *Dimension Films* (now part of *The Weinstein Company*, abbreviated as *TWC*). The

Ghostface name and mask is owned by *Fun World*. When the script for *Scream* was written, the killer was described as in a mask and black cloak. The specifics weren't figured out until the film's pre-production phase. During this phase, the team found a "Ghostface" mask by *Fun World* that looked like a "ghost in pain." *Dimension* signed an agreement with *Fun World* to license the mask. The team changed the mask and the version they settled upon replaced the old mold originally licensed by *Dimension* due to the film's popularity.

The *MTV* series was considered the new direction for the franchise. The producers of the *MTV* series opted not to license the *Fun World* mask and instead had a new mask designed for the production. Universal Orlando licensed the film and masks, but the final approval of the maze was with *Dimension/TWC*, who owned the property.

There were disagreements between the Universal and *Dimension/TWC* on the direction of the maze. It should be noted that Universal Hollywood had difficulties with *Dimension/TWC* when they used *Scream 4* for the *Terror Tram*. Interestingly enough, *Scream* and *The Purge* were left off the merchandise. The announcement of that Sprung Tent maze was delayed until they were able to secure *The Purge*.

The Purge was retrofitted into the Sprung Tent in less time than A&D had to construct Universal's *House of Horrors* in 2012. One interesting thing to note is the abundance of "empty" space with projections overlayed. In these places, A&D ripped out entire set pieces. All of the remaining set pieces were meant for *Scream*. The original maze would have been based on the first film and taken guests throughout an abridged version of the movie, much like the *Halloween* maze.

Some of the *Purge* actors still used the knife Ghostface uses in *Scream*. The eviscerated corpse inside the *Purge* was intended to be Drew Barrymore's character. The scene where guests walk through a garage had an empty space for a corpse of Rose McGowan's character. *Scream* likely won't be licensed again for use at Halloween Horror Nights. Perhaps this will change in a few years depending on the state of the franchise."

Whatever happened, it can be said that Universal's endeavors to work with and gain new IPs for the event shows just how much work and how complex such a negotiation can be, particularly on exceedingly tight timeframes. Regardless of what may or may not have occurred, the house was a sure hit for vast majority of the paying guests. An interesting fact about the house was the use of 'fake guests'. A popular technique that had returned for 2015 would see guests within the queue selected at random (though obviously they were scareactors in disguise) who would be thrown into the action and receive throat-slices. This was an added level of terror that had not been seen for many years at the event. The throat-slice would also go on to become a theme that would run through every house at the event, where at least one victim in every house would receive this painful treatment – did you spot them all?

It was August and the final reveal occurred, showcasing all the other additional houses, scarezones and shows. The next house that receive great reviews was *Asylum in Wonderland 3D*, which, in an event first (again), it would be presented inside the *Shrek* attraction. *Shrek*'s second theater is an overflow theater for busy park days, and the theater was taken out of use some months previously while the house was quietly constructed inside. The house effectively was built as a self-contained shell within the theater. Other than the fixed chairs, no other *Shrek* features or effects were removed to accommodate the house. The carpets would be protected, the curtains wrapped and the walls lined with timber boarding; this way the house would be demolished quickly without damage to ensure the second theater could quickly be reopened for the attraction. In reality, the night of the event's final day would see the construction crews enter to begin the striking, and within 3 days the theater had reopened.

The 3D technology (or Chromadepth to give its proper name) would again be deployed for an ultra-decorative and intense house. This replaced the laughs of previous years with an interesting background story that left guests questioning what they had seen. Was this an imaginative world from the Alice book or was this the twisted mind of a demented girl named Alice? The house would feature a dayglow color palate that mixed creepy versions of the popular children's story and had the odd nod to event's past by featuring Tweedle Tweek and Tweedle Foon for example. This was all delivered via an impressive entrance façade through the pages of Universal's Ultra Violent Comics handle.

The next house would be a return of a much loved but updated classic, *RUN: Blood, Sweat, and Fears* and would be located in the *Disaster* overflow queue, a location that would see this house end up as the very last inhabitant for HHN. Universal billed the house as, "You've just been selected as a contestant on *RUN*, a brutal TV show where everyday people are stalked by skilled assassins. Just remember: the more horrifying your death, the higher the ratings."

The house would prove to be the weakest link of the nine presented this year (in our opinion), though the competition would prove to be one of the strongest house line-ups ever.

The next house to return would be *An American Werewolf in London.* The house would see a recreation of the incredibly popular past house, but with one hugely notable difference: different puppets. John Landis, the director of the original movie, was said to have disliked the puppets that were built for the first house. It was rumored (though never confirmed) that he agreed that the house could return on one condition: that the puppets be updated to look more like the original movie. For, this Universal had to turn to just one man: Rick Baker. Universal reached out to Baker via a mutual friend who agreed to lend Universal his original 1980s plans/designs that showed Universal how to build the puppets exactly like-for-like. This process raised the authenticity of the house to exceptionally new high levels. The puppets were staggering in their appearance, truly frightening. Universal never released how much the puppets cost to completely recreate, though when I pressed them on the matter they quipped off-the-record "as much as your car", and this author happens to drive a nice car too!

The event would be crowned by a centerpiece that was *Jack Presents: 25 Years of Monsters and Mayhem* and would technically be one of the longest in the event's history (though this is disputed), with 15 rooms and 15 corridors. The house would see our ever-popular host present some of the best and most frightening scares from the 25 years back catalogue of HHN. Past houses, including *The Freightantic, The Forsaken, Scary Tales, Nightingales,* and *Gothic,* along with appearances from nearly every icon and every iteration of Jack would be present, from 90s Jack to 2015's haggard Jack. The house would also provide a social media phenomenon, that of HHN Bear (who you can still follow on Twitter). The Bear would provide updates on his official (unofficial?) twitter page, and was also rumored to do specific dances if the right catchphrase was said upon entering his hut.

The last house in the line-up would be one with the most impressive façade and would be a solid fan-favorite: *Body Collectors – Recollections.* The house would actually feature a composite of two HHN fan franchises; that of *Body Collectors* and the inmates of Shadybrook (*Psychoscareapy*). The house would be located in Soundstage 24 and would feature an almost full-sized façade of the Shadybrook Institute covered in snow during an almighty blizzard. The house would again feature many highlights from *Body Collectors* houses of the past, including the infamous backbone rip scene, a scene that was also recycled for a movie that was shot on the lot at Universal called *Scare Zone* (2009). It is apparently available via some on-demand movie rental sites online. It would also feature a great 'Easter egg' of baby Jack and his brother Eddie being born amongst the carnage and terror within the corridors of Shadybrook.

Think Fear was not featured at HHN25? Think again, eagle eyed fans of the grotesque overlord were quick to spot that Universal setup his famous lantern within the entrance of the 'Evil's Roots' scarezone, right opposite Animal Actors

Many had expressed concerns that the increased number of houses combined with the massive potential of each house could lead to the streets becoming a bit of a damp squib. The level of how wrong people could be was staggering; the streets would, for the first time in years, prove to be as popular as the houses. The first would be *Scary Tales – ScreamPunk* right at the front of the park in the Plaza of the Stars. It would feature classic fairy tales with sinister twists that would be presented in the popular 'steampunk' tradition. The bottleneck aspect of the run combined with the entrances of the soundstages proved a difficult location for the scareactors to perform, though the area would ultimately provide some of the best scareactors performances.

Next up would be *Psychoscareapy – Unleashed* in the New York Streets, which was a fantastic, multifaceted experience, with multiple sideshows mixed in with a creepy block party gone wrong. Universal billed it as, "The criminally insane inmates of Shadybrook Asylum have escaped and stumbled upon a Halloween Block party in the streets of New York. They quickly decide they'd kill for some costumes of their own." The mix of comedy and scares proved to be a winning formula for the event, so much so that the scarezone was incredibly popular with the public at large. The next most popular scarezone would prove to be neighboring one, with the *All Nite Die-In – Double Feature* located in the short San Francisco/*Disaster* area of the park. The zone would be a recreation of the popular 2009 scarezone of the same name based in the infamous *Carey Drive-In Theater*. The zone would feature ghosts, goblins and monsters from past HHNs that would be delivered in a clever way. At the beginning of the night, the monsters from the classic Universal area would be presented (Dracula, Frankenstein's Monster, the Invisible Man etc.), all of whom would be seen in classic black and white. These would soon make way for color versions, followed by more recent incarnations and modern classic horror movies, such as Chucky. All of which would be topped-off by the appearance of recent characters towards the end of each evening, including Freddy and Jason from their nearby house.

The HHN icons would all be back (except Bloody Mary) and would be located in the Hollywood area of the park. The scarezone would be less scarezone and more sideshow. Each icon would be set up on a specific platform with a complete setting (such as a cinema for the Usher or a library for the Storyteller). They would interact with guests all night long, in-between short shows where they would perform for the guests followed by plucking more 'fake guests' from the crowds to provide ritualistic deaths for all to see. The final scarezone would be *Evil's Roots* located in the popular corridor of Central Park. It would see a hotchpotch of returning nightmares who, with distractive sets and bellows of dry-ice, would pop-out to the flows of people to provide some nice scares.

Two shows would be presented this year, including the stalwart *Bill and Ted's Excellent Halloween Adventure*, which for many was unremarkable this year There was also a new (though technically a repeat) show of *The Carnage Returns*, which was a fantastic addition for this year. Located in the Mel's Drive-In area it would feature everyone's favorite clown flanked by his murderous partner-in-crime Chance, both of whom were played excellently by the same original actors. It would feature a combination of horror and comedy that only Jack knows best (and if you disagree then you know Jack). It would include murderous and elaborate murder that would be the envy of any mad magician, combined with dancing and musical numbers. It was probably one of the best shows the event had put on for years, and to see the original actors once again was truly brilliant.

Other event firsts included: a much-expanded musical presence with a soundtrack for the streets that was over three-figures in total tracks. The next addition would prove to be wildly popular: a brand new exclusive store for HHN. The Twister attraction by this time was earmarked for demolition straight after the event's run to make way for a Jimmy Fallon attraction and whilst the store lay empty, the Universal Creatives put it to good use. The new store featured all the regular HHN merchandise such as lanyards, tees, cups, shot glasses etc., but would also provide limited edition prints and props, made especially for the store. The event would surely be a mixture of retrospectively celebrating the past 25 years of HHN history but also brought event-firsts for nearly every aspect of HHN in Orlando. The mixture for which was so successful that the ability for Universal to surpass this will prove to be a real challenge for HHN26.

Halloween Horror Nights 26 - You Don't Have A Chance!

It was the very last night of HHN25 on November 1st that the dates for the following year's event would be released. The 2016 event was to run from September 16th to October 31st. The event hadn't even finished and fans were already speculating and looking forward to another year of horror goodness. And they didn't have to wait long either, as it was February 18th when packages, tickets and tours went on sale to the general public. They also released the specific dates, that ran to a record 31 nights. HHN news throughout the year would be pretty quiet until the spring, when the first house announcements occurred. These would, however, be overshadowed by tragedies at both home and abroad that would make the horrors of real life all too real. Due to these, the Orlando Sentinel reported that guest numbers at all nearly all Central Florida tourist attractions were lower than expected.

The first announcement came on April 14th when Universal declared that the original *Texas Chainsaw Massacre* from 1974 would be designed for the event and located in Sprung Tent 2. Mike Aiello told the Universal blog:

"As creators of Halloween Horror Nights, we have the privilege of bringing to life many popular horror films. Every now and then, we are able to replicate one that forged the reason horror has become such a factor in many of our lives. The original The Texas Chain Saw Massacre is undoubtedly on that short list. Like all of you, the horror fan in me is looking forward to reliving this story and entering that dilapidated Texas farmhouse. The anticipation of coming face-to-face with a horror legend and having my screams drowned by that saw blade is just as prevalent now as when I first witnessed this amazing horror film decades ago."

Leatherface and his warped family would be featuring in the event putting guests right at the heart of the action. Leatherface had featured at the Orlando event before but from the rebooted version and not the original source material. This 2007 house was located in the outdoor and airy queue building formerly holding *The Earthquake/Disaster* extended queue. This house featured outdoor portions and gave Leatherface the space to run and charge at guests through the iconic hanging linen sheets. So it was a surprise to the fan community that the house would be positioned in the almost entirely indoor close quarters of one of the Sprung Tents. Aiello took to Twitter to quash any concerns that people had by informing everyone that the house would be nightmarish with its attention to detail but also in claustrophobic feeling, where multiple Leatherfaces would be getting up close and personal with all guests daring to enter his family house.

It was two weeks later and Universal released another huge surprise to fans of horror everywhere with the announcement that they were building *The Exorcist* houses on both coasts. Aiello again took to the blog to make the big announcement:

"As with any horror property we collaborate with, our job is to create an attraction that adapts that property into a fully realized experience. That adaptation is a creative challenge in every case.

But translating *The Exorcist* presented us with many unique tests and questions. One big question was, "How do you adapt a film where most of the story takes place in a single bedroom?" The answer we landed on was first to break down and assess all the visuals and moments from the film. Piece together every moment within that bedroom and examine why it was intense, scary or even vile. What textures can we reconstruct differently, sometimes in an incredibly abstract way? The famous "pea soup" scene for instance. What if we were surrounded in the materials of the retch-covered bed? What if those layers of mattress padding literally enveloped us? And let's be honest, traversing through a vomit-covered bed is pretty horrifying and disgusting by itself. Now add a possessed girl into the mix!"

The house at Orlando would go down in history as being one of the most brutal on our five senses and be unique in that instead of everyone being terrified by the same aspect, everybody would be seen to leave that house being terrified by a whole manner of different factors. This author was interviewed by *Fox News* at the time, describing the dank hanging mattresses covered in sticky pea soup with the smell of fresh vomit pumped in. Still to this day, it terrifies me to think about it. The team at Universal would work tirelessly to make what is essentially a one-room-movie into a whole house, taking every shocking detail and manifesting it into terrifying real-world scares. The house was a huge success in scaring guests, so much so that it perhaps it received shorter queues with many people shaking their heads and refusing to enter! Chickens...

The story of how the house came to be is fascinating. The property had been unofficially seen in the very early days of HHN (look before the internet!) where unnamed girls on beds covered in green slime would be wheeled around the event to scare guests. After a few close shaves with IP holders, the park decided to keep any further such moves to a minimum and instead go after the rights to these outside IPs using the proper channels. Many were, and still are, applied for every year with the successes making their way to the event as the houses and scarezones we all know and love. *The Exorcist* was one of many that the event tried to obtain the rights to in the 1990s when the franchise was still alive and being made into various sequels; all such attempts however failed to get the franchise at the event. Aiello would tell the *ScareZone Podcast* that year that the property had become "something of our white whale for us as it was something we had wanted to do for years." John Murdy from Hollywood's HHN would say at *ScareLA* convention that the formal discussions to bring the house to HHN had been started in earnest all the way back in 2005 (some 11 years!).

The deal to make the iconic movie into a house would spring from Universal's excellent relationship with the IP holders, *Warner Bros*. Universal had continually exceeded all expectations with the Hollywood based company with their partnership to bring the *Wizarding World of Harry Potter* to their Universal parks and resorts around the world. This partnership of excellent financial returns for hyper detailed attractions and environments would ensure that Universal could gain more and more access with *WB*. Eventually, Universal was in a place to ask for this franchise and permission, after a couple of years of discussions was fully granted. The majority of the discussions would fall onto how the house could be conceived to make it fit the haunted house format, this was a concept that Universal took time and money to develop to ensure the finished product was its usual world class standard.

A week later and Universal announced the return of *The Walking Dead* to the popular event with a house that would serve as a 'best-of' house replicating a number of scares from past houses and scarezones that had all been within the banner of *TWD*. The house was arguably one of the best houses from this TV franchise and had a much-increased number of walkers stalking the tight corridors of the house in Soundstage 24. Fans weren't so impressed to see the franchise return for a fourth year but the mixture of past scares and the increased walkers made up for what could have been "just another" *TWD* house.

A month later on June 9th and the main tickets are put on sale along with the first glimpse of our icon for this year, Chance. Last seen in the previous year as the sidekick girlfriend to the maniacal Jack, the creatives behind HHN decided to give Chance her own chance to take the spotlight:

"For us, Halloween Horror Nights 26 literally takes place where we left off. The aftermath of the carnage is still fresh and Chance finds herself incarcerated for the crimes of last year. With the "Jack in the Box" on an evidence shelf somewhere waiting for someone to turn the crank once more, Chance bides her time within her cell. But this is not a tragedy for her. This prison is a toy box. It's within the confines of her cell that she enters her horrific "theatre of the mind". She knows that the acts committed inside her mind will manifest in the real. Both equally deranged and gothically beautiful."

It was rumored that Chance would dominate the event but with news that Chance would not, like Jack before her, have her own show this puzzled fans. Many speculated that her presence in the park may, for one reason for another, have been scaled down. Instead, she would have her own house and scarezone where actresses made-up in full costume would goad and pose with guests much to the satisfaction of all. Her house would be *Lunatics Playground 3D: You Won't Stand a Chance* which had the working title/codename of *ABBA* (*Take a Chance On Me* – get it?) and would be located in a brand new house for HHN next door to the popular *Men in Black* attraction. A temporary building purposely built for HHN inside the extended queue area (much akin to the Sprung Tents) would house the event's only 3D maze for the event. The house would divide fans, with some loving its fun and playful presentation, whereas other complained that the 3D use took away from the storyline. Whatever your opinion it would set a precedent on the number of houses with this new location. Her scarezone *A Chance In Hell* would be located at the front of the park and feature mini-shows all night with deranged Chance followers lurking amongst the hordes of guests flooding into the park from the main gates. The look of Chance was changed this year to a more meaner costume with more detailed makeup – the design would be the first redesign of the character since her debut in 2007 which was overseen by Evan Moore who had also worked on her makeup every year the character has been seen at the event.

Moving into early July and the next big announcement was the return of another popular horror franchise with *Halloween: Hell Comes To Haddonfield*. The house would see the return of Michael Myers in a recreation of his second movie *Halloween 2*. Located in the parade building, the house would literally start off where the movie does in the closet and take guests through every iconic scene -even the fire at the movie's epic climax. The previous Myers house was a huge hit, winning house of the year in 2014, so to see him return ramped up the excitement for the horrors that awaited.

A month later on August 4th and the next house was announced with a recreation of the popular recent movie *Krampus*. The movie had long been rumored for the event and would be built inside *Shrek theater 2*. The house would follow the story of the movie and take guests inside the family home being ransacked by murderous snowmen, knife welding gingerbread men and the big horned Krampus himself. One of the event's main writers and show directors, Charles Gray said:

"The Engel home is decked out for the holidays and all of you are invited to join them. From the myriad of dark elves, gingerbread men wielding nail guns, and the engorged Jack-in-the-Box, to my favorite... the Teddy Bear, each room is full of its own horrifying moments pulled from the film. You'll not only try and dodge the invading dark elves around every corner, but will also have to keep your holiday spirits up, while sneaking past the looming presence of Krampus himself. Each encounter with Krampus holds its own unique perspective, as he gathers more souls for his sinister workshop. The excitement for this property, and what it adds to this year's event, is the same excitement as waiting to see what Santa has left under the tree. Mixing two cups of horror with humor, a tablespoon of trick, with a dash of treat, and you'll receive the most gruesome holiday gift ever. Remember, it's better to give than receive... unless you're Krampus. He only takes!"

Krampus would feature a huge assortment of purpose built monster puppets throughout. Three full-size 7 foot tall Krampuses were built. Hollow fiberglass shells for the scareactors to await unsuspecting guests plus figures overhead. They were created in a joint venture with *Dynamic Designs* who built the creatures allowing specialist makeup and hair by Universal's extraordinarily talented Michael Burnett and his Universal team at Art and Design. The costumes were also all designed and prepared by the great Universal artisan Danielle Burnett.

It was then a few days later on August 10th that the rest of the houses and scarezones were announced. Or at least we thought that was the final announcement! *Tomb of the Ancients and Ghost Town: The Curse of*

Lightning Gulch would be built; the former in Sprung Tent 1 and the latter in Soundstage 24. Both houses would be original houses using wholly new storylines and concepts to terrify guests. Ancients would be a mash-up of ancient ruins being explored for the first time, mixing in elements of a certain popular archaeologist along with a claustrophobic setting that actively put SIF (Stuff In Face) on the map. All of which came to a fateful climax with the introduction of the crocodile-come-lion puppet (crocolion!) that lunged for guests as they exited the popular house. Ghost Town would also prove immensely popular with its use of water effects for the rain (though these were toned down after the first few nights as guests complained of getting too wet) along with wind effects, lightning effects, a great storyline and huge, highly detailed full-sized sets.

The *American Horror Story* House had a 'cameo of the future' with a scene that featured carpeting from *The Shining* FUN EAR FACT

It had been assumed by this point that the houses for the year had all been announced bar one. It was then Universal threw us all a massive curve ball and instead of announcing the remainder house, they announced an additional upcharge house. A house that would mix 1-2-1 storytelling and virtual reality to create a house that had never been seen before on any *Halloween* haunted house event, let alone HHN. The Repository would be built and located away from the main park next to the *Blue Man Group theater* in the event's first ever upcharge house. It would be TJ Mannarino Senior Director of Art & Design who would explain the wholly new concept:

"This is one of the most electrifying Halloween Horror Nights' project I've ever worked on – primarily because it is the culmination of 8 years of experimental story-telling, drawing on feedback from our vast HHN audience to learn what thrills and chills them the most. Throughout this heart-pounding, psychological journey, guests' most personal and intimate fears will be tested as they encounter real-life characters in highly themed physical environments, while working together in teams of four to uncover a paranormal mystery told through the use of the cutting-edge technology.

All of this is set in a centuries old warehouse where paranormal and supernatural artifacts have been collected and stored for hundreds of years. Recently though, the secretive organization behind this practice has installed state-of-the-art technology that allows spectral transportation into paranormal realms."

The website was updated to include:

"You and three others will find yourselves isolated in an ancient warehouse, left to your own skill and quick thinking to solve this haunting real-world horror experience's mysteries: Why is a former Scottish armory built in 1775 just before the American Revolution still in use today? What does a tragic fire in Scotland in 1795 have to do with events more than two centuries later? Is the "Grimslew Curse" real? Do you dare risk finding out? Learn for yourselves just what The Repository holds in its inventory. The bizarre relics gathered here have absorbed the energy of the horrific events with which they are associated. Some say they are infected by these dark circumstances. Others believe the objects were actually the cause of these misfortunes. Once you escape from The Repository you will know the haunting truth. Enter this rich, deeply themed physical environment, where you'll interact with both live scareactors and cutting-edge technology, get thrust into an original, terrifying story and face the challenge of a cryptic, daunting escape puzzle. This extensive, immersive experience goes beyond horror, beyond virtual reality and beyond anything you have ever imagined."

The upcharge house would be priced reasonably at $49.99 plus tax per person and would give guests a more personal experience than the usual conga lines of the other houses. Working in pairs, guests would have several challenges to complete to move onto the next area. Portions of the experience were in VR, and the whole experience was timed and would last most people between 1 to 2 hours. The house had been in development with an outside provider of VR for many years with super fans of the event secretly testing the technology in the previous year within the extended area of *The Mummy* ride. This is where this year's HHN merchandise store would be based following the construction of the *Jimmy Fallon ride*.

The final announcement on August 16th would be the addition of *The American Horror Story* franchise coming to the event. The popular franchise had never been done at HHN before and would be located inside Soundstage 19. The house would be a huge hit with guests, with people lining up for the house in their hundreds. The house would primarily focus on three different seasons of the popular TV show, these were: *Season 1: Murder House*, *Season 4: Freak Show* and *Season 5: Hotel*; all of which, unlike *The Walking Dead* would feature the characters from the show. Universal's hyper-detailed set design and effects were combined with scareactors playing very close representations of the classic

291

characters from the show, and played enormously well with the public. The huge demand for the house and the seamless way in which the house worked ensured the house would win 'house of the year' for the sheer awesomeness that it provided.

One of the biggest dramas behind the scenes this year occurred when Hurricane Matthew formed in the seas to the south of Florida. As soon as it was upgraded to a category 5 'major hurricane' status Universal had to think seriously about the effects on the event. As the hurricane left Cuba and gathered strength over the ocean it was projected to hit Central Florida, that's why on October 6th the decision was finally made to cancel that weekend's HHN (this also included the park). Luckily, the storm soon passed and did not cause as much damage and disruption that had been projected by the meteorologists. Universal then took the unprecedented step of adding an additional week to the end of the event bringing the dates well into November, along with honoring select tickets and frequent fear passes too. Behind the scenes it caused a number of logistical problems, no less the fact that the Scareactors contracts would expire the weekend before and many had plans to not work that extra weekend. Luckily, the reduced number of scareactors was met with a reduced footfall through the gate. My colleague Logan Sekulow attended that last weekend and said that the low visitor numbers really ramped up the scares and made him feel like he was back at old school HHN. Some of the houses such as *Tomb of the Ancients* and *The Exorcist* decided to pulse groups through as the lines were so short, these small groups entering at one time, instead of the conga lines, was said to enhance the scares ten-fold.

> The last show of the *Bill and Ted show* on the last night is always the best. Often, the actors add new lines and in-jokes from the run and do their own dance numbers. Want to see it? Get there earlier! This is a very popular tradition for uber HHN fans. FUN FEAR FACT!

Other than the hurricane, the event did make international headlines, making it 'the' place to go that Fall. Universal's Marketing Department headed to London to speak to the various outlets in Britain, along with various big pushes in Mexico. This vastly increased media attention for what was being dubbed "the greatest Halloween event in the world" also attracted an increased number of celebrities to the event. Many were rumored and many were spotted privately going on tours (from A-list Hollywood types to infamous rappers!). No celebrity made more of an impression than Steve Tyler from *Aerosmith*, who for the first time in HHN history, was allowed to attend the event on a private *RIP tour* but dressed as Rhett Butler from *Gone With The Wind*. The famous musician who got equally famous this year for a certain hand gesture in his ride at Disney's Hollywood Studios was making his annual pilgrimage to his ride and decided to see what "all the fuss was about" at Universal; he was alleged to have had "the best time" one Universal Team Member told me.

Uncharacteristically, the scarezones would all be announced in one large bunch via Universal Orlando' blog on August 10th, they included the usual assortment of varying themes all highly detailed and located in highly considered locations. The number this year had been reduced to afford more detail per zone. Possibly the weakest of the offerings was *Survive or Die Apocalypse* located in Central Park which was dubbed as:
"A Global catastrophe has ruined Earth's atmosphere. Now three warring gangs fight for control of a machine that provides clean air. All three gangs are looking for new members to help them destroy the others. Join them, or feed their starving ranks."
Not as gripping as the area had been for the previous year the zone acted as a great buffer for unexpecting patrons waiting to choose which house to venture in next or those that were looking for the new merchandize location (it had moved to the extended *Mummy* queue for this event whilst *Twister* was in construction with *Jimmy Fallon*); also located here was *Layer of the Banshee*, which also did not provide the scares. Further down the way in San Francisco was *Dead Man's Wharf* which was highly themed featuring dead zombie-like seaman rising from their watery graves to stalk victims within the fog. The impressive set and character design allowed for highly anticipated scares but also in great photo opportunities; talking of which, our next two zones provided a lot of opportunities for the scareactors to act up to the cameras; it was also awarded Scarezone of the year by Universal's management. The bottle-necking Plaza of the Stars would feature our icon Chance's own zones which acted as more of a show. *A Chance In Hell* would see our icon engage with guests on her own purpose made stage providing gags and goads in equal quantities. The icon however, was not played by Erin the main Chance actress – must to everyone's disappointment, however the actresses who played the character on the nightly stage did a good job. The final scarezone would be *Vamp 55* and would be located around the corner in Hollywood. 'Grease meets Dracula' as one commentator put it. The highly popular zone was described as:
"Welcome to Hollywood High School's 1955 Homecoming Parade. Everything is perfect until the greasers roll into town with fangs as sharp as their switchblades. The festive scene has turned to chaos as vampires attack from all around." Popular with HHN fans and public alike the zone became a mini internet sensation inspiring its own hashtags and

catchphrases.

As previously mentioned, the fans this year were slightly disappointed that Chance did not get her own show as Jack had in the previous year. Having her relegated to a mini show freed up the main purpose built stage outside Mel's. Rumors quickly spiraled that the stage would be occupied by a dance group. By August these rumors had been confirmed when *Academy of Villains: House of Fear* was announced. The ousting of the icon and the installation of an untested dance group initially brought moans from the fans; the fans couldn't have been more wrong. Dressed as Shadybrook inmates and dancing to the sounds of the recent *Suicide Squad* soundtrack the dance group provided a fantastic display of modern dance within a horror theming. Bill and Ted were also back this year with their irrelevant take on pop culture, politics and celeb lampooning, many of the gags of which had been at the expense of the both Clinton and Trump whom were both running for the presidency at the time. The script was actually very funny this year, where active pop shots were centered on the Millennial generation and a final poke at Disney's super long construction project of *Pandora* "they have sex with their tails!?" The show had been penned by Jason Horne who on one night of the run was sporting a *ScareZone Podcast* tee-shirt (the man obviously has good taste).

Halloween Horror Nights 27

Soul Collectors

Halloween Horror Nights 27 would start its program of speculation almost as soon as the previous year had finished. Rumors abounded of big name houses and franchises, along with many returning favorites that kept the HHN fan community satisfied for many months. Then it was mid-December when everyone else in the world was focusing on the festive period HHN Hollywood via their art director supremo John Murdy teased the first house codename. This sent the fans into a frenzy at how early this was, which meant that Orlando had to respond in kind and announce their own codename as 'checkmate'. A few months passed and as fans poured over every possible deviation of the word 'checkmate' we got our very first announcement in March with, not so unsurprisingly, *American Horror Story* was to return to HHN Orlando (with no mention of Hollywood, yet). Billed as *American Horror Story: Volume 2*, it would debut in Soundstage 21 and would feature the seasons not previously represented in the 2016 house of Seasons 2, 3 and 6 (Asylum, Coven and Roanoke) of the popular show.

Guests would enter via Briarcliff Manor where a nun statue sets the scene and distracts you as a scareactor jumps out. After that guests walked further into the asylum where they see Leo Morrison jumping out with his arm ripped off and Bloody Face jumping out soon after. The rec room of the asylum is presented next where guests would see Frank jumping out with his throat slit. Walking further into the room guests would see Leigh Emerson jumping out in his Santa Costume seemingly out of nowhere. They would then enter a short hallway where Sister Mary Eunice jumps out. The house would feature many great jump scares! Guests would then enter one of the Asylums hallways with many doors, out of one of these doors an asylum patient jumps out – not knowing which door was the scary part. Shortly after guests would soon transfer into the next portion of the house with a corridor announcing the change with projectors.

To get the house just right Universal actually worked with series creator Ryan Murphy and 20th Century Fox, to perfectly captured the environments, moments and scares that this house entailed. HHN's own Patrick Braillard said at the time, "If you've seen the show, you're going to constantly be in a state of 'look at that, and if you've never seen the show at all, you're just going to get scared!"

Immediately inside The Coven guests would see one of the walls where Delphine LaLaurie's head is on a plate. After that guests went into a room with three tall masked witches. One of which was a scareactor on stilts. The attention to detail and ensuring each scareactor looked like a direct copy of the actor from each episode was truly breath-taking for its accuracy. Before long guests would transfer into another transformation corridor where Roanoke would be presented (Hollywood was also later announce that this season would have a full maze at their event). As soon as guests made it in a Butcher would jump out. After that guests saw the Piggy Man being roasted on a fire and Ambrose White disemboweling Cricket Marlowe. Polk Farm was up next where guests saw two kids sucking on a pig for its milk. After that guests would enter another room where you see the Mama Polk hitting a guy with a hammer and Jether Polk shooting at you with a shotgun; the sound was deafening and made people jump as the sound was triggered each time. Later on, guests would enter the final room where they saw the burned corpses of Milo and Sophie Green impaled on sticks as the Piggy Man jumps out for one final scare, to scare people literally out the door.

During the American Horror Story announcement, it was also revealed how long and for what dates the event would run. Starting on September 15th (incredibly early) and running to November 4th, the event would be presented in its longest run ever with three further nights than it had in 2016. As fans and prospective guests readied their travel plans, a huge announcement was down the track on May 2nd with news that the classic horror movie *The Shining* would be presented for the first time at HHN. Running up to this some eagle-eyed techno wizards had looked (once again) at the code inside the updated HHN website to find that many references to 'Jack' could be found. This immediately sent the fandom into meltdown as they assumed it would be for Jack the Clown; the clown prince of HHN. However, they didn't have to wait long before the Jack was unmasked to be the titular character from this classic movie - Jack Torrance.

The house would be presented on both coasts with each HHN taking their own spin on the synonymous movie. Charles Gray, one of the main show directors for HHN said at the time, "We cast the Overlook Hotel as the aggressor and view it as if you have the 'shining'. Our goal is to have you constantly doing a double-take and give you that 'did I just see that?' feeling. After watching this movie for the first time, I remember saying, 'I would never go into room 237'. So, of course, that's where we're going to take you: all the places you shouldn't go. You'll come face-to-face with the murderous, ghostly entities around every corner. And, of course, the best part will be trying to escape the sharpened edge of an axe." Built inside the massive Soundstage 22, the house would enter you right into the action by taking you into the infamous Overlook hotel via it's maze. As you navigate the maze, Dick Halloran tells you stay 'the hell out' before a sneaky Jack jumps at you through a perfectly hidden boo-hole inside one of the hedges (a great unsuspecting scare!).

Inside the hotel you see 'REDRUM' painted on a door before Wendy comes swinging her bat into the conga line of people. The gimmick here is that you are not only being chased by Jack but you also falling into the 'shining' and become as mad as he is. Guests would be inducted into this at the very start with the classic iconography of this movie and the twisting nature of its path. Inside the lobby and it was too late for Dick, blood now pours out of a mannequin on the floor as Jack comes swinging with his axe ahead of the guests. Before long guests would enter into the dreaded Room 237 where a shower scene was presented using clever projections of a naked young woman, and as you become transfixed with this scene the haggard old witch version of the lady springs from behind the curtain to scare guests into the next scene. The Grady Twins were up next followed by Danny on his tricycle. More twist and turns later brought guests into possibly the most interesting scene of all with the whole 'how the heck are they gonna do this?' with the elevator scene and that notorious river of blood. The effect was achieved using a glass wall between guests and the dyed red water to simulate blood rushing from the elevator doors only be collected underneath and repumped back behind the doors on a never-ending cycle; it was a neat effect, though guests had no time to take it in as Jack was soon on you by smashing the hotel door down and yelling his famous line "Here's Johnny". The haunted party was featured next before more twists and turns led guests to another scene where the 'shining' had properly taken hold where a corridor of mirrors disorientated guests before a recreation of the bar is found. Floyd the bartender was there with Jack sipping scotch. Finally, the climax of the house fast approaches where guests are sent back into the maze. Jack after Jack would jump at the guests before finally a frozen mannequin of him was seen as guests swiftly left the house.

It was June 7th when the tickets officially went on sale, including all tours and special experiences such as dining with the scareactors. By the end of the month the website updated with 'our souls are requested'. A

297

nifty trailer showing some skeletal hands grasping at an unfortunate victim followed by a voodoo like backdrop, would entice fans to sign up to the revised website, where a timer would countdown the days, periodically revealing wallpapers and sweepstakes opportunities; eventually however, the countdown would countdown to nothing. A month later on July 27th the Starz Network favorite *Ash Vs the Evil Dead* was announced for both coasts. Braillard was on hand again to discuss the scares that awaited us all, "We're going to take you, regardless of your awareness of the show or the characters, and throw you into the loud, brash, and very bloody world of Ash. There are Deadites to kill and evil to stop, let's get to it. The house will feature various locations from the first two seasons of Ash vs Evil Dead and lots of blood. And for those 'in the know,' the answer is yes... We'll be going back to the cabin; with a few other surprises along the way. This is our blood-soaked, milk-eyed, crass, rock n' roll amped, chainsaw-wielding felt puppet, love-letter to everyone and everything connected to Ash vs Evil Dead." The house would be presented in the Parade Building way over the back of the park. The uncertainty surrounding the possible refurbishment/replacement of the Kidzone area ensured that guests had to get to the house via a long queue that started near the Sprung Tents and wrapped around to the far back of the park.

The previously mentioned website timer on the Orlando HHN site ran out on August 3rd to reveal nothing. Fans gave mixed reactions which were only heightened further as by this time the slow announcing

Orlando event was overtaken by the West coast who were making up ground and were releasing maze after maze which appeared to take the attention away from Orlando; this however would be short lived. August 14th rolled around and both coasts did a dual announcement of the popular SAW franchise coming back to both coasts to tie in with the recently released latest addition to their horror franchise.

A short while later on the August 18th the scarezones were all announced and the return of now firm fan favorite, *Academy of Villains* in a new show entitled, *Afterlife*. It would be this show and the zones that would be most affected when Hurricane Irma came to town in early September, even closing the theme parks for a few days from 9th to 13th September. The stage which had been built opposite Mel's for AOV had to be swiftly taken down and all the zone dressings removed before the storm hit the peninsula. Some 6.5 million Floridians would be evacuated during this time due to the hurricane causing devastation in the Caribbean. The 180 mph winds did little damage in comparison to the poorly hit Caribbean islands where collectively 52 people lost their lives and damage totaled around $64.76 billion. The main stage which could not be fully taken down during the storm suffered damage rendering it unusable for the run of the show. Instead, the creative bunch that AOV were they altered their show to a condensed version and still performed every night but outside the *Horror Makeup Show* area. Other than this change, the event would run smoothly. In fact, the show would be so popular that the kiosks selling AOV T-shirts near to the performance location would be the first to sell out (in week one too!).

Five scarezones would be presented in 2017. *Altars of Horror* in the Plaza of the Stars was billed as "Enter the nexus of evil, where all the most fearsome characters and nefarious creatures from each of the Halloween Horror Nights haunted houses lie in wait." The decorations for the scarezone consisted of five large themed pillars, topped with skulls, that each held a frame with the logo of one of the IP houses on it. Front to back, *The Shining, SAW: The Games of Jigsaw* and *Ash Vs. Evil Dead* were on the right side of the Plaza of the Stars walking into Universal Studios while *American Horror Story: Volume 2* and *The Horrors of Blumhouse* were on the left. *Festival of the Deadliest* was in Hollywood Boulevard and would feature our mascot for the event, Bones, where a frenzied party of death and hell was being frown. Everyone who had committed their soul to the event (via the website) were expected at this ghoulish gathering. Next up we had *Invasion!* In the San Francisco area where the year was 1955, and a UFO has crashed onto the wharf. Their goal: to conduct experiments upon you to prepare to invade Earth, but with some very cool photo opportunities! Next up, you can't keep a good franchise down as *The Purge* returned to the New York area with typical mini shows and chaos we all expect from this zone. But the best scarezone by far and winner of the team member voted 'zone of the year' went to the iconic *Trick 'r Treat* in the Central Park area. It was beautiful and so lovingly recreated, literally everyone had a selfie with Sam before ploughing into the rest of the event. It was so well undertaken it is easy to see why this fan favorite came back for HHN28.

August became a good month for announcements as after the zones were announced a very well-produced commercial from horror god Eli Roth was released nationwide. The commercial had Easter eggs throughout highlighting the duo houses of both coasts along with great horror scenes all wrapped up in some demented party setting; it truly has to be the best commercial HHN has ever created. Just days after this and the Blumhouse house was announced. *The Horrors of Blumhouse* would be presented in the newly formed MIB tent and would feature scares from a variety of their movies including: *The Purge, Sinister*, and the *Insidious* movies. The façade was quite impressive as it was a giant recreation of their famous production house logo but with a series of projections that kept the people in line entertained. Rumors hit the internet that the line-up inside had changed through production but they have never been confirmed. The movie *Sinister* was first up with an assortment of different rooms recreated from the movie, this was followed by trashed domestic type settings where the characters of *The Purge* had setup business before various scares from *Insidious* were presented. The final portion of the house acted as a trailer for the then forthcoming *Insidious 4* where a few teaser scenes had been recreated. Gray said at the time, "What excites me most about this house is the access we were granted to use and recreate elements of Insidious: Chapter 4. That's right, you'll be walking through a living trailer of the upcoming film. Insidious: Chapter 4 doesn't hit theaters until 2018, so this is a big deal for us and the guests who will meet the newest villain of the franchise. I can't give anything away yet, but I will say that we dive into the Further and see some very horrific…imagery."

It was a few days later via USA Today (who had the exclusive announcement) that the event would feature four original concept houses. The first of these was a firm favorite with *Scarecrow: The Reaping* in Sprung Tent 1 where a long-abandoned Depression-era farm, vengeance takes root, and the only harvest that will be reaped are the guests entering it. It would also feature the first house in HHN history to be staffed fully with 6ft 3 and over scareactors crammed into this claustrophobic nightmare inducing house. Many fan veterans of the event and this author remarked at the time that the reason the hurricane

300

hit was because this house existed as Universal had spent the last six months growing real corn out the back of the Studio to fill the entrance to this house. The reason the hurricane hit 'must have been the corn', we all remarked tongue-in-cheek, as we could remember the last time they grew corn for 2004's *Field of Screams* and a hurricane came through and flattened it all. Next up was *Dead Waters* in Soundstage 24 which brought back a little known HHN character of the Voodoo Queen. The façade of which was so impressive. After entering the soundstage guests would walk down a long hallway where you hear the Voodoo Queen talking about her kingdom and how everyone who entered her kingdom are still there. Guests then walked into a room where a half-sunken steamboat is right in front of you. The boat was impressive to behold and it was so highly detailed, surely one of the best they have ever created.

Next up was *The Fallen* also in Soundstage 24. A cathedral setting where a number of demons were doing battle thrust guests into the action; and there was action aplenty! In fact, the scareactors were so energetic and performed so many stunts in this house that they had to build into the house space for three sets of actors to perform everything that was needed to make it work seamlessly. Finally, in Sprung Tent 2 was *The Hive* where, "The crumbling house on 19 Hemingway Lane harbors a nest of bloodthirsty vampires. If you awaken them, you will face a savage, bestial hunger." The house was rumored to have been developed as a movie property before a supposed fall-out led to this vampire house being created. It was quite a gnarly house where vampires of different shapes and sized were seen feasting on a variety of human prey all to varying levels of success. The house was also the first house in Sprung Tents history to not have a façade, reasons behind that decision are unknown though the possible rumor of a cancelled IP house would fit this theory. Interestingly, the house was the first to see all team members shave their heads to play the vampire roles and the first house for many years to use its real name as its codename: 'Hive'.

It was around this time, not long before the event opened, that perhaps the saddest news in HHN history was released; Bill and Ted would be cancelled. *Bill & Ted's Excellent Halloween Adventure* would be billed as the 'farewell tour' and would feature a number of gags and numbers from some of the best shows they have ever performed. The show opened with a very teary recap of the past 26 years of fun that the duo and performers brought to so many visitors, all edited to a soulful rendition of *I Lived* by *One Republic* (there wasn't a dry eye in the house). Popular returning actors came back for one more year recreating some of their famous characters and jokes, before *We Will Rock You* brought the house down one last time, old school style. Set around a music festival, and involving the Grim Reaper (from the movie) threatening to kill the dudes before the duo saved the day. Some redrafting of the script occurred due to the horrific real-life events in Vegas at the time. In the end, the duo had to save the day by finding something redeeming about pop culture (and boy did they struggle!) in order to save themselves from being dragged to 'hell'. At the very end of the show Rufus (from the movies) would appear to bring the boys home and announce 'gentlemen, we are history'. A final blast of pyro led to a sign depicting their famous catchphrase being left on stage as fans wiped their tears away, it simply read, "be excellent to each other."

The event would be another incredibly popular year where the park was alleged to be capacity on select nights. Hollywood even announced that the first two weekends of their event fully sold out. Fans lapped up the mixture of original houses to IP houses and loved the scarezones. In all, Universal managed to undertake a great event that was shaken by the hurricane and outside events but still managed to pull-off another sterling year that will surely go down in the history as a fan favorite.

The Future of Halloween Horror Nights

"What we think is coming next..."

One of the most important deals that has been struck behind the scenes that will actively have a huge positive impact on the future years of the event will be Universal's partnership with *Legendary Pictures*. This is a partnership that had started in July 2013, which had weathered stormy times but has recently been cemented by the huge successful release of 2015's *Jurassic World*.

The partnership began with Universal as the production company's partnership with *Warner Bros* ended. The company had made many successful movies with the former partner, including the wildly popular *The Dark Knight* franchise, *Pacific Rim* and *The Hangover* franchise (to name a few). Universal has found a solid partner who is keen to build on their former successes and to open their impressive back catalogue to explore exciting new creative possibilities. Universal and *Legendary* said at the time, "Comcast and NBC Universal's global assets in film, television and theme parks offer Legendary unmatched breadth and opportunity to grow our business," *Legendary* Chief Executive Thomas Tull said in a statement. "We are delighted to be in business with this exceptional team and look forward to a successful partnership."

The deal with *Legendary* would not only tie together the companies for the purposes of production and release of movies but it will also explore other avenues that would be mutually beneficial for both. The deal has specifically detailed the possibilities of cross-promotion that can be enabled from building haunted attractions at both of its American theme parks for Halloween Horror Nights. The deal has enabled Universal to part-fund *Legendary's* movies along with distributing and marketing them. *Legendary* will then co-finance some of Universal's own in-house productions and have access to their iconic back catalogue of movies and TV shows. And although the exact terms of the deal have not been released, the driving force of the deal would be to create cinematic experiences unlike anything ever released before.

From a fan's perspective, we can now see from this 2014 deal that a number of items from this partnership have already been brought to the parks for this synergy. *Kong: Skull Island* opened in 2017 (though in partnership with *Warner Bros*) with a ride of the same name opening in Islands of Adventure in 2016. Other items have included the installation of the *Raptor Encounter* at Islands which ties neatly in with *Jurassic World* movie (it was also revised for the *Jurassic World 2* release with Blue) and also the very first partnership house of *Dracula Untold* at 2014's Halloween Horror Nights.

The *Dracula* house of that year, as discussed in a previous chapter, was a house that utilized the whole Universal idea of 'immersive preview'. The idea of bringing guests into the house for a preview of a coming attraction in order to build anticipation for the movie, in a direct expectation of better returns at the box-office, is something pretty new for the event, particularly when it is planned this way. Note that in 2009 the *Wolf Man* movie came out after the event due to production issues, when it was originally planned to be released during the event.

Crimson Peak was made into *Guillermo del Toro's Crimson Peak: Maze of Madness* at Hollywood for 2015. It was a highly detailed and immersive maze (note in Hollywood they call houses 'mazes'), which provided a great pre-release introduction into the creepy blood clay filled ghost world of *Crimson Peak*. *Legendary Pictures*, also brought us *Krampus* for HHN26.

Universal, with the partnership with *Legendary,* has an impressive run of movies coming out soon that would possibly lend themselves to future houses for our event. Let's consider a few of them:

• *Jurassic World 2: Fallen Kingdom* (2018) – In theaters summer 2018.

• *Godzilla: King of the Monsters* (2019) – which is in post-production.

• *Godzilla vs. Kong* (2020) – a sequel for a movie that is not even released yet.

• *Mass Effect* (2018): A movie based on the popular sci-fi video game.

• *Bad Blood* – a horror movie still in development.

• *Gremlins 3* – currently being scripted.

• *Trick 'r Treat 2* – currently being scripted.

• *Carnival Row* (2016): A TV series that is being co-produced by horror auteur Guillermo del Toro. Not much is known at the time of writing but supposedly it is a new twisted take on popular fairy tales.

• *Offworld* (TBC): A sci-fi horror movie.

• *The Join* (TBC) A sci-fi thriller movie.

Could any of these be houses for 2018, 2019 or 2020? This writer hopes that the third most financially successful movie at the box-office ever, *Jurassic World*, will one day become a haunt! Whatever the outcome, mixing these high-profile movies into houses by utilizing Universal's own world-renowned expertise and flair for creating wholly new and exciting content will ensure we fans will never be disappointed.

This synergy of cross marketing is obviously desirable to outside production companies too, who can be approached by the event's organizers to say, 'look at what we can do' and 'look at how they could help your movie's box office'. It all creates a win-win situation for all involved; that's why the future of the event cannot be safer.

A new development that has yet to be fully realized is the upcoming Universal Monsters Cinematic Universe or *Dark Universe*. Borrowing heavily from Disney's handling of the *Marvel* Universe and now *Warner Bros'* setup of a new *DC* universe, Universal is set to create its own Monsters universe using characters that the corporation have owned for decades. Starting already with *Dracula Untold* in 2014 this will be followed by *The Mummy* film in 2017, an untitled *Wolf Man* film in 2019 with a *Van Helsing* film, a *Creature from the black lagoon* film, a *Bride of Frankenstein* film and an *Invisible Man* film respectively being released yearly from 2020. We know that *The Mummy* (2017) was not as successful as hoped but this may still lead to some of the future planned pictures being released.

The proposed 'Monsters' production schedule (pre-Mummy release) looked like this:

• *The Wolf Man* (2018): A modern take on the popular movie

monster, written by Aaron Guzikowski.

• *The Invisible Man* (2018): Written by Aaron Guzikowski who brought us the original *Men in Black* movie. The title role is rumored to be played by Johnny Depp.

• An Untitled Universal Monster Project (2019): Little is known about this movie, possible an early crossover movie. It is currently being written by the same writers as the new *Mummy* movie.

• *Frankenstein* (TBC): Currently being written and directed by horror expert Guillermo del Toro.

• *Dr. Jekyll and Mr. Hyde* (TBC): A movie being produced by del Toro, updating the Victorian story to modern times.

• *Van Helsing* (TBC): Currently being written by *Star Trek* and *Mission Impossible III* writer Alex Kurtzman. Kurtzman and others appear to be working on every script for this new universe.

• *Bride of Frankenstein* (TBC): Currently being produced by *The Da Vinci Code* producer Brian Grazer.

• *Creature from the Black Lagoon* (TBC): A modern take on the original horror picture.

Other Universal Pictures currently in production include:

• *The Something* (2018): The film will follow a crew of astronauts who, after being stuck in space for years, eventually come across another space ship.

• *The Birds* (TBC): A remake of the original Hitchcock masterpiece.

• *Chucky 7* (TBC): A sequel to the popular possessed foulmouthed doll franchise.

The other significant partnership that appears to be working the background at HHN is Universal's close relationship with *Warner Bros*. The partnership has seen a number of supposedly "impossible" movies make their way to the event. Starting with *The Exorcist* in 2016 and now *The Shining* in 2017 the movies have had both technical hurdles to achieve their specific purpose but also legal hurdles where *The Shining* for example has taken over 10 years to agree (a direct quote from Hollywood's John Murdy). The partnership with *Warners* probably started when the pair worked together to bring *Harry Potter* and his *Wizarding World* to the masses. Universal's dedication to the IP holders ensures that this close working is likely to continue and could be used to raid *Warner's* back catalogue to bring some of the best cinematic horrors to the event. A back catalogue that does include *Castle Rock Entertainment* and New Line Cinema the latter of which is well known for their impressive horror collection (Freddy, Jason etc).

Other than these possible future inclusions, Universal has also been said to looking more long-term at the event. The two phrases that we are hearing a lot recently are "Marquee Events" and "Next-Gen". So what are these and how do they affect HHN? The name "Marquee Events" appears to be a focus from Universal to becoming more event centric to drive families, tourists and fans back to the resort as much as possible by offering more and more seasonal attractions. And whilst the Macy's Parade or our own beloved HHN event are both nothing new, the company is seeking to actively enlarge their runs and include far more to see and do.

Take the announcement in early Spring 2017, Universal Orlando is extending their Christmas offerings with a brand new Potter show (that had been rumored for months) along with seasonal decorations and new additions to the Macy's parade. "Marquee Events" now has a dedicated webpage which over time will be populated with more and more events to ensure that 365 days a year there will be some kind of additional hard-ticketed event taking place within the resort.

In many ways, the addition and extension of the events at Universal are in reaction to Disney who have relied more and more on *Food Festivals* and Halloween attractions to help drive gate numbers. The difference that Universal wants to install within their roster of events is to ensure that everything they do is more refined, tailored, annually different and world-class. If you've been to *MNSSHP* (*Mickey's Not So Scary Halloween Party*) in 1996 and then in 2016 the event would be more or less the exact same with the same decorations, same rides, same attractions, same shows (more or less). *MNSSHP*, Epcot's *Food Festival* and now HHN are all starting much earlier than they have ever before, with *MNSSHP* even starting in August!

Universal doesn't appear to want same old same old; they want experiences that are so great they'll make you want to return again and again to see their exclusive offerings throughout each year. In corporate speak "repeat business customers", people who are prepared to vacation not just once a year at the same resort but multiple times.

So what's Next Gen HHN? Nobody knows for sure and from what we've heard it is still being defined. The idea from what has been muted is to ensure the event runs successfully for another 27 years but with a focus on maximizing the gate numbers but ensuring the products offered are globally the best you could possibly see anywhere in the world. Some have told us that it would mean dropping areas of the event that aren't as successful (what those are we have not been told) or bringing new aspects into the event. Increasing spend on the things people want to see and creating something that you just can't get anywhere else are all being mooted for these early days talks.

The focus seems to be on the houses and how these can be bigger and better but also how their accessed physically, as in better line management to prevent the huge lines of people waiting hours and hours but also to ensure some connectivity can occur via our smart phones in terms of marketing, line management and interfacing with the event year round. *The Tampa Bay Times* had estimated that HHN's daily attendance for 2016 was around 600,000 for the entire run, which is allegedly double that of Busch Garden's Halloween events and still more than MNSSHP, saying that the footfall was increased from the year before. If this trend is to continue, Universal will need to consider carefully how they ensure they manage this year-on-year increase to best advance their financially but also the experience on each and every guest through those gates.

We've heard that some people within the company want to see a radically different HHN that is very unlike what we have today, whereas others want to see the same award winning formula continue. Whatever the decision they go with, we can expect a little of both and that the event will always continue to be the world's greatest Halloween event constantly lifting its own bar.

The event is in the hands, now, of some of the best creative haunt professionals in the industry. They are backed up by one of the most forward-thinking can-do companies in the world. This aspect is essential in these days of huge corporates, combined with their partnership with *Legendary* and the corporate friends they have made over the years from their successful handling of other IPs. Located on both coasts of the US and now in Singapore and Japan, the event is more popular now than it has ever been; that's why this award winning unique experience will continue to grow and grow. It will always be the world's number one Halloween event, that has always been compared with but will never be equaled or beaten.

The End...

Reading/Watching List for 2017

Not much is currently known about which houses and street scares we will experience for 2018 just yet. At the time of writing this last year we had a whole list of houses leaked to the net, all of which became true. However, for this year not so much is known as of yet just rampant rumors that we won't go into (see *hhnunoffical.com* for more info).

Preparation is the key for enjoying Halloween Horror Nights, so much so that we fully recommend the following movies to help prepare you for the horrors that may be coming this year. The list has been compiled from general atmospheric movies that are very detailed and have a vague resemblance to the various icons of the event, along with a selection of movies to remind us all of past events.

General:

• *Sharknado 3: Oh Hell No*: As it mixes horror and comedy right inside the very theme park that you will be attending.
• The *It* movie from 1990 would give most guests a taste for Jack's persona.
• *The Thing* movie from either 1982 or 2011 would be a good idea, as this house was wildly popular in years past and could be presented again.
• *Something Wicked This Way Comes* (1983) is good for the Caretaker.
• *The Gingerbread Man* (2005)
• *Jack Frost* (1997)
• *Rumpelstiltskin* (1995)
• *The Tooth Fairy* (2006)
• *Snow White: A Tale of Terror* (1997)
• *The Maze Runner* (2014)
• *Jack the Ripper* (1988) Michael Caine version.
• *From Hell* (2001)

The smash-hit *Netflix* original *Stranger Things* has been announced for HHN28. The show combines 1980s popular culture favorites with a rich and suspenseful storyline that'll leave you hooked. Seasons 1 and 2 are already out ready for your bingeing with Season 3 confirmed for this Fall.

Trick 'r Treat is returning to HHN but not in the streets but in a whole house of its own. This must-see (annually if pos too!) is a great watch every haunt season. Expect each tale from this cult classic to be represented in the house in some way.

Which witch is which… is a common problem for the event organizer's makeup department

Touring Plans

"The people that wanna see everything in one night Touring Plan…"

Touring Plan 1: All in one nighter

Premise: The person who wants to see everything in one night at all cost.

When: Avoid Fridays and Saturdays. Wednesdays are best, followed by Thursdays and then Sundays. The event seems to be busiest in the first weeks and the last week – so pick a week in mid-October.

Required: An express pass and a day ticket for either the Studios or Islands Park. Note that the best location would be the Studios Park.

Starting point: Universal usually pens guests into two groups when the Studios Park shuts for the day. These are typically held in the New York area or Kidzone. Islands of Adventure guests can typically queue up inside the Seuss Landing area of the park and enter via a small gate when the event opens. The best starting point used to be the New York area. Guests cannot choose which area they will be in if they are not in these areas before close, so check the time that the park closes first. Typically, most fans of the event will hang out inside Finnegan's Bar and Grill waiting for the event to commence if in the New York area. On occasions the park may let guests out of the penned area before the park gates open. If they do, make sure you check which houses nearby are open, as some have staggered openings to meet the footfall on busy nights. Guests in the Kidzone area can queue as early as 4pm for the houses here, and are usually allowed into the houses before 5.45pm, but I have excluded this for the one nighter plan as sometimes this perk can be for annual passholders only. So we must start at the New York holding area first. You will be given wristbands at both locations.

First house: Walk straight to the entrance of whichever house is located next to the Twister ride entrance near the New York Public

Library façade. This way the house should empty out in Production Central.

Second House: Now in Production Central there are usually two houses that enter and exit here, with a third that will exit by the *Twister* location. Ensure to queue for both houses that enter and exit in Production Central.

Top Tip here: Remember that your express pass is valid for one-house-per-event, so if on these first three houses if there is no queue, then do not use your express pass! You can then use your express pass later on in the evening instead, when the queues build up.

Third House: As above.

Show:The first and last performances of each show are always the less crowded. This means you can see the show and then exit without losing too much time. A good tip would be to see the *Bill and Ted show* first. Upon exiting make your way to Sprung Tent 2.

Fourth House: Make your way into the queue for this house which should be nearby, next to the *Men in Black* attraction. Following the queuing for this house you should be perfectly positioned in the Kidzone area.

Fifth House: You should now be near the entrance to the Parade Building, find it and queue for it.

Sixth House: You should empty back out in Kidzone. Walk back up to the Men in Black area and find the queue for the Sprung Tent 1 house.

Seventh House: Walk back to New York via the Diagon Alley area and now queue for the final soundstage house. You may have to queue up a bit for this house. Note that although you have an express pass, the time to check and then scan each pass takes time. Peak night express queues can be as long as 30 minutes for the busy times.

Eight House: You should exit right near the *Disaster* attraction, quickly break away from the crowds and find the nearby queue for this house.

Ninth House: If there is an eighth house it will either be next to the Shrek attraction or it will be in another soundstage. Whichever it is you can easily walk to both from this point.

Ending: With time to spare (hopefully), either enjoy the scarezones, grab a bite to eat or use your express pass on the rides. Noting that although your express pass is good for one-house-one-entry, you can go as many times as you like on the other rides and attractions. After the event closes you can usually use your event ticket to get free access to most of the night clubs in City Walk (if you are over 21) but that is if you have any energy to do so! The top tip here would be to book a room beforehand with Universal at any of their resorts, so that once the event finishes you can have a short stroll back to you room. The closest resort for this is *The Hard Rock Hotel*, which is a mere 7 minute walk from the front gates of the Studios.

Staying onsite guests:

Touring Plan 2: Guests staying at an onsite resort

Premise: For guests who have chosen to stay onsite. Note that some guests will have free express pass for the parks, but this does not work for Halloween Horror Nights. If you need it (recommended), you must buy it separately from your resort or online from Universal.

When: Avoid Fridays and Saturdays, Wednesdays are best, followed by Thursdays and then Sundays. The event seems to be busiest in the first weeks and the last week – so pick a week in mid-October.

Required: Separate event tickets

Starting Point: Assuming you are coming from your room or City Walk, guests need to head to the far right of the main arches where a separate queue for resort guests only is found. Like all guests, you will have your bag checked and you will walk through an airport-style scanner. Note that no weapons or costumes are allowed at the event. If you have day passes for the parks, either go to Islands and use the small entrance in *Seuss Landing* (where you are still scanned but it is quicker) or stay within the Studios in the New York area, penned in.

Plan: Follow the steps in the 'one nighter' touring plan.

Frequent Fearers:

Touring Plan 3: For guests who have purchased a frequent fear pass of any kind.

Premise: Guests who have either the 'Frequent Fear' pass or 'Rush of Fear' pass will likely be attending the event more than once.

When: Avoid Fridays and Saturdays, Wednesdays are best, followed by Thursdays and then Sundays. The event seems to be busiest in the first weeks and the last week – so pick a week in mid-October. 'Rush of Fear' owners can only attend on the first few nights as per your terms. Some passes exclude the weekends, so please do check before heading out.

Required: Just your pass, with or without express

Starting Point: This assumes you are not an annual passholder. If you are, you need to start in the park as per Touring Plan 1. If you are not you need to start at the park gates. Typically, the event starts at 6.30pm with the security lines opening at 6pm. Make sure you are there either by 5.30pm or after the initial rush around 7pm – its ok, you're not missing anything as you can come back multiple days. Follow your instincts and take it easy!

Must do: The 'old' must-do for all fans of the event was a nightly ride on Jaws or 'the shark in the dark' ride, though unfortunately old Bruce is no longer with us (RIP Bruce), so instead create a new tradition. Perhaps have a meal in the Monster Café or ride *The Mummy*.

Exiting: To avoid a traffic jam, leave the park at least 45 minutes before closing, or continue enjoying the houses right up until the last scare. Note that using valet parking can get you ahead of the jam if you can collect your car without a wait.

"Taking a chicken a person who might get scared at the event..."

Touring Plan 4: For guests traveling with a person who is scared of the event.

Premise: Guests traveling with a person who has never been before or has been and is still terrified of the prospect of attending.

When: Avoid Fridays and Saturdays, Wednesdays are best, followed by Thursdays and then Sundays. The event seems to be busiest in the first weeks and the last week – so pick a week in mid-October.

Required: Separate event tickets, though express passes are highly recommended to cut down the anticipation or suspense felt in the queue.

Starting Point: A great starting point to help anyone with anxiety about the event is to first take them around the park during the day - either the day of or before the event, so they can familiarize themselves with the layout.

Pre-start step 1: Next you need to take them on a day-time tour of the houses, maybe an afternoon tour after a light lunch and let them see for themselves the artistry that goes into the event without any of scareactors being present. If they can't stand that level of inclusion, then I would recommend they not attend the event. The tours are always led by several extremely knowledgeable tour guides that can extinguish any fears while still showcasing the artistry and complexities that go into building every single house. If they can hack that, go to the next step.

Pre-start step 2: Once you have done a tour, you need to be the studios park before closing and be in one of the designated areas as the park prepares for the event. Allow your guest to see the setup process and feel comfortable that it is still daylight outside. Perhaps have a snack and a drink and relax. Assume you are in the New York area.

First house: As soon as the event opens, take your guest to one of the houses that have opened from your tour. The likelihood is that on your tour you probably visited one or more of the soundstage houses. Taking your guest to a house they are already familiar with will hopefully build confidence. If after the first house, your guest is feeling ok you can proceed to the next step.

Show: Halloween Horror Nights isn't just about the scares, it was started as a party, and party on down we shall do. Teach your guest that some of the best adult/tween orientated shows can be found during the event, so take them to see Bill and Ted.

Scarezones: Now they've seen a show and should feel more relaxed, take your guest through a couple of scarezones. Advise your guest of the following secret, 'if you make eye contact and appear not scared, the likelihood is that the scareactor will leave you alone'. And always remind them that scareactors are here to make the event enjoyable, they won't touch you or overly try and make you get scared, they want you to have fun!

Second house: Now your guest has familiarized themselves with the streets, it is now time to take them to another house. Try choosing the comedy house of the year (if there is one) or an IP house that they might be familiar with.

Show:Now walk over and see whichever show you didn't see earlier, it will probably be *Rocky Horror*, *Beetlejuice*, the event icon's show or a magic show.

Third house: Straight after the show walk to the closest house queue and enjoy.

Ride: End the event early with a ride on another favorite ride.

Leave: Leaving slightly earlier you should reward your guest with an ice-cream on City Walk or a drink from one of the bars. If they enjoyed themselves due to this touring plan, then you need to come back again the next day and finish off the houses and scarezones that you didn't see. If they were scared all the way round and could not possible see themselves coming back... then you need to come back solo buddy!

Top Tips

Tickets:

1. Always buy your tickets from Universal Studios, no matter where you live in the world.

2. Purchasing your tickets ahead of time will save you having to queue up again once you have cleared security. Purchasing your tickets ahead of time can be undertaken by calling Universal, going onto their official website or attending any onsite ticket window or resort concierge before the event.

3. If you plan on attending more than once, then a Frequent Fear pass will always work out the best value.

4. Express passes have a history (though not recently) of selling out. Therefore ensure you purchase your express pass as soon as you know when you are going or upgrade your Frequent Fear pass to enable this option.

5. Universal usually does some great offers for guests wanting to spend the day in Islands of Adventure on the day of your booked event. Go to Guest Services or any park ticket window and enquire.

6. A huge rookie mistake that appears quite often at the event are people turning up at the gates with tickets for Hollywood's HHN. Hollywood tickets do not work at Orlando, and neither can they be exchanged. This also counts for Orlando tickets purchased for Hollywood. Ensure before you go to buy the appropriate tickets that you are on the correct website before doing so.

7. If you are visiting from abroad and have purchased your tickets in your home country, the chances are that your tickets have been sold to you via an approved third-party vendor. If you have a problem with your tickets, such as you have lost them, there is little that Guest

Services can do to help you. Instead, as soon as you have purchased the tickets take photos of both sides with your phone. That way, should they get lost, Guest Services should be able to help you; this goes for day tickets purchased abroad too. The best place to buy tickets is always the official Universal Studios site.

8.   If you stay on site and your package includes fast-passes for your day tickets these cannot be used in the evening for HHN. This question comes up a lot and a number of people can be caught out with this. Universal does change things from time to time, however right now (as it has been for years) your daytime free fast passes issued to hotel guests cannot be used for HHN.

9.   If you're going on a busy night and want to ensure you see everything, then a way great way might be to book a RIP tour. These tours sell out very quickly, however these ensure you see EVERYTHING in just one night. They can be booked for exclusive parties or as individual tickets in mixed groups. They often take you to places not seen by the public and provide a guest lounge with cash bar. Though this is not guaranteed until future details are announced, they also include direct entry rides and the shows. There is usually little-to-no waiting for each attraction, including preferred seating for Bill and Ted's. If you are interested in booking these tours you must contact Universal directly via their website.

10.   Taking a post attendance *Behind-the-Screams: Unmasking the Horror Tour* is a great way to see how the event is designed and managed. The popular tours describe in detail about how the event comes together and can be an excellent way for "chickens" to experience the houses whilst the lights are on. Again, various options are offered and they must be booked directly with Universal. They too are highly popular and generally sell-out, for 2017 they are already on sale for guests booking resort packages.

Entry and when to go:

1.   Get there as early as possible. Probably enter the park during the day and 'stay and scream' as per the touring plan in this guide.

2.   If you are a hotel guest, ensure you keep right at the park gates, as you will have a separate entry.

3.   To speed up the process at the security check area, ensure you

have all your belongings out ready for inspection.

4.   When to go to the event can vary each year. However, a rule of thumb is to avoid any weeks that coincide with local school and college vacations. Typically, the first two weeks and the last in October are the busiest, with the final week being the busiest. The third - sometimes fourth - weekend in October is usually referred to as 'Hell week', due to the schools that have let out combined with both local and international vacations that are all held then. The event can sometimes sell-out during this period.   See our busy days guides for more information.

5.   The best time to visit is within the first fortnight of the event (though the weather can be bad then) or in the middle of the month of October. Universal usually offers deals like 'Rush of Fear' tickets that enable guests to attend the event in the first two weeks at a lower cost, in an effort to push up attendance.

6.   Note that parking isn't free for the event, so queues can build up at the parking garage. Therefore, ensure you leave plenty of time to park and then get through security before the event. On select nights the valet parking option also becomes congested, so don't rely on this option if you have the money to do.

7.   As the event and the express passes can sell out, it is always the best policy to buy your tickets early. They typically go on sale in June of every year for this very reason.

8.   A top-tip for many seasoned HHN-goers is to purchase express passes but not to use them right away. If you attend on a not-so busy night, you can probably see every house with just minimal queuing. Once you have seen every house, you can then go around again and use your express pass; this way you will see every house twice!

9.   Note that express passes will mean that you will still have to wait in line. It's just that your time in line will be shorter than the standby. Express passes rarely provide instant access to a house; the only way to get true instant access would be to a book a *RIP tour*.

10.   Bring your wallet! The event sells a huge range of exclusive merchandise (and food items!) that you cannot get anywhere else. Plus, once the event merchandise sells out, that's it: if you miss getting the hoody you desire or your favorite tee, you will have to rely on internet auction sites and likely pay twice the price!

General tips:

1.   Do not despair if you don't have an express pass and the queue for a certain house is over 3 hours in length; the chances are the later you stay the shorter the queue will get. Some nights, the event stays open until 2am, providing enough time to see any selected house.

2.   The event is scary and not recommended for anyone under 13. That's exactly why they do not sell kids' tickets. So think twice before paying out for the tickets as to whether your children will actually enjoy this event.

3.   Whether you have an express pass or not it is always worth attending the event more than once. Many people say that you can truly appreciate everything that is on offer at the event unless you attend at least two full nights. It is also good to attend on dry nights, the dryer the day the better the street experiences; so always check the weather forecast before heading out.

4.   If you see a red button inside a house – press it. It will nearly always trigger some kind of effect or scare that will be worth seeing. Look out for these buttons as they are always hidden within plain sight.

5.   Not only does Universal design some unique scares every year, but they also try to come up with unique activities and food options too. In the past the unique activities have included: Fortune telling, dance parties, henna tattoos and various meet-and-greets with actual celebrities. Unique food options have included 'twisted-taters' and 'shark attack' cocktails.

6.   If you wish to drink alcohol at the event, ensure you have appropriate ID with you and register just inside the park gates.

7.   Remember to have fun and not get drunk. Sheriff Deputies along with park security are stationed at every house and scarezone, so if you or your friends get too rowdy you can get expelled from the event.

8.   If you are feeling unwell or too scared during a house, you can leave the house by speaking to one of the house chaperones that are stationed after every scene. They are there to direct the guests to the next scene and ensure everybody is having a good time; they typically stand in a corridor where an exit sign is located.

9.   It is always handy to wear sunglasses for the September nights, as what with the late setting sun and the walking from darkness to light when exiting the houses it can cause some people to get disorientated. Having a pair of sunglasses handy when exiting the houses allows the eyes to adjust more quickly.

10.   Bring plenty of money with you, as the event provides a number of unique purchasing opportunities that are only on offer during each night.   Special event merchandise can include: t-shirts, hoodies, vinyl toys, fridge magnets, shot-glasses, pins and other collectibles.

The two sides of the icon Chance from 2016

HHN Park Map

Bill & Ted Show

Sprung Tent 2

Sprung Tent 1

MIB Tent

Parade Building

Shrek Theater

Soundstage 24B

Soundstage 24A

Soundstage 19

Soundstage 22

A, B, C & D are typical scarezone locations.

Halloween Horror Nights 2019 Crowd Level Guide

We all get thoroughly bummed-out when we attend the event and the first thing that greets us is a huge crowd of people shuffling through the security cameras; well grimace no more! We have put together a comprehensive guide below showing the days that are best avoided and the days that are the least crowded. To provide this guide we have surveyed: Historical attendance records, local theme park opening and closing times, school and college term times, Disney events and other significant local events (including sporting events). The guide runs from 1 to 10, with 10 being the busiest. It would appear that the best times to go would be after the first few nights near the start or near the end of the event. Most non-school nights are also good for the duration, excluding 'hell week', see the definitions at the start of the book for what this means.

Month	Date	Day	Crowds	Notes
SEPT	14	Fri	8	
	15	Sat	8	
	16	Sun	6	
	20	Thurs	3	
	21	Fri	3	
	22	Sat	5	
	23	Sun	6	
	28	Fri	3	
	29	Sat	4	
OCT	3	Wed	5	
	4	Thurs	3	
	5	Fri	4	
	6	Sat	9	Hell Week
	7	Sun	9	Hell Week
	10	Wed	9	Hell Week
	11	Thurs	7	Hell Week
	12	Fri	9	Hell Week
	13	Sat	9	Hell Week
	14	Sun	9	Hell Week
	17	Wed	9	Hell Week
	18	Thurs	4	
	19	Fri	6	
	20	Sat	8	
	21	Sun	8	
	24	Wed	8	
	25	Thurs	3	
	26	Fri	5	
	27	Sat	9	
	28	Sun	8	
NOV	1	Thurs	4	
	2	Fri	6	
	3	Sat	8	

When people ask 'what does the future hold for HHN?'
Surely this maniacal clown is the answer!

Historical House Wait Times

We've also looked at how busy each house has been over nearly every event night for both HHN 24, 25, 26 and 27. We assessed wait times from the times provided at the entrance of each and from actual spot checks we made whilst we waited in line. We then added this data for each night to find the average time for each house at every 30 minute interval. We also stopped the clock before 1am, as most nights last year finished at 1am and we added Shrek from 25, though it did not appear as a haunt location for 2014. Again, 10 would be the busiest with 3+ hour waits and 1 just a walk-on.

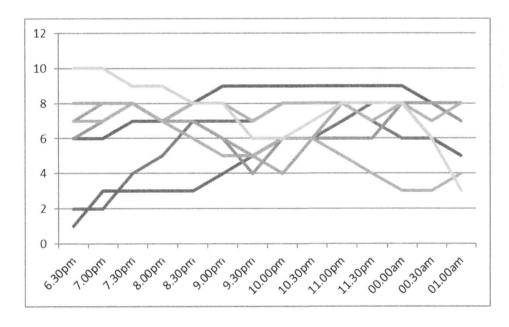

Please also note that for 2017 The *Disaster* Queue Building was out of use due to construction and will likely never return as a haunt location.

From the data collected, we found that although the anticipation for the house would have a bearing (hence why we collected three years' worth of data), we found that the biggest factor affecting wait times would be geography, as in where the house is located. The next biggest factor for any event night would be the size of crowds attending. See above for the best nights to go.

We found that the houses closest to the early-bird holding pens would fill up the quickest, with the houses located at the entrance filling up the fastest after this. It would appear that the Sprung Tents would be consistently busy all night. This would probably be due to the Simpsons holding pen being near to the entrance of these houses. These will fill up early, and then when these crowds are moving to the front of the park, the people who started at the front will be moving towards the rear. This almost rotational level of attendance ensured that the two Sprung Tents enjoyed some of the most consistent wait times over the events for the last two years. It was even noted that Insidious for one night had an express line that had nearly an hour wait time – which is wholly unheard-of for recent times.

Many of the other houses such as *Shrek* and Soundstage 21 (Jack's house from HHN25) would fill up early due to their proximity to the entrance, and then would cool-off steadily throughout the night. It was seen on one night that before closing both were a walk-on.

As with the Sprung Tents, it would appear that the soundstages are constantly busy throughout each event night. We believe that this is two-fold; the first is the fact that the soundstages are clustered together, which is annoying and confusing from a queue perspective, however it makes for easy admission to a neighboring house if the entrance is next to where the exit from the previous house is. We also believe that due to their sizes and setups, Universal usually reserves the houses that need the most space (so the largest houses) or the houses that are the most detailed or decorated to be in the soundstages (not always, but more than often so). This means that typically the houses located here provide the most anticipation, so this will add to their consistently busy level throughout each event night. They are also next to where the *Scareactor Dining Experiences* were held in 2015 and 2016, so this might have some bearing on the data collected.

HHN Tickets Guide

Halloween Horror Nights offers a variety of tickets. If we are asked one thing more than any other at our blog hhnunofficial.com and social media sites is which ticket is best? The answer purely depends on how often you'll be going and what days are best for you. So ask yourself now, am I likely to go more than 3 times and can I go weekday nights? This will impact on which ticket you have.

Before deciding, here's our rundown of the tickets available and who should buy them.

If in doubt, we strongly recommend that you ask Universal directly or us before proceeding with your purchases.

General rules:

• HHN is a separate ticketed event that occurs after hours at Universal Studios.
• Tickets for Orlando cannot be exchanged for Hollywood, so please don't buy from the wrong site.
• Tickets are best purchased direct from Universal.
• Tickets can be date specific, so check which dates you are buying to ensure they fall within your diary.
• Most importantly, things change, what we are printing here was good for 2015 but some of these may have changed for 2016.

General Admission:

These tickets will be for one day only and you will be asked which day you will be attending. The price per night always differs depending on the day you wish to attend. Typically, weekends are the busiest, so they demand the highest price. Tickets per day are usually around $100 plus tax, plus fees.

General Admission Add-On:

The day guests who are experiencing the two theme parks of Universal Orlando, they can purchase separate discounted add-on tickets to allow them to stay in the parks that night for HHN. These can be purchased in advance via the main HHN website or in the park at Guest Services. The add-on ticket can work out quiet cheaply if already visiting the park during the day; it is typical for these passes to range from $50 to $60 plus tax and fees. So if you're going to the event and the theme park on just a Saturday it will pay to get this ticket added on.

Coca-Cola Local's Day Tickets:

Discounted day passes are often offered for Florida locals. These can only be purchased directly with Universal and require a coke UPC code from any coke product that displays the HHN logo. Sometimes Universal will sell discounted tickets to locals without the UPC code, please check with Universal if you live locally on what deals they offer.

Annual Passholder Day Tickets:

Some annual passholders will have specially selected days when they can venture into HHN whilst using their own pass, please check your tickets' terms and conditions. For all other passholders, Universal usually offers discounted tickets on select nights. Please check with them closer to the event.

Express Passes:

If required, express passes can be purchased for day tickets. The passes must be used the night they are purchased for and they usually entitle the user to one express entry per house per night, with unlimited entry to any rides that are open. Note that the free express passes handed out to guests staying onsite are not valid for HHN. These typically range from $60 for quieter nights to twice that for the busier nights.

Frequent Fear Pass:

This pass enables guests to experience HHN on more than one night but on select nights, which are usually weekday nights. Express pass for every night can be added as an optional extra.

Rush of Fear:

This is a type of Frequent Fear Pass that enables the user to attend a select of different nights at HHN, usually within the first two weeks. Express pass for every night can be added as an optional extra.

Plus Passes:

This is a premium version of the Frequent Fear Pass, know as the Frequent Fear Plus Pass, this adds more premium nights to the ticket and express for every night booked as an optional extra.

RIP Tours:

Groups of around 12 can opt to tour the park with a tour guide. You and 11 others will tour together with zero wait on all houses and rides that your group goes to. If you are going one night and want to ensure you see everything, then this is the pass for you. The price is usually around the $150 mark and this is in addition to your general admission ticket. The tour includes:

• One entry to every house for that night with zero to literally no wait.
• Reserved seating at one seating of the popular *Bill & Ted's Excellent Halloween Adventure*. The seats are usually the best in the house.
• A stop midway to a special RIP Lounge with cash bar, this was held in the *MIB* attraction building's Immigration Room last year.
• Following the tour, your pass is good to be used as an express pass on all open rides.
• Complimentary valet parking for one vehicle.

Private *RIP Tour*:

A private *RIP Tour* is given for guests who wish to tour the park with a tour guide but without any strangers. A group of up to 10 can be assembled for this experience. The tours are identical to the above with these additional pointers:

• It's your tour, so you can visit multiple houses over again.
• Free photopasses are often offered.
• Often start earlier than the stand tour and can finish at anytime during operational hours.

The prices vary but are usually around $1,500 plus tax and fees, in addition to your general admission.

Unmasking the Horror Tour:

These daytime tours vary every year. Small groups are led daily around select houses to see how the houses were designed and built for the event. All tours must be booked directly with Universal. Park admission is not required, however, if no day park admission you will be escorted to the park gates on completion.

Gory Getaway / Hotel Packages:

Packages vary, some include admission and tours, please check with Universal.

Scareactor Dining Experience:

A dining experience that is held while the park sets up for night has been held historically at the Monster's Café. The experience included a themed buffet, free soda refills, scareactor photo opportunities, and one free digital download of a photo taken during your meal. This ticket is in addition to your general admission ticket and is not known whether it will be held in 2016. Details subject to change.

Please check all details with Universal prior to purchasing at universalorlando.com or call 407-363-8000.

Fantastic HHN Facts

- The average maze length is 370-400 linear feet from beginning to end.
- The lead creatives on both coasts write treatments for the mazes and these go through numerous iterations before being approved. Once finalized, they're fleshed out with concept art and full layout walkthroughs are constructed with a 3D modeling program. Once that's finalized, they draw up construction plans with all of the walls, structures, and actor placements noted.
- The length of a maze from your perception depends on the nature of the layout. Compact maze layouts tend to feel longer in nature whereas more open maze layouts tend to feel shorter.
- Halloween Horror Nights prior to 2007 didn't officially license most of the intellectual properties it used aside from what was used in marketing, such as The Crypt Keeper. 2007 was noteworthy because it was the first year Universal Orlando made a major push to license intellectual properties. In the past, they'd either use properties they didn't have the rights to or they'd make original mazes heavily inspired by intellectual properties. Attendance took an inordinate increase in 2007 and they tried to go with a mostly "original" line-up of mazes in 2008. Attendance dropped that year. 2009's line-up was mostly intellectual property mazes whereas 2010 had all original content. The majority of 2011 was original content. The trend in attendance showed a greater increase when Universal used intellectual properties.
- 2012 was a major departure in that Universal Creative got involved with several of the mazes. All of the mazes are usually created by A&D. *Silent Hill* and *The Walking Dead* were designed by Universal Creative. Alice Cooper was a collaboration between A&D and Creative with some of the material taken from Hollywood's Alice Cooper maze. The

remainder of the mazes were constructed by A&D. From what I understand, Creative haven't contributed to the event again since 2012.

- 2013 initially had original scarezones planned thematically around the mazes in each area with an original icon in charge of the event. For example, *Raccoon City* was going to be the zone most proximate to *Resident Evil* and *The Walking Dead* was going to stay contained in the Central Park/Kid Zone portion of the park. Marketing and Corporate rejected it for *The Walking Dead* in the entire park.

- 2014 was again all *Walking Dead* in terms of marketing because of Corporate and Universal's Marketing department. A&D didn't offer an icon pitch because they were told it wasn't going to be used.

- 2015 jump-started a new era. The 2012-2015 years weren't liked as an era by the scareactors and creatives involved because of the abundance of *Walking Dead*, the saturation of intellectual properties, and no icon.

- 2015 is a new era in that A&D now is using an icon for marketing, a special logo is made each year to thematically match the icon, the scarezones have more original content, and there's a balance between original and intellectual properties in the maze line-ups.

- Orlando and Hollywood collaborate to an extent and borrow concepts and technology from each other. Their philosophies differ as do the park-goers (Hollywood is basically a "dry" event aside from the finite drinks offered to VIP guests) so there are differences in terms of scare tactics, set design, and the general layouts.

- The Internet changed the event dramatically. It connected A&D with the fans in a more intimate way and allowed for things to be archived. Universal kept internal documents, such as house plans, videos, pictures, and media clippings, but they didn't take to it as intently until fan sites became more prominent and social media eclipsed the fan community pages.

- Abstract mazes like *The In-Between*, *Dead Exposure*, and Universal's *House of Horrors* (2012) are harder to accomplish because they require more lighting and completely fabricated parts to work without breaking the illusion. It doesn't always work, but you'll find interesting design choices in these mazes.

- Employee Preview is viewed as a dress/technical rehearsal

night. It's for everyone involved to figure out their roles, timing, and responsibilities and identify weaknesses that can be corrected. It's why it's the messiest night. The feedback is usually mixed because of this, as the event is technically not finished until opening night. It gets revised every week until the final weekend. The houses and props are the most pristine opening weekend, but the actors and ops crew don't hit their stride until a couple weeks into the event.

- Universal has never employed child actors at the event, instead where child appearing characters are required, as with Cindy, smaller actors are always deployed.
- Universal has over the years used true disabled actors. Some wheelchair bound actors have been used in various houses and scarezones. But also actors who may have limbs missing have also been used in house scenes where it appears body parts are being torn from the actors.
- Back in 2006, the Jaws skippers created their own script for the ride that was more adult and profane, which they hoped that they would be able to use during the event. However for reasons unknown, the script ended up getting shot down by management.
- Many of the creatives who build HHN every year started off as actors and performers at the event. Mike Aiello for example was a member of the Chainsaw Drill Team.
- Over the years many scareactors have had to undergo physical changes for their characters, but the most extreme example would be 2010's Havoc: Dogs of War and its 2013 sequel Havoc: Derailed, where every actor (male and female) shaved their head bald to play the sadistic super soldiers.
- Latin' pop singer Gloria Estefan is a long-time fan of the Orlando event, which has reportedly attended every year since its inception. In 2012, they even hired her as a scareactor for a night. Likewise, pop star Ariana Grande has reportedly being attending the event every year since she was 15.
- An *American Horror Story* house was originally planned for 2013 but on-going talks with the IP holder supposedly put the project on hold.
- Back in the late 90s of the event, Universal wanted to build a house inside the *ET* queue, and although it had been used before, news reached Steven Spielberg's house who forwarded a memo to park management reportedly saying "forget it!" The idea would have created a house where a

rogue alien (akin to the alien from Alien) would chase guests through the forest and into an extended house section in the outside queue area.

- Although houses based on *Psycho* have been seen, a house based on the works of Alfred Hitchcock has been planned many times but has never been seen. The closest the event has had was a lagoon clip show that appeared without notice in 2012 featuring clips and music from some of his most famous movies.
- 2016's *Ghost Town - The Curse of Lightning Gulch* is a sequel to 2004's *Ghost Town*.
- Original plans for 2003 had the event's icon being a demented animator (complete with Walt Disney style moustache, ahem), which would have created an army of animated monsters who had come to life to terrorize the paying public. The idea would subsequently be shelved to go back to the drawing board (sorry, not sorry!).
- In 2013 the Art and Design Dept gave a talk at a popular charity show, they hinted with props and displays that the event would be based around a forest theme, however, Universal Creative supposedly stepped in and altered the plans when the green light was given to use *The Walking Dead* to market the event that year.
- Early plans for 2002 would have seen Eddie be the main icon once again with a stage show featuring the character in the best homage to *WWE* where he is de-masked to the crowd to expose that he was in fact Jack all along!
- Despite the fact that scareactors main job is to scare the living daylights out of you, they are on the whole a nice bunch. Past scareactors have included: Doctors, nurses, fire-fighters, lawyers, accountants and even a few aspiring Hollywood actors.
- A nighttime show called *Danse Macabre* had been planned for the lagoon during the late 90s but has never come to fruition.
- In 2011, both Halloween Horror Nights and Howl-O-Scream had houses based on the author Edgar Allan Poe, and both houses were even titled *Nevermore*.
- The Thing (1982) was originally going to be at this event for its 20th anniversary, but fell through due to budget cut backs. It would however make it to the event a few years later in 2007.
- The original finale for the *Project Evilution* house would've included a giant Tyrannosaurus puppet. Due to technical difficulties, the idea was never put into production.

- 2004 had originally been planned to feature an icon called "Dr. Payne", who also would've been involved in the *Disorientorium* house as the icon's house for that year.
- In 2014 the icon was originally planned to be "The Prop Master" who was the minion of The Director and the Usher – the idea was that the Prop Master would work for the other icons in a bid to bring them back from the dead.
- A house based on the legend of the Chupacabra has been planned but not seen a few times. Rumor has it that the house got very far down the development process in 2012 before being cut. Several of the early props and masks used for the event have since been recycled in other houses.

The Rat Lady welcomes you to HHN!

House Locations at Universal Studios Orlando

Locations inside the soundstages:

Soundstage 18:

This location was originally the main production space for *Nickelodeon Studios*, before they relocated their productions to the West coast. It is now occupied by the *Blue Man Group* and has been retitled 'Sharp Aquos Theater'.

Where Evil Hides (HHN 15)

Soundstage 19:

American Horror Story (HHN26)
The Repository (HHN26)

Soundstage 20:

This location has been used to film various shows for *TNA Wrestling* and *Nickelodeon*.   It is one of the largest soundstages on the lot and can often house two mazes back-to-back inside.

Scream House (HHN 12)
Scream House Revisited (HHN 13)
All Nite Die-In (HHN 13)
Hellgate Prison (HHN 14)
Horror in Wax (HHN 14)
Cold Blind Terror (HHN 15)
Body Collectors: Collections of the Past (HHN 18)
Interstellar Terror (HHN 18)
Gothic (HHN 22)

Dead End (HHN 22)

Soundstage 22:

One of the medium-sized soundstages that has housed many of the haunts over the years.

Universal's Museum Of Horror (HHN 7)
Museum Of Horror: Chamber of Horrors (HHN 8)
Museum Of Horror: Unnatural History (HHN 8)
Psycho...Through the Mind of Norman Bates (HHN 9)
Insanity (HHN 9)
Anxiety (HHN 10)
Total Chaos (HHN 10)
Scary Tales (HHN 11)
Pitch Black (HHN 11)
Ghost Town (HHN 14)
Blood Ruins (HHN 15)
Psychoscareapy: Maximum Madness (HHN 16
Dead Silence: The Curse Of Mary Shaw (HHN 17)
Creatures! (HHN 18)
The Wolfman (HHN 19)
Legendary Truth: The Wyandot Estate (HHN 20)
Winter's Night: The Haunting Of Hawthorn Cemetery (HHN 21)
Silent Hill (HHN 22)
An American Werewolf In London (HHN 23)
From Dusk Till Dawn (HHN 24)
An American Werewolf in London (HHN 25)
The Exorcist (HHN26)
The Shining (HHN27)

Soundstage 21:

This was formerly the main production area for *TNA Wrestling* and due to this it has not been used very often for houses at the event.

The Cabin in the Woods (HHN 23)
Resident Evil: Escape From Raccoon City (HHN 23)
Jack Presents: 25 Years of Monsters and Mayhem (HHN 25)
American Horror Story: Volume 2 (HHN27)

Soundstage 23:

One of the smallest soundstages on the lot, it has been used by various television shows over the years.

The People Under The Stairs (HHN 2)
The People Under The Stairs (HHN 3)
Universal's House of Horror (HHN 5)
Castle Vampyr (HHN 15)
Scream House: Resurrection (HHN 16)
All Nite Die-In: Take 2 (HHN 16)
A Nightmare on Elm Street: Dream Walkers (HHN 17)
Psychoscareapy: Home for the Holidays (HHN 17)
Frankenstein (HHN 19)
Dracula: Legacy in Blood (HHN 19)
Hades (HHN 20)
Psychoscareapy: Echoes of Shadybrook (HHN 20)
Nightingales: Blood Prey (HHN 21)
The Thing (HHN 21)

Soundstage 24:

One of the medium-sized soundstages on the lot that has been used for the purposes of filming for various productions including: *Psycho IV*, *Ace Ventura 3*, *Superboy* (TV series), *Sharknado 3* and *SeaQuest 2032*. Therefore it has not been used for the purposes of this event very often.

Evil Dead (HHN 23)
Avp: Alien Vs Predator (HHN 24)
Dracula Untold: Reign of Blood (HHN 24)
Body Collectors – Recollections (HHN 25)
Freddy vs. Jason (HHN 25)
Ghost Town: The Curse of Lightning Gulch (HHN26)
The Walking Dead (HHN26)
Dead Waters (HHN27)
The Fallen (HHN27)

Soundstage 25:

Soundstages 25 and 19 are specially constructed soundstages for the purposes of filming TV shows, due to the additional rigs and 1st floor control room. Various Halloween Horror Nights commercials, live TV spots and other TV shows have been recorded here. Therefore it has not been used for the purposes of this event to until 2014. Soundstage 19, which is much larger, has never been used for Halloween Horror Nights.

The Walking Dead: End Of The Line (HHN 24) – the largest haunted house ever constructed by the event.

Soundstage 44 (*Hercules / Xena / Murder She Wrote* Building):

This originally housed the *Murder She Wrote* attraction when the park first opened. This made way for a *Hercules* and *Xena* attraction in 1997, before it was closed down in 2000. The building was then demolished in 2012.

Horror Nights Nightmares (HHN 14)
Unknown House (HHN 2012) – was demolished before the event started to make way for the new *Transformers ride*. Rumored to have been *American Werewolf in London*.

The Parade Building (B-79):

This was originally built to house the day-time parade. It has subsequently been repurposed for Halloween Horror Nights.

Scary Tales: Once Upon A Nightmare (HHN 18)
Silver Screams (HHN 19)
Horror Nights: The Hallow'd Past (HHN 20)
The Forsaken (HHN 21)
Universal's House of Horrors (HHN 22)
The Walking Dead: No Safe Haven (HHN 23)
Roanoke: Cannibal Colony (HHN 24)
The Walking Dead: The Living and the Dead (HHN25)
Halloween: Hell Comes to Haddonfield (HHN26)
Ash Vs. Evil Dead (HHN27)

Jaws queue:

The original haunt location that was demolished in 2012 to make way for *Harry Potter's Diagon Alley*.

Dungeon of Terror (*Fright Nights*)

344

Dungeon of Terror (HHN 2)
Dungeon of Terror: Retold (HHN 16)
Friday The 13th: Camp Blood (HHN 17)
Reflections of Fear (HHN 18)
Saw (HHN 19)
Orfanage: Ashes to Ashes (HHN 20)
Saws N' Steam: Into the Machine (HHN 21)

Sprung Tent 1:

Built solely for the use of Halloween Horror Nights, in 2006.

Psycho Path: The Return of Norman Bates (HHN 16)
The Thing: Assimilation (HHN 17)
The Hallow (HHN 18)
Chucky: Friends till the End (HHN 19)
Catacombs: Black Death Rising (HHN 20)
The In-Between (HHN 21)
Alice Cooper: Welcome to My Nightmare (HHN 22)
Urban Legends: La Llorona (HHN 23)
Dollhouse of the Damned (HHN 24)
The Purge (HHN 25)
Tomb of the Ancients (HHN26)
Scarecrow: The Reaping (HHN27)

Sprung Tent 2:

Built solely for the use of Halloween Horror Nights, in 2006.

The People Under The Stairs: Under Construction (HHN 16)

Jack's Funhouse in Clown-O-Vision (HHN 17)
Dead Exposure (HHN 18)
The Spawning (HHN 19)
Havoc: The Dogs of War (HHN 20)
Nevermore: The Madness Of Poe (HHN 21)
Penn & Teller New(K'd) Las Vegas (HHN 22)
After Life: Death's Vengeance (HHN 23)
Halloween (HHN 24)
Insidious (HHN 25)
The Texas Chain Saw Massacre (HHN26)
Hive (HHN27)

Nazarman's:

Re-purposed as a location for Halloween Horror Nights in 1993, this location was effectively taken out of use in 2007 when the area became occupied via lease by *Starbucks*.

The Slaughterhouse (HHN 3)
Hell's Kitchen (HHN 4)
Terror Underground: Transit to Torment (HHN 5)
Toy Hell: Nightmare at the Scream Factory (HHN 6)
Hotel Hell (HHN 7)
Hell's High (HHN 8)
Universal's Creature Features in 3D! (HHN 9)
Superstitions (HHN 11)
Vampyr: Blood Bath (HHN 17)

Earthquake / Disaster queue:

The outdoor queue housing for the above attractions. Most props stored within the queue had to be easily removable for the event. The building was demolished in 2016.

Dungeon of Terror (HHN 4)
Crypt Keeper's Dungeon of Terror (HHN 5)
Crypt Keeper's Studio Tour of Terror (HHN 6)
Tombs of Terror (HHN 7)
S.S. Frightanic: Carnage Crew (HHN 8)
S.S. Frightanic: Fear In First Class (HHN 8)

The Mummy (HHN 9)
Doomsday (HHN 9)
Universal Classic Monster Mania (HHN 10)
Dark Torment (HHN 10)
The Mummy Returns: The Curse Continues (HHN 11)

Run (HHN 11)
Deadtropolis (HHN 14)
Run: Hostile Territory (HHN 16)
The Texas Chainsaw Massacre: Flesh Wounds (HHN 17)

Doomsday (HHN 18)
Leave It To Cleaver (HHN 19)
Zombiegeddon (HHN 20)
H.R. Bloodengutz: Holidays of Horror (HHN 20)
The Walking Dead: Dead Inside (HHN 22)
Havoc: Derailed (HHN 23)
Giggles & Gore Inc. (HHN 24)
RUN: Blood, Sweat, and Fears (HHN 25)

The Bates Motel from *Psycho IV*:

The original sets from the 1990 movie of the same name. The motel was demolished shortly after HHN5 and then the house followed suit in 1998. These were both unfortunately located in the Kidzone area, hence their requirement to be demolished.

The Psycho Path Maze (HHN 3)
The Psycho Path Maze (HHN 4)
The Psycho Path Maze (HHN 5)

The Bone Yard:

An area in the park that used to house props and sets from previous Universal movies. The area was repurposed in 2008 to make way for the Universal Music Plaza Stage.

The Bone Yard (HHN 4)

Shrek 4-D Theater:

A current attraction within the park that closes its second theater for HHN.

Asylum in Wonderland 3D (HHN 25)
Krampus (HHN26)
SAW: The Games of Jigsaw (HHN27)

Tent 3 (*Men In Black*):

A temporary building sited next to the *Men in Black* attraction's extended queue building.

Lunatic's Playground 3D – You Won't Stand A Chance (HHN26)
The Horrors of Blumhouse (HHN27)

Beetlejuice! Beetlejuice! Beetlejuice!

Islands of Adventure Theme Park Locations

Carnage House / B285a:
A building specially erected for the event in 2012, it now serves as storage.

Maximum Carnage (HHN 12)
Disorientorium (HHN 14)
Demon Cantina (HHN 15)

Popeye and Bluto's Bilge-Rat Barges queue building:

The queue building from the popular water ride.

Scary Tales 2 (HHN 12)
Ship of Screams (HHN 13)

Jurassic Park Discovery Center:

The actual discovery center from the themed island.

Psychoscareapy (HHN 13)
Body Collectors (HHN 15)

Triceratops Discovery Trail:

A now defunct attraction that was in 2015 repurposed into a meet-and-greet with raptors from the *Jurassic Park* franchise.

Evilution (HHN 12)

Jungle of Doom (HHN 13)

Thunder Falls Terrace:

A restaurant in the Jurassic Park area of the park.

Fear Factor (HHN 12)
Funhouse of Fear (HHN 13)
The Skool (HHN 14)

Poseidon's Fury:

A current attraction at the theme park.

Terror Mines (HHN 15)

Where To Get More Information

For all official information, please see Universal's official sites of halloweenhorrornights.com or universalorlando.com. The author runs a news, rumors and speculation blog at hhnunofficial.com. We also fully recommend hhncrypt.com, horrornightnightmares.com and hhnrumors.com, as all these sites do a fantastic job at keeping fans updated all year round. Along with these we also recommend the following podcasts: *Scarezone* is a new podcast that is hosted by Logan Sekulow and the author of this book. Likewise, the Unofficial Universal Orlando Podcast run by the Mallaby family is again worth a fantastic listen, so is the *Parkscope Unprofessional Podcast*, and the *Dis After Dark podcast* which features our author. The latter two cover news and rumors from all the theme parks in Florida.

Sweet dream y'all !

About The Author

Christopher Ripley was born in the UK but has been traveling to and living in the US for many years. He has been attending both Universal Studios Florida and Hollywood for over 20 years. He authored his first book in 2015, *Halloween Horror Nights: The Unofficial Story & Guide*, which went on to become a bestseller. Since then he has set up the wildly popular HHN Blog hhnunofficial.com, become a co-presenter of the *ScareZone Podcast* (a dedicated HHN podcast) and *Dis After Dark* (the Europe/UK's number one downloaded Florida theme parks podcast). He has also ghost written a number of books and articles and has a further three books in the pipeline all related to Universal Studios coming soon.

And remember, as his pal Logan always says *"keep your eyes closed and your ears open – we'll see you at Finnegan's!"*

Other Books By This Author

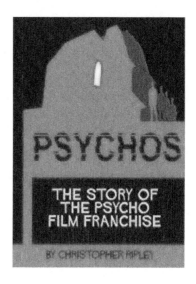

Pending
release of

The Unofficial
Story & Guide
to HHN
Around the
Globe

Printed in Great Britain
by Amazon

56016151R00210